# FRAUD INVESTIGATION

Investigating white-collar crime is like any other investigation concerned with past events. However, a number of characteristics require a contingent approach to these investigations. This book describes the process of conducting private internal investigations by fraud examiners and presents a number of reports from the United States, Sweden and Norway.

It evaluates a number of internal investigation reports to reflect on the practice of fraud examinations. Empirical studies provide a basis to reflect theoretically on practice improvements for fraud examiners. Rather than presenting normative recommendations based on ideal or stereotypical situations so often found in existing books, this book develops guidelines based on empirical study of current practice.

Internal investigations should uncover the truth about misconduct or crime without damaging the reputation of innocent employees. Typical elements of an inquiry include collection and examination of written and recorded evidence, interviews with suspects and witnesses, data in computer systems, and network forensics. Internal inquiries may take many forms depending upon the nature of the conduct at issue and the scope of the investigation. There should be recognition at the outset of any investigation that certain materials prepared during the course of the investigation may eventually be subject to disclosure to law enforcement authorities or other third parties. The entire investigation should be conducted with an eye towards preparing a final report.

As evidenced in this book, private fraud examiners take on complicated roles in private internal investigations and often fail in their struggle to reconstruct the past in objective ways characterized by integrity and accountability.

**Petter Gottschalk** is a professor in the Department of Leadership and Organization at BI Norwegian Business School in Oslo, Norway.

# FRAUD INVESTIGATION

Case Studies of Crime Signal Detection

*Petter Gottschalk*

LONDON AND NEW YORK

First published 2018
by Routledge
2 Park Square, Milton Park, Abingdon, Oxon OX14 4RN

and by Routledge
711 Third Avenue, New York, NY 10017

Routledge is an imprint of the Taylor & Francis Group, an informa business

© 2018 Petter Gottschalk

The right of Petter Gottschalk to be identified as author of this work has been asserted by him in accordance with sections 77 and 78 of the Copyright, Designs and Patents Act 1988.

All rights reserved. No part of this book may be reprinted or reproduced or utilised in any form or by any electronic, mechanical, or other means, now known or hereafter invented, including photocopying and recording, or in any information storage or retrieval system, without permission in writing from the publishers.

*Trademark notice*: Product or corporate names may be trademarks or registered trademarks, and are used only for identification and explanation without intent to infringe.

British Library Cataloguing-in-Publication Data
A catalogue record for this book is available from the British Library

Library of Congress Cataloging-in-Publication Data
Names: Gottschalk, Petter, 1950- author.
Title: Fraud investigation : case studies of crime signal detection / Petter Gottschalk.
Description: 1 Edition. | New York : Routledge, 2018. | Includes bibliographical references and index.
Identifiers: LCCN 2017046730 (print) | LCCN 2017053016 (ebook) | ISBN 9781351139069 (eBook) | ISBN 9780815352556 (hardback : alk. paper) | ISBN 9780815352563 (pbk. : alk. paper) | ISBN 9781351139069 (ebk)
Subjects: LCSH: Fraud. | Criminal investigation.
Classification: LCC HV6691 (ebook) | LCC HV6691 .G68 2018 (print) | DDC 363.25/963--dc23
LC record available at https://lccn.loc.gov/2017046730

ISBN: 978-0-8153-5255-6 (hbk)
ISBN: 978-0-8153-5256-3 (pbk)
ISBN: 978-1-351-13906-9 (ebk)

Typeset in Bembo
by Servis Filmsetting Ltd, Stockport, Cheshire

# CONTENTS

| | |
|---|---|
| List of illustrations | viii |
| **Introduction** | **1** |
| **1 White-collar crime research** | **5** |
| *Edwin Sutherland* | 6 |
| *Offense characteristics* | 7 |
| *Offender characteristics* | 8 |
| *Gender perspectives* | 9 |
| *Occupational and business crime* | 9 |
| *Convicted white-collar criminals* | 10 |
| *Special sensitivity hypothesis* | 11 |
| *Sensitivity testing* | 14 |
| *The Kerik case* | 15 |
| *Convenience theory* | 17 |
| **2 Theory of convenience** | **18** |
| *Theory development* | 19 |
| *Financial motive* | 20 |
| *Organizational opportunity* | 22 |
| *Organizational dynamics* | 23 |
| *Management control* | 26 |
| *Entrepreneurs in white-collar crime* | 27 |
| *Behavioral willingness* | 30 |
| *Occupational crime* | 32 |
| *Conclusion* | 47 |

## 3 Convenience research — 48

*Theoretical foundation: motive* — 49
*Theoretical foundation: opportunity* — 51
*Theoretical foundation: willingness* — 52
*Research propositions* — 54

## 4 Crime signal detection — 60

*Sources of crime detection* — 60
*Auditing role in crime detection* — 64
*Crime signal detection theory* — 68
*Lack of crime signal detection* — 72
*Characteristics of whistleblowers* — 74
*Crime signal sources* — 78

## 5 Investigation reports — 80

*Investigation characteristics* — 82
*Reasons for private investigations* — 85
*Private fraud examinations* — 86
*Financial crime specialists* — 88
*Certified fraud examiners* — 90
*Police versus internal investigations* — 92
*Implications from convenience* — 94

## 6 Crime investigations in Norway — 96

*Sixty investigation reports* — 96
*Betanien Nursing Home* — 106
*Furuheim Housing Foundation* — 107
*Hadeland Broadband Network* — 108
*Lunde Transportation Group* — 109
*Romerike Water Supply* — 111
*School buildings administration* — 112
*Unibuss public transportation* — 114
*SOS Racism sentence* — 115
*SOS Racism convenience* — 117
*CEOs in financial crime* — 120

## 7 Misconduct investigations in Scandinavia — 123

*DNB Bank in the Panama Papers* — 123
*Police Immigration Unit* — 130
*Dale Property Development* — 139

|   |   | Contents **vii** |
|---|---|---|
|   | *Nordea Bank in the Panama Papers* | 144 |
|   | *Regional public management* | 150 |
|   | *Tipping point decision-making* | 159 |

## 8 Crime investigations in the United States — 166

*Enron Corporation* — 166
*Philadelphia Police Department* — 168
*Chief Technology Office* — 170
*Tax and Revenue Office* — 172
*WorldCom Corporation* — 175

## 9 Misconduct investigations in the United States — 178

*Lehman Brothers* — 178
*University of Texas* — 182
*General Motors* — 184
*Coatesville Area School District* — 192
*Motorola Sales* — 194
*Save the Children* — 195
*Peregrine Financial Group* — 196
*Sandstorm banking* — 197

## Conclusion — 199

*Bibliography* — 202
*Index* — 221

# ILLUSTRATIONS

## Figures
| | | |
|---|---|---|
| 2.1 | Estimation of the magnitude of different forms of financial crime | 46 |
| 3.1 | Convenience triangle for white-collar crime | 54 |
| 3.2 | Research propositions in the convenience triangle for white-collar crime | 55 |

## Tables
| | | |
|---|---|---|
| 2.1 | White-collar criminals convicted of convenient embezzlement in Norway | 28 |
| 2.2 | Neutralization techniques applied by white-collar criminal Christer Tromsdal | 44 |
| 4.1 | Detection of white-collar crime | 60 |
| 4.2 | Comparison of journalist and non-journalist-detected white-collar criminals | 61 |
| 4.3 | Financial crime categories by detection sources | 61 |
| 4.4 | Characteristics of stimulus in detection of white-collar crime | 70 |
| 4.5 | Quality of information sources and information pieces | 79 |
| 6.1 | Summary of convenience findings in reports of internal investigations | 97 |
| 6.2 | Key issues in private investigations | 98 |
| 7.1 | Tipping points when suspects are identified | 164 |

# INTRODUCTION

When there is suspicion of fraud in organizations, private investigators are often hired to reconstruct past events. Signal detection theory may shed some light on why some fraud examiners discover and disclose more facts than other examiners. Signal detection theory holds that the detection of a stimulus depends on both the intensity of the stimulus and the physical and psychological state of the individual. A detector's ability to detect – or likelihood of detecting – some stimulus is affected by the intensity of the stimulus (e.g. how loud a whistleblowing is) and the detector's physical and psychological state (e.g. how alert the person is). Perceptual sensitivity depends upon the perceptual ability of the observer to detect a signal or target or to discriminate signal from non-signal events (Szalma and Hancock, 2013).

Furthermore, detecting persons may have varying ability to discern between information-bearing recognition (called pattern) and random patterns that distract from information (called noise).

Under signal detection theory, some researchers found that people more frequently and incorrectly identify negative task-related words as having been presented originally than positive words, even when they were not present. Liu et al. (2014) found that people have lax decision criteria for negative words. In a different study, Huff and Bodner (2013) applied the signal detection approach to determine whether changes in correct and false recognition following item-specific versus relational encoding were driven by a decrease in the encoding of memory information or an increase in monitoring at test.

According to the theory, there are a number of determinants of how a person will detect a signal. In addition to signal intensity, signal alertness and pattern recognition, there are factors such as personal competence (including knowledge, skills and attitude), experience and expectations. These factors determine the threshold level. Low signal intensity, low signal alertness and limited pattern recognition combined with low competence, lack of experience and lack of expectations will lead to a high threshold level, meaning that the individual will not detect white-collar crime.

The competence of private investigators is a concern. For several decades the public police have striven to achieve professional status, arguing that their work is a skilled activity requiring long and in-depth training. Private policing, which is not regulated by statute in countries such as the United Kingdom, the United States or Norway, directly challenges this premise. People are not required to undergo any form of training in order to set up as fraud examiners (Gill and Hart, 1997).

In his book on signal detection theory, Wickens (2001) asks us to consider what happens when a person must decide whether or not an event has occurred, using information that is insufficient to completely determine the correct answer. Without sufficient information, some errors are inevitably made. The typical signal detection situation is perceptual. The person, usually known as the observer, is presented with a noisy stimulus, and the person must decide if that stimulus contains a weak signal.

Fraud investigation is like any other investigation concerned with past events. However, a number of characteristics require a contingent approach to white-collar crime investigations, as we limit our case studies to white-collar offenders. Ever since Edwin Sutherland (1939) coined the term white-collar crime, researchers in the field have emphasized the value of preventing and detecting fraud by executives and other members of the elite in society (Piquero and Benson, 2004). The typical profile of a white-collar criminal includes attributes such as high social status, considerable influence and access to resources (Blickle et al., 2006; Dearden, 2016; Füss and Hecker, 2008). White-collar crime is committed in the course of an occupation where the offender can carry out and conceal the offense among legal activities in an organizational context (Arnulf and Gottschalk, 2013). The white-collar offender is a person of respectability and high social status who commits financial crime in the course of his or her occupation (Leasure and Zhang, 2017).

Fraud investigation endeavors to find out what happened in the past. A negative event or a sequence of negative events can be at the core of an investigation. If there is no certainty about events, or signals about aspects of events are not detected, then an investigation can become a failure. An investigation can be concerned with events that did occur or events that did not occur. Information is collected and knowledge is applied to reconstruct the past.

Fraud investigators need to have both a theoretical and empirical understanding of white-collar crime. The theory of convenience is introduced in this book to explain what white-collar offenders do. Convenience is a phenomenon that can be observed in many aspects of human life. For example, convenience stores and convenience shopping are associated with easy access to goods and services. A theory of convenience can be applied to a number of areas where people prefer alternatives that are associated with savings in time and effort, and also with avoidance of pain and problems. For example, a convenience theory of cheating suggests that cheating is a preferred alternative in certain situations.

In this book we focus on convenience theory as convenience relates to white-collar misconduct and crime. Convenience theory attempts to integrate various theoretical explanations for the occurrence of white-collar misconduct and crime; it suggests that organizational opportunity to commit and conceal financial crime is at the core of deviant behavior to avoid threats and exploit possibilities. This book presents an empirical test of convenience theory by content analysis of investigation reports by fraud examiners. Empirical evidence suggests that convenience orientation was indeed present among suspected offenders.

This book is concerned with offenders rather than criminals. To offend is to cause displeasure, anger, resentment or wounded feelings. It is to be displeasing or disagreeable. It can also be to violate a moral, a guideline, a rule or a law.

Convenience theory was introduced to integrate a number of theoretical approaches to explain and understand white-collar crime that was first defined by Sutherland (1939). Convenience theory applies the concept of convenience in terms of savings in time and effort (Farquhar and Rowley, 2009), as well as avoidance of pain and obstacles (Higgins, 1997). A convenient individual is not necessarily either bad or lazy. On the contrary, the person can be seen as smart and rational (Sundström and Radon, 2015).

Convenience theory suggests that white-collar crime is committed if crime is a convenient alternative compared to other alternatives in times of crisis and/or possibilities. Convenience can be found in three dimensions (Gottschalk, 2017). In the economical dimension, the motive is avoidance of crisis or exploration and exploitation of possibilities. In the organizational dimension, there is opportunity to commit and conceal financial crime. In the behavioral dimension, individuals demonstrate a readiness for deviant behaviors.

This book presents a study in search of empirical evidence of convenience theory by content analysis of reports of investigations by fraud examiners. Fraud examiners from large accounting, auditing, consulting and law firms are typically hired by private and public organizations when there is suspicion of misconduct and crime (Schneider, 2006). The client organization receives a report of investigation where fraud examiners describe their procedures and findings (Brooks and Button, 2011).

From a resource-matching perspective, convenience directly relates to the amount of time and effort (resources) that must be dedicated to accomplishing a task. However, convenience involves more than a simple examination of ease of use perceptions that also addresses the amount of effort in an interaction. Ease of use is the degree to which an alternative action is free of effort. Convenience addresses the time and effort exerted before, during and after an action or avoidance of action (Collier and Kimes, 2013).

Fraud investigation is often carried out by examiners from global auditing firms and local law firms. They document their work and their findings in reports of investigations. Reports are the property of the client organization and are seldom disclosed to the public; they are also often not disclosed to the police (Gottschalk and Tcherni-Buzzeo, 2017). We were able to find a number of reports in the

**4** Introduction

United States and in Scandinavia for this book. These reports represent our case studies in the book.

Chapter 1 starts by presenting perspectives introduced by Edwin Sutherland on white-collar crime. Then different perspectives on white-collar crime are discussed, such as offense and offender characteristics, occupational and corporate crime differences, and the special sensitivity hypothesis. Several convicted white-collar criminals have written their autobiographies, and an example is presented in this chapter.

Chapter 2 presents the theory of convenience as a way of understanding white-collar crime occurrences. The financial motive can be based on both threats and possibilities. The organizational opportunity is concerned with both execution and concealment of crime. The deviant behavior is concerned with the willingness to be a white-collar offender.

Chapter 3 develops convenience theory into research propositions that can further guide both theoretical and empirical understanding of white-collar crime. A number of well-known perspectives from criminology, management, sociology, psychology and other fields are integrated into the convenience hypothesis.

Chapter 4 introduces crime signal detection theory, where crime signal detection rests on four pillars. First, the intensity of the signal is important for the potential receiver of the signal. Next, the receiver's awareness can determine whether or not the receiver notices a signal. Third, the ability of the receiver to carry out pattern recognition will determine to what extent the receiver is able to allocate a new piece of information in a relevant spot in the investigation puzzle. Finally, the extent of personal experience with signals will influence to what extent the receiver is able to reflect on and interpret the new signal as well as have an understanding of the context in which the signal emerged.

Chapter 5 introduces reports of investigations by fraud examiners. Financial crime specialists and certified fraud examiners carry out fraud investigations in client organizations. A comparison of police versus internal investigations is presented.

Chapter 6 presents a sample of 60 investigation reports from Norway. Seven of these investigation reports are presented in detail as they led to imprisonment of white-collar criminals. In addition, the case of fraud by the CEO in a non-government organization (NGO) is presented.

Chapter 7 presents more investigations in Norway, in addition to a case in Sweden and a case in Denmark.

Chapter 8 is devoted to fraud investigations in the United States where internal investigations were carried out and reports possible to find for research. The case studies are all concerned with white-collar offenders who were sentenced to prison.

Chapter 9 is also devoted to fraud investigations in the United States where internal investigations were carried out and reports possible to find for research. However, none of the suspects were prosecuted in these cases.

One important purpose of the case studies is for the reader to reflect on signal detection, looking both at signals of crime and signals of innocence.

# 1
# WHITE-COLLAR CRIME RESEARCH

Ever since Sutherland (1939) coined the term white-collar crime, there has been extensive research and debate about what to include and what to exclude from this offense category (e.g. Piquero and Benson, 2004; Pontell et al., 2014; Stadler et al., 2013). In accordance with Sutherland's original work, convenience theory emphasizes the position and trust enjoyed by the offender in an occupational setting. Therefore, the organizational dimension is the core of convenience theory where the offender has access to resources to commit and conceal financial crime.

The typical profile of a white-collar criminal includes the following attributes (Piquero and Benson, 2004; Pontell et al., 2014; Stadler et al., 2013):

- The person has high social status and considerable influence, enjoying respect and trust, and belongs to the elite in society.
- The elite generally have more knowledge, money and prestige and occupy higher positions than other individuals in the population occupy.
- Privileges and authority by the elite are often not visible or transparent, but known to everybody.
- Elite members are active in business, public administration, politics, congregations and many other sectors in society.
- The elite are a minority that behaves as an authority towards others in the majority.
- The person is often wealthy and does not really need crime income to live a good life.
- The person is typically well educated and connected to important networks of partners and friends.
- The person exploits his or her position to commit financial crime.
- The person does not look at themselves as a criminal, but rather as a community builder who applies personal rules to their own behavior.

- The person may be in a position that makes the police reluctant to initiate a crime investigation.
- The person has access to resources that enable the involvement of top defense attorneys and can behave in court in a manner that creates sympathy among the public, partly because the defendant belongs to the upper class, like the judge, the prosecutor and the attorney.

However, one of the theoretical challenges facing scholars in this growing field of research is to develop an accepted definition of white-collar crime. While the main characteristics are the foundation, such as economic crime committed by a person of respectability and high social status in the course of an occupation, other aspects lack precision (Kang and Thosuwanchot, 2017).

## Edwin Sutherland

Edwin Sutherland is one of the most cited criminologists in the history of the criminology research field. Sutherland's work has inspired and motivated a large number of scholars in the field associated with his work. His ideas influence, challenge and incentivize researchers. Sutherland's research on white-collar crime is based on his own differential association theory. This learning theory of deviance focuses on how individuals learn to become criminals. Differential association theory assumes that criminal behavior is learned in interaction with other persons.

Sutherland's (1939, 1949) concept of white-collar crime has been influential for various reasons. First, there is Sutherland's engagement with criminology's neglect of the kinds of crime committed by powerful and influential members of the elite in society. Next, there is the extent of damage caused by white-collar crime. Sutherland emphasized the disproportionate extent of harm caused by the crime of the wealthy in comparison to the much researched and popular focus on crime by the poor and the equally disproportionate level of social control responses. Third, there is the focus on organizational offenders, where crime occurs in the course of their occupations. A white-collar criminal is a person who, through the course of their occupation, utilizes their respectability and high social status to perpetrate an offense. Fourth, the construction of the corporation as an offender indicates that organizations can also be held accountable for misconduct and crime. Finally, there is the ability to theorize the deviant behaviors of elite members. Many researchers have been inspired by Sutherland's groundbreaking criticism of mainstream criminology as neglecting the crime of the upper class and focusing attention on the crime of the poor. This was a major insight that began a dramatic shift and broadening in the subject matter of criminology that continues today.

Sutherland's long-lasting influence on criminological, sociological and more recently also on management thinking is observable across the globe, but in particular in the United States and Europe. Sutherland exposed crime by people who were thought of as almost superior, people who apparently did not need to offend as a means of survival. Businesspersons and professionals frequently commit serious wrongdoing and harm with little fear of facing criminal justice scrutiny. It may be true that poverty and powerlessness are a cause of one kind of crime while excessive power can be a cause of another kind of crime.

Sutherland exemplified the corporation as an offender in the case of war crime, when corporations profit massively by abusing the state of national emergency during times of war. Corporate form and its characteristics as a profit-maximizing entity shape war profiteering. It is powerful organizations that may commit environmental crime, war profiteering, state-corporate crime and human rights violations.

While Sutherland's concept of white-collar crime has enlightened sociologists, criminologists and management researchers, the concept may have confused attorneys, judges and lawmakers. In most jurisdictions there is no offense labeled white-collar crime. There are offenses such as corruption, embezzlement, tax evasion, fraud and insider trading, but no white-collar crime offense. Sutherland's contribution to the challenge of concepts such as law and crime can be considered one of the strengths of his work as he showed that laws and legal distinctions are politically and socially produced in very specific ways. For lawmakers there is nothing intrinsic to the character of white-collar offenses that makes them somehow different from other types of offense.

One reason for this confusion is that white-collar crime in Sutherland's research is both a crime committed by a specific type of person and a specific type of crime. Later research has indicated, as applied in this book, that white-collar crime is not a specific type of crime, it is only a crime committed by a specific type of person. However, white-collar crime may indeed emerge some time in the future as a kind of crime suitable for law enforcement, as Sutherland envisaged in his offender-based approach to crime, focusing on characteristics of the individual offender to determine the categorization of the type of crime.

Sutherland's broader engagement with criminological and sociological theory in general, such as his theory of differential association and social learning, has been and remains influential. One aspect of the theory of differential association – social disorganization – has had a significant influence on later researchers.

Sutherland's work is the foundation of all teaching, research and policing of white-collar crime today.

## Offense characteristics

White-collar crime is illegal acts that violate responsibility or public trust for personal or organizational gain. It is an act or a series of acts committed by non-physical means and by concealment to obtain money or property or to obtain business or personal advantage (Leasure and Zhang, 2017).

White-collar crime is a unique area of criminology due to its atypical association with societal influence compared to other types of criminal offenses. White-collar crime is defined by its relationship to status, opportunity and access. This is the offender-based perspective. In contrast, offense-based approaches to white-collar crime emphasize the actions and nature of the illegal act as the defining agent.

In their comparison of the two approaches, Benson and Simpson (2015) discuss how offender-based definitions emphasize societal characteristics such as high social status, power and respectability of the actor. Because status is not included in the definition of offense-based approaches and status is free to vary independently from the definition in most legislation, an offense-based approach allows measures of status to become external explanatory variables.

Benson and Simpson (2015) approach white-collar crime utilizing the opportunity perspective. They stress the idea that individuals with more opportunities to offend, with access to resources to offend and who hold organizational positions of power are more likely to commit white-collar crime. Opportunities for crime are shaped and distributed according to the nature of economic and productive activities of various business and government sectors within society.

Benson and Simpson (2015) do not limit their opportunity perspective to activities in organizations. However, they emphasize that opportunities are normally greater in an organizational context. Convenience theory, however, assumes that crime committed in an organizational context is to be called white-collar crime. This is in line with Sutherland's (1939, 1949) original work, where he emphasized profession and position as key characteristics of offenders.

## Offender characteristics

The white-collar offender is a person of respectability and high social status who commits financial crime in the course of his or her occupation (Leasure and Zhang, 2017). In the offender-based perspective, white-collar criminals tend to possess many characteristics consistent with expectations of high status in society. There is both attained status and ascribed status among white-collar offenders. Attained status refers to status that is accrued over time and with some degree of effort, such as education and income. Ascribed status refers to status that does not require any specific action or merit but rather is based on more physically observable characteristics, such as race, age and gender.

The main offender characteristics remain privilege and upper class. Early perception studies suggest that the public think that white-collar crime is not as serious as other forms of crime. Most people think that street criminals should receive harsher punishments. One explanation for this view is self-interest (Dearden, 2017: 311):

> Closely tied to rational choice, self-interest suggests that people have views that selfishly affect themselves. Significant scholarly research has been devoted to self-interest-based views. In laboratory conditions, people often favor redistribution taxes when they would benefit from such a tax. This self-interest extends into non-experimental settings as well. For example, smokers often view increasing smoking taxes less favorably than non-smokers do.

In this line of thinking, people may be more concerned about burglary and physical violence that may hurt them. They may be less concerned about white-collar crime that does not affect them directly. Maybe those who are financially concerned with their own economic well-being will be more concerned with white-collar crime (Dearden, 2017).

White-collar perpetrators have social power associated with different occupational activities across society. Power and authority in the hands of individuals enable white-collar crime. The power essentially comes from the positions individuals legitimately occupy.

## Gender perspectives

Research has suggested a relationship between gender and tax compliance, with men being more likely to commit tax offenses than women. Research on tax evasion has both an offender-based perspective and an offense-based perspective. Wealthy individuals have more opportunities to avoid tax compliance and to benefit more heavily from it. In addition, lack of tax compliance can be organized in a professional setting, where the business enterprise manipulates accounting for the purpose of tax evasion. Status affects the ability of individuals to avoid detection or sanctions for non-compliance and the opportunity to commit a variety of tax offenses are status based. Tax compliance can be the result of interaction between authority and expectations, where both authority and expectations are based on individual status.

The offense-based approach to defining white-collar crime is also fitting when examining tax offenses. The actions of being non-compliant dictate that the offense itself is considered a crime.

A special kind of tax offense is bank deposits in tax havens. As documented by Andersen et al. (2017: 2), banks help politicians and others transform petroleum rents and other assets into hidden wealth by bank deposits in tax havens:

> Political elites abuse public office to extract rents. Even moderate levels of political rents may have socially undesirable effects, through the adverse selection of political candidates and by distorting political incentives. In countries without strong democratic governance, political rents can be substantial and the economic and political consequences severe.

When white-collar offenders are brought to justice, Supernor (2017: 148) found that "a lot more women were given community service than men" because "women are considered homemakers for families, and the court systems do not want to punish a woman in a way that would take her away from her family".

## Occupational and business crime

A distinction in white-collar offenses can be made between occupational crime and business crime. Occupational crime is committed by persons in an organizational setting for purely personal gain and to the detriment of the organization. Business crime is committed by or on behalf of the organization for profit or enhancement (Kang and Thosuwanchot, 2017). Of course, in business crime organizations cannot commit illegal acts independently of human agents.

Occupational crime is typically committed under conditions of low levels of socialization and weak accountability. Employees may be unfamiliar with organizational goals, or simply ignore them, while at the same time making efforts to achieve personal goals due to weak restraints by the accountability system. The presence of occupational crime may be symptomatic of larger failures in an organization's system since an organization without committed and accountable employees suggests a higher likelihood of failing in the end. Occupational crime tends to be committed by privileged individuals who feel no attachment to the organization and who do so for purely personal gain (Kang and Thosuwanchot, 2017).

Business crime, on the other hand, is typically committed under conditions of high levels of socialization and strong accountability. Employees identify with not only the organization but also its goals. The pursuit of organizational goals over individual goals does not imply the absence of crime. Rather, achievement of organizational goals becomes so important that if it cannot be done in legal ways, dedicated employees do it in illegal ways (Kang and Thosuwanchot, 2017).

Both occupational and business crime are committed within the organizational context. Corporate crime is committed for business advantage. Examples of corporate crime include cartels and corruption. Illegal price fixing and market sharing occur in cartels to enable participants in cartels to achieve more profits. Bribes are offered to potential customers, allies and public officials to enable contracts and licenses (Leasure and Zhang, 2017).

## Convicted white-collar criminals

It is often argued that convicted white-collar criminals have a hard time in prison. They have to leave all their privileges and opportunities behind to join a community dominated by street crime inmates. The argument is formulated in the special sensitivity hypothesis, which suggests a relatively tougher everyday life for white-collar crime inmates compared to street crime inmates. However, empirical studies of white-collar inmates do not support the special sensitivity hypothesis. Rather, empirical studies support the special resilience hypothesis, which suggests that white-collar offenders are able to adapt to prison life more successfully than other inmates. In this section we argue that the theory of convenience can provide support for the special resilience hypothesis.

If a white-collar criminal should end up in jail, defense attorneys work hard to make prison life as easy as possible for the client. Attorneys argue that it is much worse for a member of the elite to end up in prison than for other people. After a short while, the white-collar offender typically gets most of his freedom back in an imprisonment setting to avoid too much damage (Gottschalk, 2014). However, research indicates that it is easier for a white-collar criminal than for a street criminal to spend time in prison. White-collar offenders tend to find new friends more readily and are able to sleep all night, while most other inmates may have trouble sleeping and making friends in prison (Dhami, 2007; Stadler et al., 2013).

Stadler and Benson (2012: 494) argue that the feeling of innocence is a characteristic of many white-collar criminals:

> Indeed, a distinguishing feature of the psychological makeup of white-collar offenders is thought to be their ability to neutralize the moral bind of the law and rationalize their criminal behavior.

Stadler and Benson (2012) base their argument on an empirical study that they conducted among prison inmates. Almost without exception, white-collar inmates denied responsibility for crime. They applied techniques of neutralization (Sykes and Matza, 1957). Other inmates felt to a much larger extent responsibility for crime. That the feeling of innocence is a characteristic of white-collar criminals was also confirmed in a study by Dhami (2007), who interviewed inmates in a prison in the UK.

Evidence of neutralization by denial of responsibility can be found in autobiographies by white-collar criminals such as Bogen (2008), Eriksen (2010), Fosse and Magnusson (2004), and Kerik (2015). Bernard B. Kerik was a former police commissioner in New York who served three years in prison. He seems to deny responsibility, to condemn his condemners and to suggest normality of action. Evidence of neutralization can also be found in autobiographies by people who were accused of misconduct but never prosecuted or convicted. An example is ex-Lehman CFO Erin Callan, who presents herself as a victim rather than as an offender (Montella, 2016).

In this article we argue that there is lack of evidence for the special sensitivity hypothesis for white-collar inmates. The autobiography by Kerik (2015) is used for our case study of lack of evidence. Rather, there is support for the special resilience hypothesis that we discuss in terms of convenience theory (Gottschalk, 2016c, 2017).

## Special sensitivity hypothesis

The idea that white-collar criminals are especially sensitive to imprisonment is based on the premise that they are of higher status than street criminals. They belong to the elite in society and their fall from grace is much greater, since the higher people fly, the further they fall. White-collar offenders have greater investment in the prevailing social order and have more to lose. Stadler et al. (2013) argue that a belief is commonly held by those in the criminal justice system that white-collar offenders are ill equipped to adjust to the rigors of prison life. According to the special sensitivity hypothesis, the claim is made that white-collar offenders experience the pains of imprisonment to a greater degree than traditional street offenders.

Upon incarceration, they lose their direct influence and authority over people in business and private life, they lose their direct access to resources that enable them to do almost whatever they like, and they lose their self-identity characterized by position, trust and profession. They enter a world that is foreign to them. They leave a hierarchy in society where they held positions at the top and join a hierarchy in prison where they are far from the top. Those with physical prowess and criminal connections – such as members of global biker gangs – rule prison life. White-collar offenders find few of the equals with whom they have socialized most of their lives so far. The majority in most prisons is populated by poor and minority group members. In Northern European prisons, for example, the majority consists of refugees and immigrants who ended up on the wrong side of the law.

Stadler et al. (2013) argue that the special sensitivity of white-collar offenders has been cited as a reason for the supposed leniency with which they have been punished traditionally. Their argument is based on a study by Mann et al. (1979), who found that American judges handed down lighter sentences to white-collar criminals because of an a priori assumption that they would not cope well with the prison environment. Judges apparently assumed that white-collar offenders were not socialized into the ways of the majority of the prison population simply because they come from the upper echelon of society. It was therefore assumed that the experience from arrest to imprisonment would be especially traumatic for white-collar criminals compared to street criminals.

The special sensitivity hypothesis assumes that the transition from a life of freedom and privilege to one of strict regulation and material deprivation is likely to be particularly shocking to newly incarcerated white-collar inmates. The hypothesis implies that white-collar offenders have more to lose than other offenders by going to prison. The hypothesis considers as extra burden the stigmatization experienced as a result of prestigious job loss, media coverage of the court case, asset recovery by the government, family breakup, reputation damage within the community, withdrawn professional licenses and dismissal from the elite. The hypothesis suggests that these circumstances far exceed what street criminals have to go through after detection and conviction (Logan, 2015).

The idea that white-collar offenders are especially sensitive to the pains of imprisonment was developed with high-status offenders in mind. The idea stems from the fact that they differ substantially from other offenders with respect to their social and other background characteristics, as well as their experience with the criminal justice system (Logan, 2015: 11):

> In light of these differences, members of the criminal justice community– namely judges – have argued that indoctrination to prison life is particularly shocking for newly incarcerated white-collar offenders. Similarly, these individuals maintain that typical street offenders, who often come from more disadvantaged backgrounds, are far less susceptible to the pains of imprisonment.

Stadler et al. (2013: 1092) formulate the idea in a similar way, where the special sensitivity hypothesis is based on the undeniable fact that white-collar offenders are different from street offenders with regard to their backgrounds:

> Because they would be transitioning from a life of freedom and privilege to a life with little or no liberty and possessions, incarceration is assumed to be especially shocking for white-collar offenders. In contrast, street offenders typically live more deprived lives and would therefore experience less of a culture shock upon incarceration.

Mann et al. (1979: 487) interviewed judges to explore their reasons and motivations for the special sensitivity hypothesis and got answers like the two following responses:

> A white-collar criminal has more of a fear of going to jail than this syndrome we find in the street crime. And I am not saying that if you cut everyone they don't bleed red blood. A person who commits a robbery or an assault, they don't want to go to jail either. But the white-collar criminal has more to lose by going to jail; reputation in community, business as well as social community, decent living conditions, just the whole business of being put in a prison with a number on his back demeans this tremendous ego that is always involved in people who are high achievers.
>
> It can be a major disruption for the family, for the individual. It may undermine his whole career. I can probably better understand the white-collar defendant. He is more like me and that probably – I guess I do believe that white-collar defendants are more sensitive to and more affected by the prison experience.

Defense attorneys are active supporters of the special sensitivity hypothesis. Their support comes as no surprise, since the magnitude of billable hours involved in white-collar defense far exceeds what is feasible in street crime defense. Often, attorneys are hired to contribute symbolic defense and information control, in addition to substance defense. They continue to work for their clients after conviction (Gottschalk, 2014). Stadler et al. (2013: 1094) found that

> Almost without exception, defense attorneys argue that merely convicting a white-collar offender results in enough suffering. Prison, it is argued, would be an especially difficult hardship for these individuals because of their social background.

The special sensitivity hypothesis may seem particularly relevant in prison settings that are poorly managed and marked by high levels of inmate violence and other forms of victimization. In such environments, white-collar inmates can prove attractive targets and be neglected by lack of guardianship (Stadler et al., 2013).

## Sensitivity testing

The special sensitivity hypothesis has been tested by Dhami (2007) in the United Kingdom and by Stadler et al. (2013) and Logan (2015) in the United States. None of these three empirical studies found any support for the hypothesis that white-collar offenders have a special sensitivity to imprisonment.

Dhami (2007) explored how white-collar prisoners perceived the reactions of the judiciary, media, significant others, prison staff and other inmates towards them and how these offenders perceived their own offending behavior. The study in the United Kingdom indicates that it may be easier for a white-collar criminal than a street criminal to spend time in prison. Interviews with 14 white-collar offenders revealed that they perceived the reaction from the criminal justice system and the media as negative, but the reaction of others, including other inmates, as positive.

Stadler et al. (2013: 1101) found no support for the suggestion that white-collar offenders experience more pain and cope less well within the society of captives:

> Based on a sample of 366 federal prison inmates, we assessed the special sensitivity hypothesis. The analysis revealed that white-collar inmates are not more likely to experience negative prison adjustment. In some regards, white-collar inmates had fewer institutional problems and were more likely to cope with prison life successfully. Results thus call into question the merits of the special sensitivity hypothesis and are consistent with the view expressed earlier by Michael Benson and Francis Cullen that white-collar offenders may possess attributes and resources sufficient for their successful adaptation to life in prison.

Stadler et al. (2013) measured inmate adjustment to prison by statements such as: (i) experience difficulties in prison; (ii) trouble sleeping; (iii) evidence of need for safety in prison; (iv) problems with current or former cellmate; and (v) having no friends in prison. Response analysis indicates that white-collar offenders in the United States are not more likely to experience prison adjustment problems than non-white-collar offenders. For two of the five measures, white-collar inmates were significantly less likely to experience problems. Fewer white-collar offenders experienced general prison difficulties compared to the general inmate group, and a larger percentage of white-collar offenders made friends in the prison. Fewer white-collar offenders experienced problems with former or current cellmates. White-collar offenders seemed less in need of safety in prison.

Logan (2015) used nationally representative prison data based on inmates' self-reports in the United States and studied four domains of prison life:

- Victimization: Were inmates injured in a fight, assault or incident in which someone tried to hurt them? No difference was found between white-collar and non-white-collar inmates with respect to experiencing victimization in prison.
- Prison conduct: Had inmates violated prison rules and been subject to disciplinary action? Compared to other inmates, white-collar criminals showed

significantly less substance abuse-related misconduct. White-collar offenders were significantly less likely than other inmates to be written up for carrying weapons. White-collar offenders were less likely than other inmates to be involved in verbal or physical altercations with prison staff.
- Psychological adjustment: Did inmates have feelings of negative affect, receive treatment for mental health disorders and experience symptoms of mental health disorder? White-collar offenders were no more likely than other inmates to develop feelings of negative affect while incarcerated. White-collar offenders were no more likely to be in need of mental disorder treatment.
- Participation in prison programs: Did inmates participate in employment counseling and life skills and community adjustment classes? White-collar offenders were more likely than other inmates to score higher on the program participation scale.

As an alternative to the special sensitivity hypothesis, Logan (2015) introduced the special resilience hypothesis. Resilience is the ability to cope with change. White-collar criminals may in fact fare better in prison than other inmates. White-collar offenders often have greater amounts of personal and social capital, including higher levels of education and closer ties to family than other offenders. They are more likely to adopt non-criminal identities. White-collar inmates may have greater emotional and psychological resources than other inmates. Such factors can be linked to reduced stress in prison.

## The Kerik case

Some white-collar criminals write their autobiographies in prison or afterwards. Examples include Bogen (2008), Eriksen (2010), Fosse and Magnusson (2004), and Kerik (2015). Bernard B. Kerik was a former police commissioner in New York, who served three years in prison. His book entitled "From Jailer to Jailed: My Journey from Correction and Police Commissioner to Inmate #84888-054" is an interesting object for content analysis concerning the special sensitivity hypothesis versus the special resilience hypothesis.

Content analysis can be defined as any methodology or procedure that works to identify specific characteristics within texts attempting to make valid inferences (Krippendorff, 1980; Patrucco et al., 2017). Content analysis assumes that language reflects both how people understand their surroundings and their cognitive processes. Therefore, content analysis makes it possible to determine how a white-collar offender understands personal experiences as an inmate (McClelland et al., 2010).

Chapter 18 in Kerik's (2015: 249) book seems to be the most interesting and relevant part for our study. It is entitled "From the Inside" and starts with the following paragraph:

> If you think that a federal prison camp is some kind of resort, think again. There will be no need to bring your golf clubs or swim trunks, just plenty

**16** White-collar crime research

of hand sanitizer and a big wad of cash if you want to avoid catching a flesh-eating MRS disease and you want to remain in contact with the outside world via telephone or email. The place will invariably be a disgusting shithole.

However, chapter 18 is not that interesting after all. Kerik uses the chapter to tell the nation how the prison system can be improved based on his experience. Everyone knows that you cannot generalize from a single observation. Therefore, we needed to search other places in the book for evidence of the special sensitivity hypothesis versus the special resilience hypothesis.

Former New York City police commissioner Bernard B. Kerik (born 1955) pleaded guilty to eight financial crime charges including tax evasion and corruption. He was sentenced to 48 months in federal prison and three years of supervised release. He arrived at the Federal Correctional Institution in Cumberland, Maryland on May 17, 2010.

It is hard to find evidence of the special sensitivity hypothesis. Evidence of the special resilience hypothesis, on the other hand, is easy to find. This is a typical example (Kerik, 2015: 33):

> I often stayed up until midnight or 1:00 a.m. reading and writing in my bunk. Like a lot of guys, I slept with earplugs in, just trying to shut it all out. I walked or ran most days around the grass and gravel track outside, summer and winter. Five times around was a mile (...)
>
> About a year and a half into my sentence I met a new inmate, Joe Burchfield from Rhode Island. Joe and I used to walk the track together. A former city councilman, he'd been arrested and charged with bribery. Out of all the men I met at Cumberland, he turned out to be one of the best.

One possible trace of the special sensitivity hypothesis can be found in the following paragraph (Kerik, 2015: 29):

> No matter what you have been incarcerated for, or how long your sentence, the one thing that is certain is that you will immediately be cut off from the outside world, including from those you love and anyone or anything that depended on you. No matter what problem or emergency might arise, no matter how devastating a circumstance might be for your family and children, the only thing you can do from prison is watch their suffering from afar and pray for them to get through it on their own.

Kerik's (2015) autobiography is an interesting book about his stunning fall from grace that brought him painfully through the criminal justice system and landed him in prison for several years. Overall, the book is evidence of the special resilience hypothesis rather than the special sensitivity hypothesis for white-collar offenders.

## Convenience theory

Convenience theory suggests that white-collar criminals have a strong convenience orientation (Gottschalk, 2016a, b, c, d, 2017). The theory of convenience attempts to integrate various theoretical explanations for the occurrence of white-collar crime from sociology, psychology, management, organizational behavior, criminology and other related fields to shed light on different perspectives of convenience. Convenience is a relative concept concerned with the efficiency in time and effort as well as reduction in pain and solution to problems (Engdahl, 2015; Gottschalk, 2017). Convenience orientation refers to a person's general preference for maneuvers characterized by avoidance of pain and savings in time and effort. A convenience-oriented person is one who seeks to accomplish a task in the shortest time with the least expenditure of human energy. A convenient individual is not necessarily bad nor lazy. On the contrary, the person can be seen as smart and rational in spending time and effort where it matters most for the individual or the organization (Sundström and Radon, 2015).

Inmates with a strong convenience orientation favor actions and behaviors with inherent characteristics of saving time and effort. They have a desire to spend as little time as possible on challenging issues and situations that may occur in prison. They have an attitude that the less effort needed the better, and they think that it will be a waste of time to spend a long time on a problem. They prefer to avoid the problem rather than handle it. They want to avoid discomfort and pain. They want to survive prison life in the best possible way. Convenience motivates the choice of action and behavior. An important element is avoiding more problematic, stressful and challenging situations.

Convenience can be both an absolute construct and a relative construct. As an absolute construct, it is attractive to commit financial crime as such. As a relative construct, it is more convenient to commit crime than to carry out alternative actions to solve a problem or gain benefits from an opportunity. Convenience is an advantage in favor of a specific action to the detriment of alternative actions. Blickle et al. (2006) found that if the rationally expected utility of an action by a white-collar offender clearly outweighs the expected disadvantages resulting from the action, thereby leaving some net material advantage, then the offender will commit the offense in question.

In conclusion, the special sensitivity hypothesis often argued by white-collar defense lawyers and members of the elite finds little support in empirical studies of white-collar inmates versus street crime inmates. Instead, the special resilience hypothesis finds support, where white-collar inmates have the ability to adapt to prison life without much pain. The theory of convenience provides a basis for the special resilience hypothesis, because white-collar offenders tend to have a strong convenience orientation to avoid pain and waste of energy.

# 2
# THEORY OF CONVENIENCE

As suggested by Gottschalk (2017), white-collar crime can be a convenient option to avoid threats and exploit opportunities. Convenience is a concept that was theoretically mainly associated with efficiency in timesaving. Today, convenience is associated with a number of other characteristics, such as reduced effort and reduced pain. Convenience is associated with terms such as fast, easy and safe. Convenience says something about attractiveness and accessibility (Sundström and Radon, 2015).

Convenience is characterized by some comfortable practicality. It is simple and not necessarily bad or illegal. For example, ship-owners can register their boats under flags of convenience, which is sailing under a false flag to reap economic benefits that might otherwise not be achievable. Convenience can be "tricking out" without traces of obvious crime, lying in the gray zone and exploiting the system for organizational or personal gain and pleasure. Convenience can be causing enrichment in an easy and comfortable manner without losing face or reputation (as long as the offender is not revealed). In academic research, some researchers use convenience samples – that is, readily available respondents – for their empirical studies. The selection is not random and cannot be said to be representative of the population. It is unacceptable to generalize research results based on such samples. Another example is the convenience store – the grocery shop or a gas station – where consumer goods are easily available and accessible but prices are higher and the selection is more limited (Sari et al., 2017).

Convenience orientation is the value that individuals and organizations place on actions with inherent characteristics of saving time and effort. Convenience orientation is a value-like construct that influences behavior and decision-making. Mai and Olsen (2016) measured convenience orientation in terms of a desire to spend as little time as possible on the task and the attitude that the less effort needed the better and that it is a waste of time to spend a long time on the task. Convenience orientation towards illegal actions increases as negative attitudes towards legal actions increase. The basic elements of convenience orientation are the executive attitudes to the saving of time, effort and discomfort in the planning, action and achievement of goals. Generally, convenience orientation is the degree to which an executive is inclined to save time and effort to reach goals. Convenience orientation refers to a person's general preference for convenient maneuvers. A convenience-oriented person is one who seeks to accomplish a task in the shortest possible time with the least expenditure of human energy (Berry et al., 2002).

The actual convenience is not necessarily important in convenience theory. Rather, the perceived, expected and assumed convenience influences choice of action. Berry et al. (2002) make this distinction explicit by conceptualizing convenience as individuals' time and effort perceptions related to an action. White-collar criminals probably vary in their perceived convenience of their actions. Low expected convenience could be one of the reasons why not more members of the elite commit white-collar offenses.

## Theory development

Theory is a necessary part of research in organization sciences (Ashkanasy, 2016), and convenience theory emphasizes the organizational opportunity to commit and conceal white-collar crime. Theory is a systematic, interrelated set of concepts that explain a body of data. In convenience theory, three main concepts explain the occurrence of white-collar crime: financial motive, organizational opportunity and personal willingness. These concepts are all interrelated as organizational opportunity interacts with financial motive and personal willingness. Interactions between motive, opportunity and willingness determine the extent of convenience perceived by a potential white-collar crime offender.

Theory is a way of imposing conceptual order on the empirical complexity of the phenomenal world. Convenience theory offers a conceptual order on financial crime by members in the elite in society who certainly do not need to commit crime for their survival. Theory offers a statement of relations between concepts within a set of boundary assumptions and constraints. Convenience theory makes assumptions about human behavior, such as individuals' motives and desires as well as individuals' behaviors in organizational contexts. A theory reflects the magnitude of a discipline's knowledge base. Convenience theory reflects and builds on a knowledge base from criminology, psychology, management, strategy and many other disciplines.

Theory does more than abstract and organize knowledge. It also signals the values upon which that knowledge is built (Suddaby, 2014). In white-collar crime research, a number of values are at stake. For example, not all are equal before the law. Some are simply too powerful to jail (Pontell et al., 2014). Ever since Sutherland (1939) coined the term white-collar crime, researchers in the field have emphasized the value of preventing and detecting elite crime. Therefore, an important value signaled by convenience theory is that white-collar crime is just as bad as – and maybe even much worse than – traditional street crime including rape, murder and theft, since offenders' motive is found in their choice of convenience with no regard to harm and victims. This signal from white-collar crime research is still controversial today. It seems that many consider white-collar criminals as individuals who were unlucky, who made a mistake that was not intentional, who made a short cut in a stressed job situation and who should not be considered crooks. According to Leap (2007), white-collar crime imposes a degree of physical and emotional trauma on its victims that far exceeds the trauma inflicted by street criminals.

Developing theory is neither easy nor ever completed. Theory development is defined by Weick (1989) as disciplined imagination, where theory is an ordered set of assertions about a generic behavior or structure assumed to hold throughout a significantly broad range of specific instances. The generic behavior in white-collar crime can be found in the abuse of power, influence and trust by offenders, and the generic structure is visible in the organizational context among convicted offenders.

There are a number of interactions between dimensions in the theory of crime convenience. For example, opportunity enhances temptation (Steffensmeier and Allan, 1996: 478): "An illegitimate enterprise, being able tends to make one more willing, just as being willing increases the prospects for being able".

Thus, the organizational dimension of opportunity influences the desire for financial gain in the economic dimension. Opportunity also influences the behavioral willingness, while the behavioral willingness in turn influences abilities in terms of organizational opportunities.

## Financial motive

Threat of bankruptcy or threat of other kinds of financial loss is a frequent economical motive for white-collar crime. According to Piquero (2012), the fear of falling is strong among members of the elite. Kouchaki and Desai (2015: 362) found that the threat of falling may lead to unethical behavior: "Perceived threat engenders self-protective defenses that cause people to focus narrowly on their own needs, which interfere with adherence to moral principles and encourage unethical acts". They also suggest (Kouchaki and Desai, 2015) that people experiencing anxiety, nervousness and worry are likely to behave selfishly and engage in self-interested unethical acts in an effort to restore the threatened self. Individuals experiencing threats tend to focus inward and acquire resources as a means of compensating for threats. In threatening situations, the brain tends to shift into a state that facilitates mobilization of defense mechanisms. Threats are typically characterized by the salience of risk of loss. Threats tend to bring about socially undesirable actions geared towards self-protection. To cope with threat, people rely on a variety of potential mechanisms to shield themselves from negative experiences and unpleasant feelings and, ultimately, to protect their self-esteem.

Threats can create moral panic. Moral panic is used to characterize reactions that do not accurately reflect the actual danger of a threat. During a moral panic, sensitization processes generate an escalation in the individual disturbance (Kang and Thosuwanchot, 2017).

Chattopadhyay et al. (2001) studied organizational actions in response to threats. They found that threats are associated with urgency, difficulty and high stakes. Threats involve a negative situation in which loss is likely and over which one has relatively little control.

A possibility implies a positive situation in which gain is likely and over which one has a fair amount of control, which is at the same time characterized by urgency, difficulty, and high stakes (Chattopadhyay et al., 2001).

When an organization develops and maintains a strong systematic socialization program, employees identify with not only the organization but also its goals. When personal promotion or dismissal, as well as bonuses and benefits, are connected to achievement of goals, then employees identify even more strongly with organizational goals. When the socialization process is coupled with strong accountability systems, employees are regulated to achieve organizational goals. The pursuit of goals does not at all imply the absence of crime. The bottom-line focus within an organizational context might increase the frequency of financial crime on behalf of the organization for profit or enhancement. A strong emphasis on goal attainment might indeed lead organizational members to engage in illegal acts (Kang and Thosuwanchot, 2017).

Kang and Thosuwanchot (2017: 501) tell the following story:

> Philip R. Bennett joined Refco Inc. in 1981, becoming the chief financial officer (CFO) in 1983 and heading it as the chief executive officer (CEO) since 1998 following the retirement of Thomas Dittmer, the stepson of the company's founder. Bennett was asked to leave the company when federal prosecutors accused him of a "massive securities fraud, charging him with a scheme to hide a debt of as much as $545 million that he allegedly tried to keep secret from investors". In 2008, Bennett pleaded guilty to the charges and was sentenced to 16 years in prison.
>
> Having been in Refco Inc. for more than 24 years and coupled with the helming of two high-ranking positions – CFO and ultimately CEO and chairman – Bennett's identification with the goals of Refco Inc. can be considered to be high. In other words, having spent sufficient time in a position of power in Refco Inc. with the ability to influence the company's direction, Bennett was highly socialized into the goals of the company.
>
> One of Refco Inc's key goals was to go public to raise funds. The company engaged reputable institutions (i.e. Credit Suisse First Boston, Goldman Sachs Group, and Bank of America Corp.) to underwrite its IPO in 2005. However, Bennett committed illegal acts to make Refco Inc. more attractive as an investment option in the public listing.

## Organizational opportunity

Persons at the pinnacle of a corporate hierarchy (or just about any hierarchy, for that matter) who have considerable authority are not often challenged, insist upon results and are accustomed to getting their way. Therefore, various forms of dishonest and illegal behavior that elite members engage in seem to be convenient for the offenders. They believe they can ignore various reservations they would have if they were lower down in the power structure and if they were expected to demonstrate leadership and achieve ethical results. Greed, self-importance, immunity from criticism, fondness for getting one's way and fear of falling all contribute to the convenience of white-collar crime in the organizational setting. An offender is in a position to point to the importance of one's place in the organizational hierarchy, one's ability to cover one's tracks, blame others or insist on deniability, and the pressure to achieve results. White-collar criminals tend to engage in various rhetorical strategies to make it sound to their subordinates as though they have done nothing wrong.

Organizational dynamics is an interesting perspective on white-collar crime. Organizational dynamics can cause a downward spiral, leading to misconduct and crime. In the downward spiral, the tendency to commit white-collar crime increases. It becomes more convenient to commit crime than pursue alternative actions when crises or opportunities emerge. Convenience theory suggests that white-collar crime can be an attractive option for executives and others in the elite. In this section, negative organizational dynamics is explained by institutional theory, social disorganization theory, slippery slope theory, neutralization theory and differential association theory.

As argued by Ashkanasy et al. (2017), organizations are intrinsically human entities. Processes that drive human thought and behavior also drive organizations. If deviant behavior is preferred by some and accepted by others, then deviance may drive an organization. When a leader implicitly or explicitly defines misconduct and crime as acceptable, followers will tend to do the same. In the organizational setting, there is no organizational or corporate crime that is not driven by human thought and behavior.

The opportunity perspective is thus more than just an organization lacking control over its members. There are dynamics among members, where some prefer convenient solutions to problems and challenges even when the solutions imply breaking the law. The organization is a community of practice where individuals merge into groups and departments to complete tasks and reach goals in ways that establish themselves over time through dynamic interactions among organizational members.

In their article on organizational dynamics as a way to understand the causes and effects of top management fraud, Zahra et al. (2007: 128) emphasize organization-level pressures: "Without stockholder monitoring, some executives may act opportunistically and enrich themselves while foregoing stockholder-desired, long-term value creating activities for their firms".

## Organizational dynamics

Organizational dynamics may over time create a culture for misconduct and crime (Zahra et al., 2007: 129):

> Over time, some organizations can develop deviant cultures in which wrongdoing is rationalized and institutionalized. These organizations are often led by leaders who tolerate unethical behavior and conceal corrupt practices. These leaders might also encourage gamesmanship and political maneuvering as a means of getting ahead.

As argued by Uhl-Bien and Carsten (2007: 189), it is difficult to be ethical when the boss is not:

> The eye-opening results of the Milgram studies of authority in the early 1960s show the pervasiveness of this dynamic. These studies, which have received widespread attention from both social scientists and the general public, demonstrate that individuals are willing to inflict negative, even harmful, treatment on others simply at the request of an authority figure. Milgram found that when individuals see another as an authority figure (in position of power) and / or having expertise the individual does not have, they will blindly obey commands – even those that lead to blatant negative consequences.

In his discussion of the dynamics of white-collar crime, Leap (2007: 42) also emphasizes organizational culture:

> Corrupt organizational cultures have been cited as a root cause for major corporate scandals. Among the most significant causes of this corruption are executives and managers who fail to serve as ethical role models and set a bad example for others. When the CEO and other top executives engage in fraud or the misappropriation of assets, some lower-level managers and employees will take notice and follow suit.

Institutional collapse is one kind of organizational dynamic that makes it possible for white-collar crime to occur more frequently. According to institutional theory, the organizational context, behaviors and processes may support white-collar crime. Organizational behaviors reflect a culture that evolves over time and becomes legitimized within an organization (Itzkovich and Heilbrunn, 2016). Corruption and other kinds of financial crime become entrenched by the legitimizing process (Pillay and Kluvers, 2014; Rostami et al., 2015).

While the theory of institutional collapse is concerned with breakdown caused in interaction with external forces (Shadnam and Lawrence, 2011), the theory of social disorganization is concerned with collapse caused only by internal forces.

Social disorganization leads to the breakdown of conventional social norms. The gradual erosion of conventional relationships weakens the organization and makes it unable to satisfy the needs of its members. The organization gradually loses the ability to control the behavior of its members. There is no functional authority over potential white-collar criminals in the organization (Wood and Alleyne, 2010). As a consequence of social disorganization, organizational opportunity to commit white-collar crime increases (Hoffmann, 2002; Swart and Kinnie, 2003).

Slippery slope theory is a third theoretical perspective on organizational dynamics as enabler of white-collar crime. Slippery slope means that a person "slides" over time from legal to illegal activities. Arjoon (2008: 78) explains slippery slope in the following way:

> As commonsense experience tells us, it is the small infractions that can lead to the larger ones. An organization that overlooks the small infractions of its employees creates a culture of acceptance that may lead to its own demise. This phenomenon is captured by the metaphor of the slippery slope. Many unethical acts occur without the conscience awareness of the person who engaged in the misconduct. Specifically, unethical behavior is most likely to follow the path of a slippery slope, defined as a gradual decline in which no one event makes one aware that he or she is acting unethically. The majority of unethical behaviors are unintentional and ordinary, thus affecting everyone and providing support for unethical behavior when people unconsciously lower the bar over time through small changes in their ethical behavior.

Welsh et al. (2014) argue that many recent scandals can be described as resulting from a slippery slope in which a series of small infractions gradually increase over time. Committing small indiscretions over time may gradually lead people to commit larger unethical acts they would otherwise have judged to be impermissible.

The slippery slope theory is in contrast to individual theories such as the standard economic model of rational choice theory as described in the economic dimension. Moral behavior is shaped by psychological and organizational processes, where individuals are motivated to view themselves in a positive manner that corresponds with their moral values. Individuals tend to rationalize minor unethical acts so that they may derive some benefit without being forced to negatively update their self-concept. For example, a minor transgression such as taking a pen home from the office may seem permissible, whereas taking money out of the company cash drawer may more clearly be thought of as stealing (Welsh et al., 2014).

A fourth theoretical perspective on organizational dynamics as enabler of white-collar crime is neutralization theory (Sykes and Matza, 1957). For example, in religious organizations there is evidence that misconduct and crime can be rationalized by higher loyalties. When the Catholic Church in Norway was caught with a long list of individuals who were not members of the church, they refused to pay back subsidies to the government. Tjørholm (2016: 12), a professor of religion at a university in Norway, argued that in some situations the Catholic Church seems to decouple itself from the common moral and social obligations:

> The indictment against Oslo Catholic diocese was recently announced. The chief financial officer is accused of serious fraud, with a maximum possible sentence of six years. For the Oslo Catholic diocese, the allegation means a fine of one million Norwegian kroner. Bishop Bernt Eidsvig avoided indictment because there is insufficient evidence of guilt. Leadership of the Oslo Catholic diocese undoubtedly adopted reprehensible methods when it registered members as the basis for attracting state subsidies.

A fifth and final perspective is dynamics created by differential association. The essence of differential association is that criminal behavior is learned, and the main part of this learning comes from within important personal groups. Exposure to the attitudes of members of the organization that either favor or reject legal codes influences the attitudes of the individual. The individual will go on to commit crime if they are more exposed to attitudes that favor law violation than to attitudes that favor abiding by the law (Hoffmann, 2002; Wood and Alleyne, 2010).

Negative organizational dynamics can be explained by institutional theory, social disorganization theory, slippery slope theory, neutralization theory, differential association theory and other theories. Institutional collapse causes a negative spiral, social disorganization causes loss of overview, slippery slope causes ignorance, neutralization causes rationalization, while differential association causes crime identity. Dynamics are created by feedback loops that reinforce deviant behaviors.

Based on this section, there are several avenues for future research. An attractive avenue would be to conduct a longitudinal study of a business or public organization in terms of organizational deterioration caused by negative organizational dynamics. Such a case study could illustrate impacts on white-collar crime occurrence from various theoretical perspectives. Another avenue for future research could be to build a model of influencing factors on white-collar crime magnitude in causal relationships and feedback loops that represent negative organizational dynamics. A third avenue could be a cross-sectional analysis of a sample of companies where CEOs have been convicted of white-collar crime.

This section has illustrated that organizational dynamics can be an interesting perspective on white-collar crime. White-collar crime was described in terms of convenience theory, where crime is a convenient option when there is a financial motive, an organizational opportunity and behavioral willingness. Negative organizational dynamics can strengthen the financial motive and increase behavioral willingness, as well as adding organizational opportunity. For example, the willingness in the behavioral dimension of convenience theory increases as individuals notice that misconduct and crime are no longer considered an abuse of position and power.

## Management control

"That's how they taught us to do it". This is a phrase illustrating learned deviance and inadequate deterrence. Leasure and Zhang (2017) studied reports of Wells Fargo and Morgan Stanley engagement in widespread fraudulent sales practices in the retail banking industry. They found that the underlying deviance had been taught by senior management and that new employees were taught these fraudulent practices. Furthermore, they found that ethics and compliance practices and policies were largely ineffective in curtailing such conduct. Wells Fargo was fined $185 million for fraudulently opening accounts. Wells Fargo opened as many as two million fake accounts in an effort to meet wildly unrealistic sales goals.

Within the opportunity perspective on white-collar crime, we find routine activity theory that focuses on situations of crime. The premise of routine activity theory is that crime is relatively unaffected by social causes such as poverty, inequality and unemployment. The theory stipulates three necessary conditions for crime: a likely offender, a suitable target and the absence of a capable guardian, coming together in time and space (Felson and Boba, 2017). The existence or absence of a likely guardian represents an inhibitor or facilitator for crime. The premise of routine activity theory is that crime is to a minor extent affected by social causes such as poverty, inequality and unemployment. Motivated offenders are individuals who are not only capable of committing criminal activity but willing to do so. Suitable targets can be some things that are seen by offenders as particularly attractive.

When introducing routine activity theory, Cohen and Felson (1979) concentrated upon the circumstances in which offenders carry out predatory criminal acts. Most criminal acts require convergence in space and time of (1) likely offenders, (2) suitable targets, and (3) the absence of capable guardians against crime. The lack of any of these elements is sufficient to prevent the successful completion of a crime. Though guardianship is implicit in everyday life, it is usually invisible in the absence of violations and is therefore easy to overlook. Guardians are not only protective tools, weapons and skills but also mental models in the minds of potential offenders that stimulate self-control to avoid criminal acts.

When compared to convenience theory, routine activity theory's three conditions do not cover all three dimensions. The likely offenders can be found in the behavioral dimension, while both suitable targets and the absence of capable guardians can be found in the organizational dimension. While routine activity theory defines conditions for crime to occur, convenience theory defines situations where crime occurs. White-collar crime only occurs when there is a financial motive in the economical dimension.

Those who are similar to the typical white-collar offender may be less likely to be concerned with white-collar offending than those who are not similar to the typical offender. Dearden (2017) found that it was reasonable to assume that for individuals who see themselves as in some way similar to white-collar criminals, their in-group status may mitigate their perceptions of white-collar crime. Similarity makes people accept each other.

When white-collar offenders commit occupational crime they may be attracted by the strong sense of superiority coming from having beaten the system without detection. They may blame the lack of controls for their own wrongdoings. They feel no attachment to the organization and no obligation to the employer. Rather, they enjoy the lack of socialization and lack of accountability that enables them to explore and exploit the organization for personal gain. Their deviance passes unnoticed by others, and their behavior is accepted by others (Kang and Thosuwanchot, 2017).

## Entrepreneurs in white-collar crime

Entrepreneurs are often seen as important economic agents, driving forward employment, opportunities and economic development. Entrepreneurship is associated with innovation, adaptation, change and dynamism, hard work, willpower, and overcoming challenges and struggles. According to Welter et al. (2017), entrepreneurship is a broadly available social technology for creating organizations that may pursue a myriad of goals. They argue that entrepreneurship research can and should be a window into and a tool for shaping social and economic equity.

In this line of reasoning, financial crime by white-collar criminals is an alternative tool for pursuing a large spectrum of social and economic goals. A typical example is corruption, where entrepreneurs on behalf of the organization bribe vendors, public officials and others to achieve goals. Another example is embezzlement, where entrepreneurs abuse their positions in organizations to enrich themselves.

Tonoyan et al. (2010) explored the determinants of corruption in transition economies and looked at the East–West gap in corruption in Europe. They found that viewing illegal business activities as a widespread business practice provides the rationale for entrepreneurs to justify their own corrupt activities. Moreover, closed social networks with family, friends and national bureaucrats reduce the opportunism of the contracting party of the corrupt deal, thus providing a breeding ground for corruption.

Eddleston and Kidwell (2012) studied deviant behavior in family firms that violates organizational norms. Examples are theft, embezzlement and corruption. Given that only 30 percent of family firms make it to the second generation, understanding how parents encourage children to act in deviant ways in the firm seems important. Rather than focusing on the child's personality as the cause of deviance, the study shows the importance of examining family relationships.

Entrepreneurs in white-collar crime demonstrate deviant behavior. Similar to moral entrepreneurs as discussed by Ryan (1994), white-collar crime requires both "technicians", who develop techniques of business-level enforcement of rules, and "interpreters", who legitimate the work of technicians by providing expansive readings of applicable legal limitations.

Entrepreneurs in white-collar crime are different from criminal entrepreneurs when criminal entrepreneurs are defined as entrepreneurs who are mainly on the wrong side of the law in their business endeavors. Entrepreneurs in white-collar crime demonstrate deviant behavior to benefit the organization, often labeled corporate crime, or to benefit the individual, often labeled occupational crime (Kang and Thosuwanchot, 2017). McElwee and Smith (2015) argue that illegal and criminal entrepreneurship is particularly context specific when it operates in the shadow economy. The shadow economy comprises those economic activities and the income derived from them that circumvent or otherwise avoid government regulation, taxation or observation (Schneider and Williams, 2013).

In the following, four case studies of convicted offenders illustrate entrepreneurs in white-collar crime based on convenience theory. Table 2.1 lists the four cases. The two first cases are presented extensively since there are internal investigations reports publicly available.

*Are Blomhoff* was educated as a priest and became chief executive officer (CEO) at the religiously based social foundation Betanien in Bergen, Norway. The foundation operates several nursing homes, kindergartens and health institutions associated with the Methodist Church. When he was 52 years old, CEO Blomhoff was in charge of developing a nursing home in Spain for older Norwegians. He got money transferred from Spain to Norway for the project. He had exclusive responsibility for all money transfers to Spain. He embezzled some of the transferred

**TABLE 2.1** White-collar criminals convicted of convenient embezzlement in Norway

| White-collar criminal | White-collar crime | Economical dimension (motive) | Organizational dimension (opportunity) | Behavioral dimension (deviance) |
|---|---|---|---|---|
| *Are Blomhoff* CEO Priest 52 years old | Embezzlement Betanien Foundation 3 years prison | Greed for private apartment and expensive parties | Exclusive responsibility for money transfers between mother company and subsidiary | Different behavior in Spain and Norway |
| *Lars Brorson* CFO 40 years old | Embezzlement Hadeland Broadband 4.5 years prison | Greed for expensive property and consumer goods | Exclusive responsibility for money transfers between Norway and Spain | Blamed lack of control mechanisms for his fraud |
| *Marius Schatvet* CFO 50 years old | Embezzlement Aschehoug Publishing 3 years prison | Divorced and wanted to keep house and cabin | Exclusive responsibility for money transfers in chain of bookstores | Dissatisfied with his salary level (owner made much more than him) |
| *Kjell Staddeland* CEO 50 years old | Embezzlement Ugland Shipping 3.5 years prison | Greed for living in the best house with parking space for 5 cars | Exclusive responsibility for money transfers in joint venture | Dissatisfied with his salary level (owner made much more than him) |

money to buy himself an apartment in Spain and to arrange expensive parties with prostitutes in Spain.

*Lars Brorson* was chief financial officer (CFO) at Hadeland Broadband, a subsidiary of Hadeland Energy. He came from a position at Hadeland Energy and had for a long time been in charge of financial transactions between Hadeland Energy and Hadeland Broadband. According to investigators from PwC (2014), Brorson sent a total of 18 million Norwegian kroner (about US$3 million) to his own accounts from Hadeland Broadband's overdraft account. Half of the amount was transferred in 2012, divided into 42 payments. Between 2011 and 2014, 66 such transactions were recorded.

*Marius Schatvet* was chief financial officer at the publishing house Aschehoug. When he was working alone on the entrepreneurial task of refinancing the publishing house's involvement in a chain of bookstores, he was able to transfer some of the money to his own account without anybody noticing. He did this for many years. Unfortunately for him, he finally typed in his own bank account number with a wrong digit, thereby attracting attention. An employee in the accounting department noticed the transaction and blew the whistle on CFO Schatvet. Schatvet was sentenced to three years in prison (Silvola et al., 2014).

*Kjell Rune Staddeland* was chief executive officer at Ugland Shipping. The Ugland family had owned the company for generations and was rich. Staddeland made the family even richer, while at the same time receiving a modest CEO compensation. When he was handling an entrepreneurial joint venture agreement for the company on his own, he found a way to embezzle. After a while, however, he regretted his crime and told the owner, who reported Staddeland to the police (Berglihn and Fosse, 2013).

Agency theory suggests that problems occur between principal and agent when there are (i) conflicting preferences, (ii) different knowledge and information, and (iii) different attitudes to risk (Bosse and Phillips, 2016). In their entrepreneurial activities, the sample of four convicted executives abused their powers. Mr. Blomhoff at Betanien was charged with the entrepreneurial task of establishing a nursing home in Spain. Mr. Brorson at Hadeland was charged with the entrepreneurial task of running broadband development while interacting with the energy company. Mr. Schatvet at Aschehoug was to reorganize the publishing house's involvement in a chain of bookstores, while Mr. Staddeland at Ugland was to reshape a joint venture. In all four cases they were alone in their endeavors. In all four cases the executives enriched themselves by committing white-collar crime and concealing their illegal transactions among legal transactions.

Obviously, the first problem in the agency relationship occurred because no principal appreciates embezzlement by agents. The second problem in principal–agent theory is the dominating one in the cases, where the principal has little or no means to control what the agent is doing. The third and final problem in agency theory seems less relevant, as the action of embezzlement does not really involve different principal and agent attitudes to risk.

White-collar crime is a convenient alternative for privileged individuals who want to enrich themselves. Their occupational positions enable them to commit offenses and conceal them among legal activities. This is especially the case when the offender has sole responsibility for a task involving substantial amounts of money, as illustrated by the four accounts above. One simple learning point from this section is that nobody – not even chair persons, chief executives or presidents – should ever have sole responsibility for tasks involving money on behalf of the organization.

## Behavioral willingness

Deviant behavior can be learned from others. In executive successions, cultural transmission tends to occur – for example, from a retiring chief executive officer (CEO) to an emerging CEO. Cultural transmission can explain why individuals who were reluctant to engage in deviant behavior may engage in misconduct and crime. Cultural transmission models may explain the passing on of misconduct behavior with regard to white-collar crime. Generally, such models explain transfer of cultural norms, values and belief systems that are transmitted between individuals or groups within and across generations. Transmission of criminal behavior across generations of executives occurs via a learning process with predecessors as well as in delinquent associations and peers. The principles of cultural transmission and differential association can be applied to corporate offending.

The concept of deviance is here an attribute of individuals, where we focus on negative forms of deviance in relation to white-collar crime within organizational contexts. Deviance is non-conformance to a norm that refers to any type of behavior that fails to meet normative standards and may evoke a collective response of a negative type. Negative deviance is intentional behavior that departs from the norms of a referent group in bad ways (Mertens et al., 2016).

Deviance is here both behavior and outcome, as behavior leads to crime. It is a departure from organizational norms in legal organizations, where organizational norms are informal or formal rules that regulate bandwidths and boundaries for behavior (Mertens et al., 2016).

Craig and Piquero (2017) studied two personality traits that sometimes predict offending intentions. Low self-control and desire-for-control are two personality traits that can have multiple effects on white-collar offending. Findings suggest that while low self-control was predictive of intentions to offend, the impact of desire-for-control varied based on the respondent's level of self-control. In contrast to prior studies, desire-for-control reduced offending intentions, but only among those with high self-control.

Self-control reflects an individual's capacity and motivation to override desires and urges in order to act in accordance with one's norms and goals, such as maintaining positive relationships with others. Soltes (2016: 54) suggests that "people with lower self-control have greater difficulty resisting temptation and restraining reckless behavior, and eventually some of this rash and opportunistic behavior is likely to end up as criminal conduct".

Liang et al. (2016) argue that effective human functioning requires the capacity to transcend primal desires and habitual behaviors in order to behave in a socially appropriate manner. When self-control fails, individuals disregard the long-term implications of their behaviors and succumb to their desires, such as cheating and bribing.

Liang et al. (2016: 1388) suggest that self-control is determined by two forces:

> The first is a primitive impulsive system wherein desire arises and drives behaviors, and the second is a higher-order reflective system wherein the desires and action tendencies that arise in the first primitive impulsive system are monitored and restrained.

White-collar offenders rationalize their own misconduct – misconduct through which they sought fast, desirable results by violating the rules but expected to get away with it.

Behavioral willingness can be high when the subjective detection risk is low. Detection risk is a combination of likelihood of detection and consequences after detection. Subjective detection risk varies among individuals.

Subjective detection risk is influenced by a number of factors. Attitudes towards police performance or effectiveness comprise one such factor. When white-collar offenders believe that the police are unable to solve crime, then the risk of criminal behavior is low. The police do not operate in a vacuum. They rely on community members to report crime, serve as witnesses in court and act as capable guardians over person and property. Police effectiveness is also based on the level of support that the community provides. Policing practice reveals that businesses that have suffered from financial crime have lower trust, confidence and satisfaction with law enforcement (Dowler and Sparks, 2008; Telep and Weisburd, 2012). Hence, the legitimacy of the police is often rooted in the level of corporate support they receive. For this reason, confidence in the police may actually impact levels of white-collar crime within private and public organizations.

On the other hand, collective efficacy in law enforcement may increase subjective detection risk. Collective efficacy holds that organizational members and stakeholders work collectively towards a common objective, such as crime control and order maintenance. The fundamental component of collective efficacy is the notion of social trust among all actors towards a common goal (Sampson et al., 1997). All members of the relevant communities work together to control crime through mutual trust. However, when trust or confidence in the police is either lacking or non-existent, the possibility of reducing actual levels of crime will be diminished.

Some white-collar criminals suffer from personality disorders such as psychopathy. Psychopathy can be characterized by fearlessness, antisocial behavior combined with high social attention seeking, immunity to stress, egoism and self-centered impulsivity (Blickle and Schütte, 2017).

The behavioral willingness to commit white-collar crime can be reversed when fraud is detected. Especially in cases of personality disorder, a possible outcome is detection suicide. Brody and Perri (2016: 786) tell the following story:

> To outsiders, Darrin Campbell was the picture of an unassuming prosperous executive. However, records show that Campbell was at the center of a securities fraud scandal that accompanied the collapse of Tampa-based Anchor Glass Container Corporation, then the third-largest manufacturer of glass containers in the USA. Shareholders accused him and other executives of failing to disclose financial weaknesses before a public stock offering, leading to lawsuits and a multimillion-dollar settlement. As part of the settlement, Campbell did not have to admit wrongdoing. Yet, after this incident, there were speculations that perhaps Campbell and his family were having financial problems. Campbell can be seen purchasing items that he would eventually use to kill and burn their home with. Campbell, with a handgun, eventually executed his 51-year-old wife, his 18-year-old son and 15-year-old daughter before burning down the family's home and shooting himself in the head. What transformed a 49-year-old executive into a methodical killer who eventually committed suicide?

Brody and Perri (2016) reflect on this question by discussing negative life events as a major cause of most suicides. Similarly, Kang and Thosuwanchot (2017) apply Durkheim's (1952) four categories of suicide that all have aspects of negative life events for white-collar offenders. First, the egoistic suicide is filled with apathy and indolent melancholy along with complacence. Second, the altruistic suicide is filled with the energy of passion or will and with calm feelings of duty, mystic enthusiasm or peaceful courage. Third, the anomic suicide is filled with irritation or disgust, with violent recriminations against life in general or against one particular person. Fourth, the fatalistic suicide is responding to excessive regulation, to passions violently choked by oppressive discipline and a future pitilessly blocked.

Personality disorder is characterized as enduring maladaptive patterns of behavior and experience that involve at least two of four areas: cognitive, affective, interpersonal, and/or control of impulse.

Craig (2017) tested Agnew's social concern theory by examining empathy's role on white-collar offenses. As Agnew argued, social concern elements can have both moderating and mediating effects with other causes of crime and empathy can interact with low self-control. The test showed that empathy had indirect effects on embezzlement through its reduction in self-control. Furthermore, empathy mediated effects of low self-control on credit card fraud.

## Occupational crime

Occupational white-collar crime is financial crime for personal gain. A trusted position as a professional or executive is abused by an offender to the detriment of the organization. A number of cases from the United States and Norway are presented in this section. The theory of convenience is introduced to explain white-collar crime, and white-collar crime is understood as a part of the shadow economy. In an empirical sample in Norway, the main victims of occupational crime are employers, customers, banks, tax authorities, and shareholders.

Occupational crime is financial crime for personal benefit. Individuals commit occupational crime for personal enrichment. They abuse their trusted positions in an organizational context (Friedrichs, 2002; Gottschalk and Rundmo, 2014; Hansen, 2009; Heath, 2008; Holtfreter, 2005; Kang and Thosuwanchot, 2017; Peltier-Rivest, 2009). Machen and Richards (2004) report that estimated occupational fraud and abuse in organizations in the United States amounted to $660 billion, or roughly 6 percent of their revenues in 2003.

Gottschalk and Rundmo (2014) found that occupational criminals receive a more severe punishment in court in terms of prison sentence, despite the fact that corporate criminals commit financial crime for far greater amounts of money. They speculate that judges consider offenders who enrich themselves to be worse criminals than offenders who enrich the organization illegally.

Occupational criminals can find their victims both internally in the organization and externally. For example, embezzlement can cause harm to an employer, while fraudulent statements can cause harm to a bank. Insider trading can cause harm to other shareholders, while tax evasion causes harm to society at large.

This section is concerned with the victims of occupational crime committed by white-collar offenders and with the harm done. Occupational crime, type and extent of harm, and victims are introduced first, followed by case studies of two convicted white-collar criminals in the United States. A sample of convicted occupational criminals in Norway is then presented, followed by case studies corresponding to the main victim categories: employers, tax revenue, customers, banks and shareholders.

Next, the theory of convenience is introduced to explain the white-collar crime phenomenon (Gottschalk, 2017), followed by an estimation of the shadow economy that white-collar crime is part of. Harm to victims of occupational crime committed by white-collar offenders is thus not only a matter of frequency but also a contribution to the underground economy, which causes damage to society both locally, and globally (Edelbacher et al., 2016).

## *Crime characteristics*

Occupational crime is committed for personal benefit. Hansen (2009) argues that the problem with occupational crime is that it is committed within the confines of positions of trust and in organizations, which prohibits surveillance and accountability. Heath (2008) found that individuals who are further up the chain of command in the firm tend to commit bigger and more serious occupational crime. According to Hansen (2009), individuals or groups commit occupational crime or elite crime for their own purposes or enrichment, rather than for the enrichment of the organization on a whole, in spite of supposed corporate loyalty. Occupational crime is offenses committed through opportunity created in the course of a privileged occupation in an organizational context. It involves abuses of structural systems in the workplace in order to accomplish various forms of white-collar crime (Sutherland, 1949). It is violation of the legal codes in the course of activity in a legitimate profession (Friedrichs, 2002). Occupational crime is committed on behalf of the individual offender. It is the use of one's occupation for personal enrichment through the deliberate misuse or misapplication of the employing organization's resources or assets (Holtfreter, 2005). It is committed by persons in an organizational setting for purely personal gain and to the detriment of the organization (Kang and Thosuwanchot, 2017). Any fraud committed by an employee, a manager or executive, or by the owner of an organization where the victim is the organization itself may be considered occupational fraud (Peltier-Rivest, 2009).

Occupational criminals tend to feel no attachment or loyalty to the organization (Kang and Thosuwanchot, 2017). They socialize with colleagues superficially, but they do not feel connected to their colleagues. Occupational criminals lack accountability and integrity. They are unaware of, ignore or disagree with, organizational goals. They claim that organizational failures, lack of controls, institutional collapse, management incompetence and other factors make them stimulated to crime. They may suggest that they are not fairly paid and therefore have to add something by themselves. Even though they are trusted and privileged individuals in the organization, white-collar criminals commit occupational crime because they feel no attachment to the organization.

Holtfreter (2005) finds that occupational crime is clandestine, it violates the perpetrator's fiduciary duties to the organization, it is committed for the purpose of direct or indirect financial benefit to the perpetrator and it costs the employing organization assets, revenues or reserves. Occupational crime is a violation of trust.

Holtfreter (2005) distinguishes between three mutually exclusive categories of occupational crime: asset misappropriation, corruption and fraudulent statements.

## *Types and extent of harm*

Kempa (2010) found that victims of fraud in Canada report high incidences of stress, anger, depression, loss and isolation – especially among those that lost more than $10,000. Further, trust in others is also often undermined because fraud is often initialized through an existing relationship of trust.

In a study of financial fraud in the private health insurance sector in Australia, Flynn (2016: 155) found present and future harm to the integrity of the insurance system:

> Fraud comprises the integrity of the private health insurance system, leaching from it millions of dollars every year. These losses are significant but given little public attention. A culture of denial exists among most politicians, health administrators, staff in insurance companies and the general public about the scale of the problem.

Otusanya (2012) studied financial criminal practices of the elite in developing countries and found that the questionable practices of the political and economic elite increase their capital accumulation but harm citizens. Harm to citizens occurs because the state–civil society relationship is distorted and because any accountability that the state might have to its citizens is eroded. State policy and state institutions tend to favor the particular interests of the elite rather than the general interests of society.

Peltier-Rivest (2009) found that the median fraud loss was $187,000 in Canada after fraud was committed by an employee in occupational crime. While asset misappropriations was the most frequent schemes, fraudulent financial statements were the most costly, with a median loss of $1 million and a mean loss of $2 million. The results also suggest that private companies and not-for-profit organizations suffer relatively larger fraud losses, with a median (mean) loss of, respectively, 7 percent (11 percent) and 11 percent (14 percent) of their annual sales. The results also indicate that organizations employing fewer than 100 employees sustain fraud losses representing a median of 11 percent of their sales and a mean of 19 percent of their sales. The smaller the organization the more likely fraud losses will be relatively larger.

Leasure and Zhang (2017: 2) found that the most common type of occupational crime is embezzlement, which is the appropriation of money for one's own benefit: "The use of computers has increased the amount of embezzlement as they make this crime easier to commit". Arrests for embezzlement in U.S. banking rose significantly as computers became the preferred way of doing financial business. Occupational crime can also be the simple theft of company supplies and products.

Leasure and Zhang (2017: 2) suggest that occupational crime can also be classified as professional occupational crime, which is committed by professionals such as lawyers, lawmakers or doctors in the course of their jobs: "For instance, doctors may steer patients to specialists or laboratories in which they have a financial interest or bill insurance companies for procedures that were not performed".

## *Crime victims*

Reisig and Holtfreter (2013) studied elderly victims of shopping fraud in the United States. They found that two forms of remote shopping – telemarketing purchase and mail-order purchase – increase the probability of becoming a victim of shopping fraud. The probability of becoming a target and victim of shopping fraud was affected positively by reduced levels of self-control.

Holtfreter et al. (2005) conducted a similar study of consumer fraud, where they looked at consumers' vulnerability. They found social vulnerability, where socially determined lifestyles and patterns of daily activities have an impact on vulnerability, especially interesting. Social status can potentially influence their attractiveness as fraud targets, and may also contribute to successful victimization once targeted.

Golladay (2017) studied victims of identity theft and found that victims are often much older than victims of violent and property crime. Identity theft victimization is most common between the ages of 25 and 64. Unlike many kinds of crime, identity theft victimization is not significantly different for men and women. Victimization varies based on income. Households that report an income of over $75,000 a year reported higher rates of victimization.

Lokanan (2017) studied the demographic profile of victims of investment fraud in Canada. The findings indicate that the victims were not particularly rich and a significant proportion borrowed money and opened margin accounts to invest. Those most vulnerable were investors who were retired and had limited investment knowledge. Many also dipped into their savings to fund their future retirement needs. Kempa (2010) suggests that one million adult Canadians (nearly 5 percent) have lost money to some kind of investment fraud.

Peltier-Rivest (2009) found that the most frequent victims of occupational fraud were private companies, followed by government entities and public companies.

Holtfreter et al. (2010) found that offending and victim populations overlap to some degree, suggesting that a common underlying factor partially explains both outcomes. They found that low self-control is associated with fraud offending. The findings also show that individuals with lower levels of self-control report that they are more likely to behave in ways that increase their exposure to fraud victimization. The overlap between fraud offending and victimization exposure is partially explained by low self-control. A similar result is presented by Holtfreter et al. (2008).

## *Yusuf Acar*

Yusuf Acar, a mid-level manager at the District of Columbia's office of the chief technology officer (OCTO) was arrested on March 12, 2009 and charged with bribery, conspiracy, money laundering and conflict of interest related to procurement improprieties. He was sentenced to two concurrent terms of 27 months in prison. During his guilty plea, Acar admitted that he accepted bribes on at least 59 occasions from Sushil Bansal, who owned a company called Advanced Integrated Technologies Corporation (AITC). Bansal paid Acar a total of more than half a million dollars. Sidley (2010) conducted an internal investigation of the case, while FBI (2010) conducted a criminal investigation of the case.

The main victim of Acar's scheme was his employer in Washington, DC. Other victims included AITC's competitors as well as employees at OCTO whose jobs were negatively influenced by the services provided by AITC. "The residents of the District of Columbia deserve an ethical government with ethical employees, and have the right to know that their money is being spent honestly and for the public good," said U.S. Attorney Machen (FBI, 2010).

The harm was not only overpriced IT services from AITC. The harm was also underperforming computer software supplied by AITC people. Because of the bribes, Acar made several procurements of both computer software and consulting services from AITC.

OCTO had 231 full-time employees and employed 267 contractors; most of them were full-time. OCTO had a longstanding contractor culture where contractors draw a salary from a third-party vendor that contracts with the District government. Contractors played a key role in managing numerous, simultaneous, one-time modernization projects.

Acar's occupational crime involved a series of loosely related fraudulent schemes that were not particularly complex according to fraud examiners Sidley (2010). They all escaped detection and would likely have remained undiscovered but for the cooperation of an informant.

Yusuf Acar had ample organizational opportunity to commit convenient white-collar crime:

- He was in charge of hiring consultants.
- He was in charge of buying software licenses.
- He was able to monitor emails by others.

Over time, Acar's schemes had grown more brazen, reflecting his growing confidence that there were no mechanisms in place to detect the fraud. The initial plan was a basic corruption scheme with kickbacks from Sushil Bansal's company, AITC, who had been awarded a contract to provide temporary contractors in the security division. Bansal had tendered a number of candidates, but Acar and his co-workers had initially rejected them as unqualified.

## Harriette Walters

Harriette Walters served as a tax assessments manager for the District of Columbia. She was convicted of being the central participant in the largest fraud scheme ever perpetrated by a government official in the District. In September 2008, Walters pleaded guilty to federal charges related to the theft of over $48 million of district funds. Counsel from Wilmer Cutler Pickering Hale and Dorr and forensic accounting advisors from PricewaterhouseCoopers were hired to investigate how Walters was able to embezzle 48 million of funds from the District of Columbia (WilmerHale and PwC, 2008).

Walters masterminded a nearly two-decade-long scheme in which she processed fraudulent real property tax refunds and arranged for the proceeds of those funds to be deposited into bank accounts controlled by her and her friends and family. For example, she cashed refund checks that were returned when the taxpayer recipient had died. She also fabricated several tax refund checks. It appeared that Walters had figured out that she had the last eyes on the tax refund check and operated with little monitoring (Stewart and Nakamura, 2007).

Because of the lack of monitoring, four managers were held responsible for failing to catch the fraud. The four managers resigned: deputy chief financial officer Sherryl Hobbs Newman, her deputy director Matthew Braman, the director of real property tax administration Martin A. Skolnik, and the chief assessor Thomas Branham (Stewart and Nakamura, 2007).

The investigation by WilmerHale and PwC (2008) had a mandate of determining how Walters was able to embezzle over nearly 20 years and recommending changes in controls, work environment and oversight structures that could help prevent future fraudulent schemes. The investigation should not attempt to trace the stolen money or determine how the money was distributed or spent. Nor did the mandate seek to determine the guilt or innocence of any participants in Walters' scheme. Federal authorities had addressed those issues.

The WilmerHale and PwC (2008) investigation involved three phases: (i) document and data collection; (ii) document and data review and analysis; and (iii) witness interviews. The investigators reviewed and analyzed more than 680,000 electronic and hard copy documents. They reviewed emails and other electronic documents associated with 87 current and former employees.

The second phase of the investigation involved a review of the collected documents and an analysis of the data included in the documents. WilmerHale and PwC reviewed documentation for manual real property tax refunds, including all refunds dating back to 1998, no matter the amount. Some 1,600 documents required more in-depth review because: (1) the identity of the refund recipient was fraudulent; the voucher packets reflecting the refund were issued to a legitimate business or entity, but the check was addressed to "care of" address related to several of Walters payees; (2) there was a lack of authorizing signatures; and (3) documentation did not correspond to the property or taxpayer listed as the recipient of the refund or was missing. In addition, WilmerHale and PwC closely scrutinized the following types of real property transactions:

- refunds over $10,000
- refunds that were to be held for taxpayer pick up and those issued to taxpayers that did not appear to own property in the District
- refunds ordered by the court for which an original court order with a raised seal did not accompany the refund documentation

Following the review of the refunds, WilmerHale and PwC analyzed the data in various tax systems, where they identified "refunds with characteristics consistent with refunds previously identified as fraudulent in court documents filed by the U.S. Attorney's Office". The analysis also identified suspicious refunds where hard copy documentation was not available, unclear or incomplete. The analysis of the Financial Management System ("FMS") revealed several refunds to entities or individuals involved in the Walters' scheme; unfortunately, hard copy records were unavailable. FMS was a system that processed refunds manually. It was replaced in October 1998 with the System of Accounting and Reporting ("SOAR"), which also required that refunds be processed manually.

A similar analysis of data in SOAR was conducted. Real property tax refund payments in the general ledger, which was housed in SOAR, were isolated and searched for refunds characteristic of fraud (i.e. known entities involved in the fraud scheme, refunds sent to "care of" addresses or coded "hold for pickup", etc.). Lastly, WilmerHale and PwC analyzed documentation for real property tax refunds processed through the Integrated Tax System, in order "to identify patterns of data and activity indicative of Walters' scheme". The system is an automated system that was introduced in 2005. It is composed of several applications, which supported the district's various tax types (i.e. personal income, business and real property tax). This system interacted with some of the District's relevant computer systems but not all. There was no direct interface between the system and SOAR, which meant entries from the system had to be manually entered into SOAR. The private investigation team discovered that Walters "manipulated the system to process fraudulent refunds at least twice".

In addition, WilmerHale and PwC requested copies of cancelled checks associated with the refunds previously identified during the review and those associated with all other real property tax refunds of $100,000 or more. Reviewing the cancelled checks allowed WilmerHale and PwC to determine whether the refunds were legitimate or illegitimate and to identify checks that "had been deposited at bank branches where known fraudulent refunds had been processed based on account information on the back of checks". They also compared endorsements to confirm or identify additional fraudulent refunds.

Finally, the private investigation team compared refunds in the SOAR general ledger with those from other databases. WilmerHale and PwC identified refunds that did not coincide with actual properties or property owners contained in the various systems. Furthermore, they "obtain[ed] additional information regarding the fraudulent nature of certain previously identified suspicious payments". This concluded the document review and data analysis.

The final phase of the investigation process was witness interviews, which supplemented the previous reviews and analyses. WilmerHale and PwC conducted interviews of over 70 individuals including: current and former Office of the Chief Financial Officer ("OCFO") employees, representatives of the Office of the District of Columbia Auditor, the Office of the Inspector General, the Office of Risk Management, the District's current and former independent auditors, and other third parties.

Upon completing the investigation, WilmerHale and PwC concluded that Walters perpetrated her lengthy fraud scheme due to a failure of controls, a dysfunctional work environment and a lack of oversight. The reliability of real property tax refunds process could not be ensured because no policies or procedures could be found within the Office of Tax and Revenue ("OTR"), which formally documented how real property tax refunds should be processed. If policies and procedures did exist managers and employees did not follow them consistently. Managers in the OTR did not test the refund process or take basic steps to examine real property tax refunds. In fact, when Walters began her scheme her managers in the Real Property Tax Administration ("RPTA") signed off on these refund vouchers without reviewing the attached documentation for legitimacy. "Worse, Walters' direct supervisor in 2003, evidently made clear in words or deeds that she no longer wished to sign off on real property tax refund vouchers at all". This failure of managers to exercise responsibility allowed Walters to process all real property tax refunds without review and approval from upper management. In addition, there was lack of automated controls.

WilmerHale and PwC (2008) formulated the following recommendations:

- Controls Improvement. Walters' scheme went undetected for such a long time in part because of the lack of sufficient controls, the failure of existing controls to operate effectively and the lack of management oversight of those controls.
- Systems Improvements. The vast majority of Walters' fraudulent refunds were processed manually.
- Work Environment Improvements. A culture of compliance was lacking in the organization.

When evaluating this investigation, it can be assumed that the starting point for the examination was good. FBI had already identified the who, what (i.e. fraud) and how (processing fraudulent real property tax refunds) of the crime. Evidence was already collected and Walters was already arrested. At this point Walters already knew she had been caught. According to her attorney, Walters wanted to cooperate and tell the truth. She told investigators that loopholes in software allowed her to carry out her scheme and lax internal controls allowed her to go undetected. Walters revealed her role in the scam, how she did it, how it could have been prevented and who did not pay attention to their job.

The investigating team focused on the mandate: how did the fraud occur? Why did the scheme go undetected for so long? What changes can be made to reduce risk of any recurrence of similar fraudulent activity?

The investigative process seems professional. For example, the report makes clear what the investigation was and was not: it was not to determine guilt or innocence, but it was an audit of the administration of real property tax refunds. They do not only blame Walters (rotten apple), they also blame management (rotten barrel). Evidence and interviews back up report statements. Investigators cooperated with criminal investigations. For example, they accommodated the request to hold off on witness interviews. They invited attorneys to sit in on interviews they conducted. They informed individuals they interviewed of rights (i.e. if truth would incriminate, no answer). They hired independent attorneys to represent certain interviewees. Interviews were optional, and many refused. Investigators could probably have made it more attractive to participate in interviews.

In addition to Walters, ten more individuals pled guilty in connection with her scheme. None were district employees, they were bank manager, relatives and friends. The chief financial officer for the District of Columbia asked several high-ranking managers to resign for their failure to prevent or detect Walter's scheme. More than 30 individuals lost their jobs due to the fraud. Law enforcement officials recovered $10 million. Walter's assets were seized and sold (i.e. house, car and handbags). Managers and employees were replaced. New guidelines were introduced.

## Norwegian sample

Between 2009 and 2015, a total of 408 convicted white-collar criminals were reported in Norwegian media. I collected court documents for each of them and developed a database of white-collar offenders. In the database there are 63 corporate criminals and 345 occupational criminals (85 percent). The following categories were applied to classify victims of occupational offenses:

- A total of 109 offenders caused harm to their employers as victims (31.5 percent)
- A total of 73 offenders caused harm to society at large by tax evasion (21.2 percent)
- A total of 53 offenders caused harm to their customers as victims (15.4 percent)
- A total of 43 offenders caused harm to banks as victims (12.5 percent)
- A total of 29 offenders caused harm to shareholders as victims (8.4 percent)
- A total of 38 offenders caused harm to others (11.0 percent)

In the following we will review case studies where offenders caused harm to an employer, the revenue service, customers, banks and shareholders, respectively.

## *Victim: employer*

Are Blomhoff was a priest in the Methodist Church. He had a business education and became chief executive officer in the Betanien Foundation that was linked to the church. The foundation operated child care facilities and homes for elderly. Because of the climate in Norway, Betanien wanted to help snowbirds move to Spain in the winter season. The board at Betanien decided to build a nursing home in Spain and CEO Blomhoff took on the task. Money was transferred from Norway to Spain and Blomhoff was in charge on both sides of the transactions. He embezzled some of the money and bought himself an apartment in Spain. In addition, he spent some of the money on parties with friends and prostitutes in Spain. When two colleagues blew the whistle on Blomhoff, the chairman at Betanien did not believe them. When the two whistleblowers threatened to tell the media, the chairman hired global auditing firm BDO (2014b) to investigate the matter. The fraud examiners found evidence of embezzlement of more than two million euros. In the district court later that year (Drammen tingrett, 2014), Blomhoff confessed to the embezzlement and was sentenced to four years in prison.

The harm to Betanien was not only financial loss. The whole foundation came to a standstill when the chairman had to resign from his position. Trust deteriorated and the two whistleblowers became extremely active in accusing others of involvement in the fraud. Rumors and accusations went back and forth in the organization and sponsors and donors became reluctant to support it.

## *Victim: tax revenue*

Isa Gerbeshi was running Wara Painting Service, which went bankrupt in 2014. Bankruptcy lawyer Anne Helsingeng in the Wara bankruptcy reported the case to the police, but the case was dropped. Later, Oslo police followed his moves and got him convicted to five years in prison for money laundering and tax evasion (Haakaas, 2015).

Gerbeshi and his family from Kosovo were involved in a number of bankruptcies, leaving behind unpaid taxes of more than 22 million Norwegian kroner (three million US dollars). This amount represents lost income tax to fund government activities. Society at large is thus a victim of Gerbeshi's scam. Another victim is the law-abiding part of the Norwegian construction and painting industry that loses in competition with companies from the shadow economy.

The shadow economy is defined as market-based production of goods and services, whether legal or illegal, that escapes detection in the official estimates of the gross national product. The shadow economy comprises those economic activities and the income derived from them that circumvent or otherwise avoid government regulation, taxation and observation (Schneider and Williams, 2013).

The society at large is a victim of the shadow economy, since the shadow economy causes damage to the financial interests of the country, performed by legal and illegal businesses. The shadow economy is sometimes labeled the informal economy or the underground economy (Edelbacher et al., 2016: 1):

> The informal economy is emerging worldwide as an antipode to the formal economy. Although only partially visible and parallel to the formal economic system, it is manifested in social and cultural activities in European cities in the tourist trade, in the form of vendors in the streets and squares or those selling flowers in restaurants. It has links to drug trafficking and prostitution, but also provides economic opportunities for immigrants, young people, and students. It has links with the formal economy, contributes to the forces of formal and informal social control, and is an important factor in the economies of European countries.

The shadow economy is illegal economic or non-complying economic activity within legal businesses existing alongside a country's official and legitimate economy – for example, transactions such as under-declared income, undeclared work and over-declared costs.

The Gerbeshi family now owns a number of houses in Kosovo that look like palaces (Haakaas, 2017).

## *Victim: customers*

Odd Arild Drevland was an attorney at law in his own law firm. He registered billable hours on February 29, but that date does not exist. In the trial against him, he was, among others in the indictment, accused of having falsified an agreement. He referred to an alleged understanding he had with a deceased entrepreneur. The contract was completely open, which gave Drevland the opportunity in the future to take out whatever he wanted to claim in connection with work for the entrepreneur's company. For a number of years Drevland was chairman of the company (Buanes and Valland, 2015).

In court, Drevland admitted to losing control over his finances. He admitted embezzling the funds of a major client when he was in charge of a large property transaction. He admitted embezzlement in relation to another client who had money in a client account in his law firm. Drevland was sentenced to two and a half years in prison (Pettersen et al., 2015).

The main victims of Drevland's fraud were his customers, who trusted his legal work for them. He abused their trust by embezzling some of their money. He did not only cause harm to his clients. He also caused harm to the legal profession, since every fraudulent attorney is one too many for the legal profession. A fraudulent attorney raises the question of whether lawyers should continue to have their client–attorney privilege and be able to deny government access to information about money deposited in law firm client accounts.

## *Victim: banks*

Christer Tromsdal was labeled a finance acrobat. He used various firms and associates to commit bank fraud. He asked banks to finance property developments and property procurement where the values were misstated, based on fake estimates from corrupt consultants. A total of 15 defendants were convicted in court to imprisonment. Banks lost hundreds of millions of Norwegian kroner (about $50 million).

The direct victims were the banks. The indirect victims are bank customers who have to compensate for the bank loss, either by higher interest rates on bank loans or by lower interest rates on bank deposits. Tromsdal has been convicted several times for white-collar crime, his latest sentence of six years in prison being from Oslo district court in 2015 (Oslo tingrett, 2015).

Consistent with the behavioral dimension of convenience theory, as explained later in this section, Christer Tromsdal applied neutralization techniques when blamed for crime. Table 2.2 shows neutralization techniques applied by Tromsdal, as they appeared in numerous media reports and court documents this decade. 'Yes' means that Tromsdal applies this neutralization technique, while 'No' means that there is no sign of this neutralization technique in the many interviews in the media with Tromsdal.

As illustrated in the table, there is no direct sign of victim denial or harm denial by Tromsdal as an occupational crime offender. However, he presents himself as a victim, where he claims that others are responsible for the harm that he considers has been inflicted on him.

## *Victim: shareholders*

Rune Brynhildsen was a partner in the firm Woldsdal Public Relations. He was sentenced to ten months in jail for exploiting inside information about a company where he was a PR advisor. Brynhildsen was sentenced for violation of the Securities Act. In his job as a PR consultant he learned about future plans, including mergers and acquisitions that would influence stock prices. Brynhildsen also leaked information to allies who traded stocks accordingly (Høyesterett, 2011).

**TABLE 2.2** Neutralization techniques applied by white-collar criminal Christer Tromsdal

| # | Neutralization technique | Yes/No | Explanation |
|---|---|---|---|
| 1 | Rejects responsibility for the crime and disclaims leadership role in the action. | Yes | He blames others and says he only tried to help some friends. "It is not my responsibility" (Bjørndal and Kleppe, 2013). |
| 2 | Denies injury from the crime and refuses to accept that harm has been done. | No | There is no sign of this neutralization technique. |
| 3 | Dismisses victims of the crime and rejects that anyone has suffered harm. | No | There is no sign of this neutralization technique. However, he seems to consider himself as the main victim of the crime. "I have let myself be used by others" (Bjørndal and Kleppe, 2013). |
| 4 | Condemns the condemners and is skeptical of those who criticize his action. | Yes | He feels that he has been a victim of a witch-hunt by Økokrim for more than ten years, and he condemns investigators and prosecutors at Økokrim. "I choose to call the whole process a witch hunt" (Hultgren, 2012). "People say he is a crook who cheated all the old people" (Kleppe, 2015). |
| 5 | Invokes appeal to higher loyalties as a reason for his action. | Yes | He had to do it for his friends and acquaintances. "I have helped friends and acquaintances" (NTB, 2015a). |
| 6 | Alleges normality of action and argues that action is quite common. | Yes | "When someone hears the word 'straw man', it sounds scary, but to me it is like an assistant" (Meldalen, 2015). |
| 7 | Claims entitlement to action because of the situation. | No | There is no sign of this neutralization technique. |
| 8 | Notes legal mistake and considers infringement irrelevant because of error in the law. | Yes | "In my head it is not illegal to do business with others" (Kleppe, 2015). |
| 9 | Feels entitled to make mistakes and argues action is within acceptable mistake quota. | Yes | Since he once was a police informant, he feels entitled to do business his own way. "I was shot at work for Oslo police" (Dahle, 2011). |
| 10 | Presents dilemma tradeoff by weighting various concerns with conclusion of committing the act. | No | There is no sign of this neutralization technique. |

Insider trading victimizes other shareholders. When an insider trader makes extra profit by the purchase or sale of stocks, others lose, because the value of the company has not changed. Furthermore, insider trading undermines the capitalistic market for allocation of financial resources among companies registered on a stock exchange.

Brynhildsen initiated illegal insider trading prior to price-sensitive announcements. He and his associates capitalized on finance and industry information that he had privy to, in advance of public notice.

McInish et al. (2011) found that insiders are more likely to trade on high-volume days, which indicates an effort to hide their trades. Hansen (2014: 29) found that the regulatory system in the United States is faulty, with some prosecuted and others getting away with civil actions, "much as the regulatory systems that are expected to control all types of underground, black market activities".

## *Convenience theory*

The theory of convenience explains white-collar crime in three dimensions (Gottschalk, 2017). First, there is a financial motive for illegal profit. Next there is an organizational opportunity to commit and conceal crime. Finally, there is willingness for delinquency in the behavioral dimension. Occupational criminals have a personal motive for financial gain that can be caused by both threats and possibilities. Divorce and separation, collapse of the housing market, gambling debts and large hospital bills are just a few examples of where threats can create a motive for financial crime at work. Greed on the other hand, defined as a lack of satisfaction with whatever you have already, is possibility driven. A greedy person always wants more (Goldstraw-White, 2012). Facing strain, greed or other situations, an illegal activity can represent a convenient solution to a problem that appears to the individual or organization as otherwise difficult or even impossible to solve.

In the organizational dimension, Benson and Simpson (2015) suggest that organizational opportunity to commit white-collar crime manifests itself through the following three characteristics: (1) the offender has lawful and legitimate access to the premises and systems where crime is committed; (2) the offender is geographically separated from his victim; and (3) criminal acts appear to be legitimate business. While corporate crime typically satisfies all three criteria, occupational crime may not satisfy the second criterion, because the most frequent victim is the employer. A fourth characteristic of both corporate and occupational crime is the availability of resources to conceal the crime and delete all traces. Concealment is an important aspect of white-collar crime. In traditional crime, criminals go into hiding. In white-collar crime, the offense is hidden. Concealment is also important in another context for occupational offenders, which is not the case for corporate offenders. Since the occupational offender makes personal financial gain, they have to avoid its detection and possible confiscation. Tax havens and faithful family and friends are sometimes the means to succeed in such efforts to make crime convenient.

In the behavioral dimension, neutralization is a key component of willingness to commit occupational crime (Sykes and Matza, 1957). Offenders claim that they cause no harm at all to any victim. In addition to neutralization, lack of self-control stands out as a key characteristic of offenders (Gottfredson and Hirschi, 1990).

## *The shadow economy*

It is often argued that detected offenders are just the tip of the iceberg of all white-collar crime. Estimating the magnitude of white-collar crime is an even greater challenge than estimating social security fraud or tax evasion, as illustrated in Figure 2.1. The only known size for the scope is the total of convicted white-collar criminals. As illustrated in the figure, this is a small circle within the larger circle of total white-collar crime. When estimating social security fraud or tax evasion, there are two known sizes, not just one: there is the detected fraud as well as the total payments in social security, and there is the detected evasion as well as the total tax revenues in tax collection.

Based on the research method of expert elicitation, the tip of the iceberg of white-collar crime in Norway is estimated at 9.4 percent. We know that the magnitude of convicted white-collar crime is 1.1 billion Norwegian kroner (approximately $138 million). Given that these convicts represent less than 10 percent of the total offender population, the total magnitude of white-collar crime in Norway is 12 billion Norwegian kroner (approximately $1.5 billion). With a population of five million compared to the United States' 321 million, the equivalent of $1.5 billion detected in Norway would be $96 billion in the United States. Ninety-six billion is less than estimates from the FBI and the Association of Certified Fraud Examiners, who approximate the annual cost of white-collar crime as being

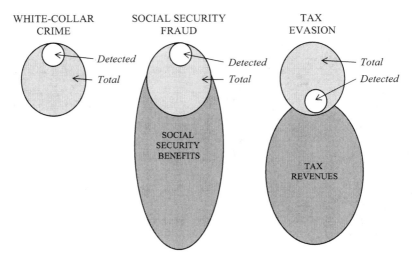

**FIGURE 2.1** Estimation of the magnitude of different forms of financial crime

between $300 and $600 billion, according to the National White Collar Crime Center (Huff et al., 2010).

We return to the shadow economy and this figure when we discuss social conflict theory later in the book.

## Conclusion

White-collar crime comprises occupational crime and corporate crime as well as government crime and state-corporate crime, all of which involve privileged individuals abusing their positions of trust in a professional setting to commit financial crime. Occupational white-collar crime is characterized by personal enrichment (Holtfreter, 2005) to the detriment of the organization (Kang and Thosuwanchot, 2017).

Victims such as employers, customers and banks suffer financial harm. In addition, competitors and society at large are challenged by white-collar crime as part of the shadow economy (Schneider and Williams, 2013). In open, transparent, trust-based societies such as Norway, which is rated "best country to live in" by the United Nations, and the United States, which is number 14 on the list (Chokshi, 2017), the damage to society can be formidable.

# 3
# CONVENIENCE RESEARCH

Crime signal detection is dependent on knowledge and understanding of the white-collar crime phenomenon. Knowledge can be derived from research as presented in this chapter. Rather than applying the theory of convenience, this chapter reframes theory into a convenience hypothesis that can be tested by research propositions. The convenience hypothesis suggests that white-collar crime is committed by offenders out of convenience, where crime is relatively more convenient than alternative actions to avoid threats and exploit possibilities. Convenience orientation is the value that individuals and organizations place on actions with inherent characteristics of saving time and effort as well as avoiding strain and pain. There are three dimensions covering the convenience hypothesis: (i) opportunity to commit and conceal crime in an organizational context, (ii) financial motive to achieve personal and organizational objectives, and (iii) personal willingness for deviant behavior. Six research propositions are developed in this chapter to link those three dimensions.

The convenience hypothesis suggests that white-collar crime is committed by offenders out of convenience (Gottschalk, 2017). Rather than embarking on legal activities to exploit possibilities or avoid threats, white-collar criminals find illegal activities more attractive. Convenience is a relative concept where decision-makers chose actions that involve a minimum of effort, strain, pain and future cost. A convenient individual is not necessarily neither bad nor lazy. On the contrary, the person can be seen as smart and rational (Mai and Olsen, 2016; Sundström and Radon, 2015). For example, a CEO with a multiple of tasks and a busy schedule may have no other choice but to choose convenient solutions to challenges to handle his or her everyday life (Fanelli and Misangyi, 2006; Galvin et al., 2015; Lord, 2016; McDonald and Westphal, 2003; Shen, 2003).

The convenience hypothesis suggests that convenience occurs in three dimensions for white-collar offenders. First, the desire for illegal financial gain is based on perceived needs in the economical dimension, where the offender is strongly concerned with achievement of wealth and fame (Goldstraw-White, 2012), and with a fear of falling (Piquero, 2012). Next, the opportunity to obtain illegal financial gain is based on profession and position in an organizational context (Sutherland, 1939, 1949, 1983), where the offender has legitimate access to resources to commit and conceal crime (Benson and Simpson, 2015). Finally, the willingness to commit crime by deviant behavior is based on a number of reasons such as lack of self-control (Gottfredson and Hirschi, 1990), too powerful to jail (Pontell et al., 2014), application of neutralization techniques (Sykes and Matza, 1957) and low subjective detection risk (Gottschalk and Tcherni-Buzzeo, 2017; Telep and Weisburd, 2012).

The purpose of this chapter is to advance the idea of convenience in white-collar crime by explaining the theoretical foundation and suggest propositions for future research. The convenience hypothesis may serve as an integrated framework for future studies of white-collar offenders.

## Theoretical foundation: motive

The convenience hypothesis finds its theoretical foundation in a number of theories related to financial motive, organizational opportunity and deviant behavior. In the following, a number of theories are listed that support these three dimensions of convenience in white-collar crime. First, we look at theories that describe financial motives that make white-collar crime convenient:

1. *Theory of goal orientation* suggests that profit orientation becomes stronger in goal-oriented organizations, whose aim tends to be an ambitious financial bottom line. In such organizations, goals tend to justify means – even criminal means – to achieve the desired profit (Jonnergård et al., 2010). For example, corruption may seem acceptable to achieve long-term profit goals. In goal-oriented businesses, increased profits can be expedient both for the business (corporate crime) and for executives (occupational crime), who retain their jobs, enjoy promotion and receive bonus payments. There is a greater extent of criminogenity – that is, propensity to financial crime – in organizations that are primarily or exclusively controlled and managed by ambitious financial objectives, because failing achievement may have very negative consequences and achievement of goals may have very positive consequences for the organization as well as for executives.
2. *Strain theory* suggests that unorthodox and simple solutions are sought when a situation becomes complex and threatening. In an empirical study (2007), Langton and Piquero found that strain theory was useful for predicting a select group of white-collar offenses. Using data about convicted white-collar offenders, they examined the ability of strain theory to explain white-collar offenses. First, they found that strain was positively and significantly related to financial motivations for offending. Next, they found that individuals reporting higher levels of strain were more likely to engage in more complex types of financial crime. Third,

strain relates to negative emotions. Finally, strain among white-collar offenders was negatively related to business-type motivations for offending. Strain among white-collar criminals can be measured in terms of events such as: (i) number of legal marriages, where two or more legal marriages are assumed to imply more strain, (ii) neighborhood, where lower class or lower middle class are assumed to imply more strain, (iii) academic performance, where failure to achieve positively valued goals is assumed to imply more strain, (iv) total assets, where less wealth is assumed to imply more strain, (v) total liabilities, where more debt is assumed to imply more strain, and (vi) employment history, where failure to achieve positively valued goals is assumed to imply more strain.

3. *Fear of falling theory* suggests that people in leading positions are afraid of the consequences of failure and therefore try to survive in their positions by applying various means (Piquero, 2012). They are afraid of falling off the financial cliff and losing their wealth and status. Therefore, they work constantly to remain successful, preferably more successful than others, their fear of failure meaning that they do not have the time to relax and enjoy their wealth. It is this struggle for continued financial success that is important to them. The fear of falling leads to solutions to problems such as acute illiquidity in terms of financial crime as the preferable way out of the crises. Profit-driven crime is thus not only an issue of making even more money. Rather, it is a matter of survival, and it may be about rescuing a sinking ship.

4. *American dream theory* can be perceived as the opposite of fear of falling theory. While the dream is about climbing up the ladder of success, the fear is about falling down from the pyramid. The American dream suggests that everyone in America (and elsewhere) has an opportunity to achieve monetary success, and monetary success is the only thing that counts in life (Pratt and Cullen, 2005). The American dream theory assumes that everyone in America has the opportunity to become financially successful. A high white-collar crime rate can be attributed to the commitment to the objective of material success emphasized in the American dream. It is caused by an overemphasis on success in exposed assets (Schoepfer and Piquero, 2006) unmatched by a concurrent emphasis on what means are legitimate for reaching the desired goal.

5. *Theory of crime forces* suggest that the market is such that the only way to survive is to implement financial practices similar to the ones applied by competitors (Leonard and Weber, 1970). If corruption is the name of the game, every business has to use bribes to stay in business.

6. *Theory of social concern* suggests that individuals care about the welfare of others, that they want close ties with others, that they are likely to follow moral guidelines such as innocent people should not suffer harm, and that they tend to seek confirmation through other people's actions and norms (Agnew, 2014). That a person puts others before themselves will initially lead to less crime. But economic crime may be committed where the welfare and success of others is a motive. Misconduct and crime can occur when people have more consideration for others than for their own interests.

7. *Theory of profit-driven crime* (Naylor, 2003) attempts to provide a general theoretical model and a clarified terminology. The theory implies that profit-driven crime can be understood in economic terms rather than in sociological terms. It proposes a typology that shifts the focus from actors to actions. Rather than focusing on profit-driven crime as a logical sequence of actions, it deconstructs a profit-driven crime into its inherent characteristics, which differ radically according to whether a crime is predatory, market-based or commercial in nature. Among the principle characteristics is whether transfers of property occur by force, free-market exchange or fraud; whether those transfers involve redistribution of wealth, distribution of income or redistribution of income; whether the crime occurs in a non-business, underground network or legitimate business setting. This approach answers the "how" question, rather than the "who" question or "why" question.

## Theoretical foundation: opportunity

Next, we look at theories that describe organizational opportunities that make offense and concealment of white-collar crime convenient:

1. *Opportunity theory* suggests that white-collar crime is convenient because offenders have lawful and legitimate access to the premises and systems where crime is committed, offenders tend to be geographically separated from their victims, and the criminal acts appear to be legitimate (Benson and Simpson, 2015). Aguilera and Vadera (2008: 434) describe a criminal opportunity as "the presence of a favorable combination of circumstances that renders a possible course of action relevant". Opportunities for crime occur when individuals and groups can engage in illegal and unethical behavior and expect, with a certain confidence, that they will avoid detection and punishment.
2. *Institutional theory* suggests that misconduct and crime may emerge in organizations with a collapse of morale as a consequence of the missing flow of ideology, regulation, ideas and mutual influence. Criminal opportunities are shaped by individuals, groups and other organizations, as well as society at large (Bradshaw, 2015). The organizational context, behaviors and processes may support white-collar crime (Pillay and Kluvers, 2014; Shadnam and Lawrence, 2011).
3. *Agency theory* suggests that both principal and agent can demonstrate opportunistic behavior in their relationship. Opportunistic behavior is not detected because there is asymmetry in knowledge about what is done and how it is done (Eisenhardt, 1985). Agency theory describes problems that may arise between principal and agent because of diverging preferences and different values, asymmetry in knowledge of activities and performance, and different attitudes to risk. Principals can suspect that agents make decisions that benefit themselves at the expense of the principals.
4. *Theory of partnerships* suggests that ample opportunities for white-collar crime can exist not only within but also among organizations. In alliances and

partnerships, an ally or partner can abuse the trust on which the arrangement is based (Lampe and Johansen, 2003).
5. *Contract theory* suggests that even when partnerships and alliances are regulated by contracts, opportunism can occur, since legal contracts can prevent some, but not all, negative outcomes (Luo, 2002).
6. *Network theory* suggests that networks – which may be very different from hierarchies and alliances – can also create ample opportunities for financial crime when the core of the network does not know what people at the periphery do (Lemieux, 2003).
7. *Theory of core competences* implies that those who have access to core competencies in an organization are enabled to misuse those competences for illegal gain (Leonard-Barton, 1992).
8. *Theory of resource mobilization* implies that those who have access to strategic resources are enabled to commit and conceal financial crime (Barney, 2001).
9. *Routine activity theory* has a premise that crime is to a minor extent affected by social causes such as poverty, inequality and unemployment. Motivated offenders are individuals who are not only capable of committing criminal activity, but willing to do so. Suitable targets can be things that are seen by offenders as particularly attractive. According to routine activity theory, it is the absence of a capable guardian that enables white-collar crime (Cohen and Felson, 1979).
10. *Theory of social dominance* suggests that the white-collar offender can feel safe due to convenient domination so that followers will be loyal even when misconduct and crime occur (Judge et al., 2009).
11. *Outsourcing theory* suggests that an offender can outsource criminal acts to others so that the offender cannot be held responsible should the criminal activity be detected (Gilley and Rasheed, 2000).
12. *Theory of criminal entrepreneurship* suggests that entrepreneurs are able to mobilize followers based on a vision, several ideas and personal charisma. An entrepreneur sees possibilities where others see problems (Wright, 2006).

## Theoretical foundation: willingness

Finally, we look at theories that describe personal willingness for deviant behavior that make the offense and concealment of white-collar crime convenient:

1. *Differential association theory* suggests that whether individuals engage in white-collar crime is largely based on their socialization within certain peer groups. In an elite setting, interactions with deviant others promote criminal activity. The essence of differential association is that criminal behavior is learned (Sutherland, 1983). Offenders socialize with those who share the same values as they do, and they distance themselves from criticism and skeptical others.
2. *Theory of rational choice* suggests that potential offenders compare costs and benefits before committing crime. If benefits exceed costs, then it is considered rational to commit white-collar crime (Pratt and Cullen, 2005).

3. *Self-control theory* suggests that those lacking a minimum level of control over personal initiatives and activities will tend to commit white-collar crime whenever the situation is such that crime can quickly solve a problem (Gottfredson and Hirschi, 1990).
4. *Deterrence theory* suggests that there is not enough to be afraid of for offenders (Comey, 2009). Offenders consider the subjective detection probability to be extremely low, and they do not think of imprisonment as the worst thing that can happen to them. Furthermore, they believe that a professional defense attorney will help them get out of any problems. Whether the potential sentence is a few months or many years in prison has minimal effect on potential offenders' final decision.
5. *Obedience theory* suggests that many are followers in crime who obey their leaders (Baird and Zelin, 2009). Glasø and Einarsen (2008) studied emotion regulation in leader–follower relationships. They found that negative emotions such as disappointment, uncertainty and annoyance are typically suppressed, while positive emotions such as enthusiasm, interest and calm are typically expressed or faked. When leaders and followers referred to experienced or expressed emotions, the most highly scored emotions were "glad", "enthusiastic", "well" and "interested". The reported level of emotion regulation was higher for leaders than for followers.
6. *Theory of negative life events* suggests that events such as divorce, accident, lack of promotion, and cash problems can cause potential offenders to consider white-collar crime a convenient solution (Engdahl, 2015).
7. Some convicted white-collar criminals claim that they accidently moved from legal to illegal activities over time without really noticing. They moved down a slippery slope without anyone reacting to their actions. This line of reasoning is in line with a third theoretical perspective that is called the *slippery slope theory*. The theory suggests that it is a series of small infractions that can lead to larger ones. An organization tends to overlook each of the small infractions and accepts silently deviance that occurs in minor steps over a relatively long period of time. The theory suggests that deviant acts occur without the conscience awareness of the offender who is responsible for the misconduct. The gradual decline is so minor in its steps that no one event makes the offender or colleagues aware of misconduct and crime. The theory of slippery slope suggests that crime is unintentional, since offenders unconsciously have lowered the bar over time through minor increases in their deviant behavior. For example, small favors in the beginning can overtime develop into serious corruption.

    Welsh et al. (2014) argue that many recent scandals can be described as resulting from a slippery slope, in which a series of small infractions gradually increase over time. Committing small indiscretions over time may gradually lead people to complete larger unethical acts that they would otherwise have judged to be impermissible.

8. *Neutralization theory* is one of the best-known explanations for deviant behavior. Offenders simply think they did nothing wrong. They apply neutralization techniques such as denying responsibility for crime, denying damage from crime and denying any victim of crime (Sykes and Matza, 1957).
9. *Theory of social conflict* is based on Marxism, which distinguishes between the ruling class and the ruled class in society. The ruling class – to which white-collar criminals belong – are entitled to break laws that they have developed and implemented for the ruled class (Petrocelli et al., 2003).
10. *Attribution theory* suggests that offenders have a tendency to attribute causes of crime to everyone else but themselves. Attribution theory is part of social psychology, which studies how humans spontaneously attribute reasons, guilt and responsibility in situations that arise (Eberly et al., 2011).
11. *Blame game theory* is concerned with a group of people when something goes wrong. They all try to place the blame on each other, and one of them may end up with all the blame (Lee and Robinson, 2000). For example, a top-level executive can be successful in blaming a middle manager in the same organization.

## Research propositions

Three dimensions of the convenience hypothesis are linked as illustrated in Figure 3.1, suggesting that white-collar crime is convenient when there is a financial motive in the economic dimension, an opportunity to commit and conceal crime in the organizational dimension and a personal willingness in the behavioral dimension.

A number of research propositions can be linked to the convenience triangle as illustrated in Figure 3.2. Arrow A indicates that opportunity can influence motive, B indicates that opportunity can also influence willingness, C indicates that motive can influence opportunity, D indicates that motive can influence willingness, E indicates that opportunity can influence willingness, while F indicates that willingness can influence motive.

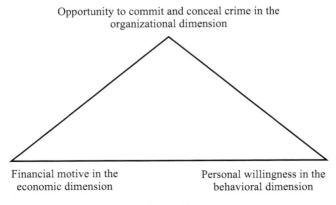

**FIGURE 3.1** Convenience triangle for white-collar crime

Convenience research 55

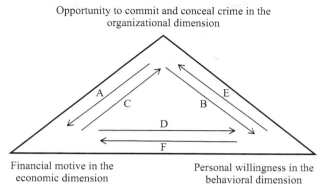

**FIGURE 3.2** Research propositions in the convenience triangle for white-collar crime

Arrow A in Figure 3.2 suggests a causal relationship from the organizational dimension on the economic dimension. Access to resources in the organizational dimension makes it more attractive to exploit opportunities and face threats through economic crime. Profession and position in the organization make it possible to commit and conceal white-collar crime (Bucy et al., 2008; Michel, 2008), which in turn makes crime more attractive to safeguard opportunities for financial gain and to prevent bankruptcy, forced downsizing or other threats. When senior executives and others in the elite are allowed to engage in economic crime without significant risk of being discovered or punished (Aguilera and Vadera, 2008; Haines, 2014), illegal gain becomes relatively more attractive. What might have been considered impossible or difficult, is now considered easy and convenient. Conversely, it becomes less attractive to secure an unlawful gain when crime is difficult to implement and when disclosure is likely. It is when the acquisition of extra profits requires little effort and involves little risk of disclosure or consequences that it become more attractive to cover personal and organizational needs illegally. When two reasons for not accessing illegal profits – lack of opportunity and obvious disclosure – are removed, illegal profits become more attractive to meet needs. Perceived needs move closer and become more important to satisfy. An obstacle is reduced and perhaps completely eliminated to access funds that can help achieve the goals of an organization and/or an individual. The extent of opportunity in the organizational dimension is predominantly determined by access, distance and legitimacy (Benson and Simpson, 2015; Pickett and Pickett, 2002). In a principal–agent perspective, the principal is unable to monitor what the agent as potential offender is doing (Chrisman et al., 2007; Li and Ouyang, 2007; Williams, 2008). This reasoning leads to the following first research proposition.

*Proposition A: Increased opportunity to commit and conceal financial crime in the organizational context increases the desire for illegal profits to cover perceived needs.*

Arrow B in Figure 3.2 suggests a causal relationship from the organizational dimension on the behavioral dimension. When a member of the elite discovers how easy it can be to carry out embezzlement, how convenient it can be to offer or receive a bribe, how easy it can be to defraud a bank, how convenient tax evasion can be, or how easy it can be to commit other forms of financial crime within the organizational context where the member has a privileged and trusted position, then the member's willingness to utilize resources to commit white-collar crime might increase. The member sees that the risk of discovery is small or completely absent. The member sees no negative consequences, he or she only notices the upside of the crime.

The circumstances in the organization may be such that a potential white-collar criminal is not noticed at all. The deviant behavior – to the extent it is noticed – is perceived as normal and does not arouse any suspicion. When nobody notices or reacts to deviant behavior and action, then the perpetrator can easily see himself or herself as quite normal – and certainly not as a criminal. The position that the person holds in or related to the business makes it easy to defend and accept any deviating actions (Sutherland, 1949). When a potential offender does not expect any personal or job-related consequences of criminal acts (Adler and Kwon, 2002), then their willingness to commit financial crime will be greater than when they are worried about future negative consequences. Furthermore, a person who has too much organizational identification can be damaging to the organization. Galvin et al. (2015) found that an executive's organizational identification, meaning the degree to which the executive's own identity and his/her perceptions of the organization's identity are tied together or overlap, is a key psychological state of mind to understand, because it may have important performance effects. The phenomenon is labeled narcissistic identification. Such strong identification with the organization can lead to an increased magnitude of white-collar crime, since there is no perceived difference between private money and company money. It is more convenient to commit financial crime professionally than privately, among other reasons because of the larger sum found in a company. An increased degree of freedom at work in the organization can also cause an individual to believe they can get away with almost anything (Bookman, 2008; Hansen, 2009; Heath, 2008; Reed and Yeager, 1996; Trahan, 2011). An example here might be the senior management at the bank Lehman Brothers, which went bankrupt. When Valukas (2010) examined the bankruptcy, his report of the investigation concluded that top management's deviant behavior was within acceptable business practices in the financial sector and, therefore, not crime. The top executives escaped any consequences of their deviant actions. They were never charged because, among other reasons, there were several individuals at the top of the organization who participated in the risky financial game (Ashforth et al., 2008) and because banking activities were generally characterized by high risk, unethical loan agreements and destructive business cultures (O'Connor, 2005; Punch, 2003). It was common to behave in a deviant and criminal manner. An excessive profit hunt and unrealistic objectives in the organization can lead to a behavior that is characterized by destructive leadership in the form of tyrannical leaders, tragic leaders, unrighteous leaders and reluctant leaders. This reasoning leads to the following second research proposition.

*Proposition B: Increased opportunity to commit and conceal financial crime in the organizational context increases the willingness to engage in the deviant behavior associated with white-collar crime.*

Arrow C in Figure 3.2 suggests a causal relationship from financial motive in the economic dimension to opportunity to commit and conceal crime in the organizational dimension. A stronger desire for profit is expected to affect the extent of organizational opportunities to commit white-collar crime. It will be easier to carry out financial crime and hide it among legitimate activities in the organization when the need for profit based on threats and possibilities increases. Threats can be handled and possibilities can be exploited when profit is secured for such purposes, where profit is a means of self-centered search for satisfaction and avoidance of pain (Chang et al., 2005; Gottfredson and Hirschi, 1990; Hirschi and Gottfredson, 1987). A strong desire for more profits will affect ways found in the organization to commit white-collar crime (Benson and Simpson, 2015). The profit hunt makes one more creative in finding ways to commit financial crime that is more conveniently hidden (Füss and Hecker, 2008), and the crime is carried out so that the risk of discovery is further reduced (Pratt and Cullen, 2005). Crime might be a rational choice that can be influenced by impulses (Kamerdze et al., 2014; Welsh et al., 2014). This reasoning leads to the following third research proposition.

*Proposition C: Increased desire for financial gain to avoid threats and exploit possibilities increases opportunities to commit and conceal crime in the organizational context.*

Arrow D in Figure 3.2 suggests a causal relationship from financial motive in the economic dimension to personal willingness in the behavioral dimension. Enhanced desire for profit to face financial threats and take care of financial possibilities can enhance the extent to which individuals are willing to commit financial crime. The need for financial gain and success makes it attractive for individuals in privileged positions to commit crime, simply because success is associated with wealth among members of the elite in society. A strong motive in situations characterized by threats (Blickle et al., 2006; Brightman, 2009) or possibilities (Bucy et al., 2008; Hamilton and Micklethwait, 2006) may lead to increased inclination to commit corporate crime and occupational crime, where the potential offender can use illegal profits to achieve respect and self-realization. Some members of the elite suffer from greed, which is socially constructed needs and desires that can never be completely satisfied or resisted (Goldstraw-White, 2012). Greed can take the form of a powerful quest to get more and more of something, and there is a strong preference for maximizing personal wealth. The more, the better. A growing perceived need for illegal profits may cause a potential offender to slip faster towards a criminal runway (Arjoon, 2008). Increasingly, the growing perceived need may lead to reduced self-control (Hansen, 2009), increased control of others (Piquero et al., 2010), increased stress related to avoidance of falling down (Agnew, 2005), more marked personality disorders, ignorance of deterrence mechanisms, and increased inclination to apply neutralization techniques (Sykes and Matza, 1957). This reasoning leads to the following fourth research proposition.

*Proposition D: Increased desire for financial gain to avoid threats and exploit possibilities increases the willingness to engage in the deviant behavior associated with white-collar crime.*

Arrow E in Figure 3.2 suggests a causal relationship between personal willingness in the behavioral dimension and opportunity to commit and conceal crime in the organizational dimension. Deviant and criminal behavior is absorbed in an organizational context where it is not noticed. The willingness of the potential offender affects how the person identifies opportunities and mobilizes resources to commit financial crime. When a white-collar offender is willing to commit financial crime, the person will develop organizational openings for crime to be carried out successfully without being detected. One reason for willingness is stress (Agnew, 2014; Gottfredson and Hirschi, 1990; Johnson and Groff, 2014; Langton and Piquero, 2007; Pratt and Cullen, 2005). Another reason for a person being willing and ready to carry out crime is that he/she slides down the slope from legal to illegal activities to achieve goals (Arjoon, 2008; Welsh et al., 2014), while a third reason is lack of fear of being exposed and punished (Benson and Simpson, 2015; Comey, 2009; Gottfredson and Hirschi, 1990). Top executives with a crazy need to control others in the organization can open up opportunities for themselves to commit crime without anyone daring to react to or report it (Piquero et al., 2010). The willing offender can engage in breaking down norms and common values, removing regulations and routines, ignoring controls, and problematizing the role of auditors before they embark on financial crime (Passas, 2007; Schoepfer and Piquero, 2006). This reasoning leads to the following fifth research proposition.

*Proposition E: Increased personal willingness for deviant behavior to commit white-collar crime increases opportunities to commit and conceal crime in the organizational context.*

The final arrow F in Figure 3.2 suggests a causal relationship between personal willingness in the behavioral dimension and financial motive in the economic dimension. Acceptance and neutralization of personal deviance make it easier and more attractive for white-collar offenders to commit financial crime. Willingness reduces the offender's personal barrier to criminal acts. The desire for financial gain to meet needs perceived by the individual and the organization is strengthened by eliminating personal barriers to crime. As a member of the privileged elite, the white-collar offender feels entitled to break the law (Petrocelli et al., 2003). Although illegal profits are not very attractive at first, the attractiveness can increase if the individual does not feel that any obstacles or suspicions stand in the way of their criminal acts. For example, the white-collar offender cannot imagine any harm resulting from or victim of their actions (Sykes and Matza, 1957). The offender perceives that the environment fully understands and accepts their actions, because they have distanced themselves from those who oppose such actions (Sutherland, 1949). Once all obstacles have been removed in the head of a potential offender (Benson and Simpson, 2015), easy profit can become more attractive for realizing personal and business goals. Willingness to commit crime is a combination of, among other things, neutralization (acceptance of own deviant actions), lack of norms (reduced self-control) and the situation (such as stress level).

*Proposition F: Increased personal willingness for deviant behavior to commit white-collar crime increases the desire for financial gain to avoid threats and exploit possibilities.*

In conclusion, this chapter has developed the concept of convenience in white-collar crime into research propositions based on the convenience hypothesis. Future empirical study may test the extent to which propositions find support in case studies and samples of white-collar criminals. Future research may also improve and refine research propositions to be tested empirically concerning the extent of convenience when white-collar criminals commit financial crime.

# 4
# CRIME SIGNAL DETECTION

In Norway, 405 white-collar offenders were sentenced to prison between 2009 and 2016. Table 4.1 lists how these criminals were detected. We find journalists occupy the top position, followed by crime victims, bankruptcy lawyers, tax authorities, banks and the police.

## Sources of crime detection

A comparison of the white-collar crime cases detected by journalists, alongside those detected by others, is presented in Table 4.2. There are some interesting differences that are statistically significant. First, the sum of money involved in crime is significantly larger in cases detected by journalists. The average amount for journalist-detected criminals is 110 million Norwegian kroner (approximately 18 million US dollars). The statistical analysis in Table 4.2 and the following

**TABLE 4.1** Detection of white-collar crime

| Rank | Crime detection source | Criminals | Fraction |
|---|---|---|---|
| 1 | Journalists investigating tips from readers | 101 | 25% |
| 2 | Crime victims suffering financial loss | 52 | 13% |
| 3 | Internal controls of transactions in organization | 45 | 11% |
| 4 | Bankruptcy lawyers identifying misconduct | 45 | 11% |
| 5 | Tax authorities carrying out controls | 25 | 6% |
| 6 | Commercial banks controlling accounts | 18 | 4% |
| 7 | Accounting auditors controlling clients | 18 | 4% |
| 8 | Police investigations into financial crime | 9 | 2% |
| 9 | Stock exchange controls of transactions | 4 | 1% |
| 10 | Other detection sources | 88 | 23% |
|  | Total | 405 | 100% |

**TABLE 4.2** Comparison of journalist and non-journalist-detected white-collar criminals

| Total 369 white-collar criminals | 97 detected by journalists | 272 detected by others | T-statistic difference | Significance of t-statistic |
|---|---|---|---|---|
| Age convicted | 48 years | 48 years | -.512 | .609 |
| Age at time of crime | 43 years | 44 years | -.893 | .372 |
| Years in prison | 2.5 years | 2.2 years | 1.659 | .098 |
| Crime amount | 110 m NOK | 26 m NOK | 4.783 | .000 |
| Personal income | 260,000 NOK | 429,000 NOK | -2.058 | .040 |
| Personal tax | 113,000 NOK | 201,000 NOK | -2.185 | .030 |
| Personal wealth | 1.6 m NOK | 3.2 m NOK | -1.050 | .294 |
| Involved persons | 5.0 persons | 2.8 persons | 8.186 | .000 |
| Business revenue | 234 m NOK | 214 m NOK | .381 | .704 |
| Business employees | 136 persons | 132 persons | .094 | .925 |

tables were implemented when the sample size was 369 convicted white-collar criminals.

Strangely enough, criminals detected by journalists are registered as having lower income, less tax and fewer assets than white-collar criminals detected by others. Not so strange, however, is that the number of persons involved in criminal activity is larger in cases detected by journalists. It is likely that external detection is easier when more criminals are involved in the offense.

Some of the characteristics are not different. For example, criminals detected by journalists have the same age as criminals detected by others. Criminals detected by journalists are associated with organizations of about the same size as those associated with criminals detected by others.

When we compare financial crime categories committed by white-collar criminals in terms of detection, results indicate that journalists tend to detect fraud rather than crime in the other categories, as shown in Table 4.3.

Since a substantial fraction of white-collar criminals are detected by journalists and very few are detected by traditional law enforcement agencies, there might be lessons to be learned from media working procedures. Journalists review information and information sources in established and developing networks of individuals located in key areas of the economy. Journalists study accounting reports and other information and receive documents from their network of sources. They

**TABLE 4.3** Financial crime categories by detection sources

| Crime category | Total detected in each crime category | Journalist detection in each category | Journalist detection fraction |
|---|---|---|---|
| Fraud | 160 | 52 | 33% |
| Theft | 17 | 2 | 12% |
| Manipulation | 127 | 28 | 22% |
| Corruption | 65 | 13 | 20% |
| Total | 369 | 97 | 26% |

interview lawyers, competitors, the police and authorities. They set a case aside for weeks and months until new information emerges. In the meantime they keep the information top secret, until publishing it for the first time.

Investigative journalists tend to develop hypotheses about phenomena and causality. They are very different from reporting journalists who only relate what they have heard or seen. Investigative journalists develop an idea via a study of potential offenders and their victims. They apply systematic analysis and treat their sources with care and professional concern.

In most criminal areas it is expected that a combination of victim and police will be the main source of criminal detection. When crime victims suffer an injury or a loss, they tend to report the incident to the police, who then investigate and hopefully find the offender(s). In the case of financial crime by white-collar criminals, it is often quite different. A victim is frequently unaware of injury or loss. For example, accounting fraud resulting in tax evasion is not a harm or damage perceived by tax authorities.

A number of angles can be explored in the process of white-collar crime detection within news media. On the one hand we have the news media (newspapers and online media) that specialize in financial information of all sorts and report on it regularly. For them, the sources of information can be traditional – for instance, tips, company reports, stock exchange information and press conferences – and less traditional, such as undercover operations, business informants, leaks in documents like the Panama Papers and Paradise Papers, and visits to tax havens. For regular news media spread out over the country, the situation can be quite different. The detection of white-collar crime can come from a tip-off by a whistleblower or from official information if the police or an economic crime prosecutor performs a local search. In many cases whistleblowers alert journalists to serious crime and they, rather than journalists or the media, may sometimes be the true detectors.

In addition, the way the news is treated in the news media is dependent on a number of simultaneous variables: do they have the right journalists in place at the time? Do they have an interest in the matter? Do they know anything or anyone related to this? There will also be a balancing of resources. The main resource perspective in leading media houses relates to knowledge management.

Not many news media outside of the larger ones will be in a position to set aside investigative journalists to work for months on a case of white-collar crime. In situations where news media have done so, the experience of some editors seems to be uncertainty as to whether it was worthwhile relative to the size and complexity of the case. For non-specialist news media, there will always be the need to balance resources against the newsworthiness of the case. If a major white-collar crime story had emerged in Norway in the weeks after the July 22 terrorist attacks in 2011, there is reason to doubt whether the matter would have received much attention in the general public press.

General news media have a constant incoming flow of news and there is a daily need to prioritize what is important and what should be published. For all news items there are some general rules of journalism that comes into play: is it important for many people? Is it really news? Is it possible to get reliable information on this? Is it possible to approach the right people with the right questions? Can both parties in a conflict be approached? And in addition to these questions there will be the question of whether the news organization at this point in time has the resources to deal with it. If the journalist knowledgeable about economic matters is on holiday, there can be doubt whether the news media organization will come back to the matter at a later point. The decision will depend on the development and the newsworthiness of the case at the second point in time. If the news organization is the first to report on the crime and it is regarded as "hot", it will probably do whatever is possible to handle the matter, knowing that other media, and especially online media, can report on it and in this way "steal" the story. News organizations always have a pride in reporting on a matter of significant interest and being cited by other news organizations.

The organizational culture also has an influence on white-collar crime detection among journalists. If journalists are driven by self-interest to win investigative journalist prizes (SKUP in Norway), there is a greater possibility that such stories will emerge via publication. But news organizations differ tremendously in this respect. Øvrebø (2004) showed in a study of the Norwegian newspaper *Dagsavisen* following a change of editor-in-chief in 2001 that the news profile and priorities of the newspaper changed in line with principles laid down by the new editor when she took up her position. It can be argued that the personal preferences of an editor influences the news priorities of a newspaper, and that this will relate to all types of editorial material, whether general, sports, cultural or financial news.

For a general news organization, white-collar crime is not a big story in itself unless it has implications for well-known persons or something happens to the organization where the crime has taken place. Nationally it can be a big story if the person involved has a well-known profile or the crime is unusual in some way. If an important local employer has to file for bankruptcy because of a white-collar crime, then the story is more than just another white-collar crime case since its wider consequences turn the world upside down for ordinary people in the area. In such a case, the white-collar crime will take the form of any other important news story and be followed and treated as such, its white-collar crime element – the starting point – mixed with other elements and consequential stories. Campbell (1997) studied the journalistic process of environmental news in Scotland and addressed the information sources that are used in the news process. The study showed the preference for human sources as opposed to library-based information and discussed the influence of pragmatic constraints like time and space on the production of news. It can be argued that the news-gathering process for white-collar crime is not dissimilar.

The status of white-collar crime detection among journalists seems to be related to the story's inherent significance, meaning that it will be treated as just another crime or news story and have the same internal process. For smaller news organizations without journalistic specialization in financial matters, the white-collar crime story will be treated according to the news prioritizing structure of that particular organization. For larger news organizations that typically have separate sections for financial and economic news, the story will be treated according to the prioritization of that particular section. And if the story is big enough, it will be moved from the specialist section into the general news of the organization. The higher the profile of persons involved, the more likely it is to have more central coverage – that is, be moved into what is often the first section of the newspaper or the prioritized areas of a website's front page.

Four of the ten detector categories made up 62 percent of the total crime detecting sources, and of these, the first two – journalists investigating tip-offs from readers and crime victims suffering loss – made up 39 percent. It can be argued that these two categories are more attractive to journalists than the others simply because it is easier to construct news stories based on these journalistic angles. Themes such as manipulation and corruption are more difficult to make into a story that is interesting for readers because they are more complex and harder to describe in layman terms. Tips from readers given to a news medium are generally accompanied by a personal story, which gives the journalist a clue as to what to work on and what to discuss internally for assigning the right news priority and angle. This is also supported by the breakdown in Table 4.3 showing that fraud is the category with the highest percentage of journalistic detection.

White-collar crime detection and follow-up seems to be related to a number of linked journalistic procedures and cultural elements. For specialized publications in the financial information area, the white-collar crime news arena is close to hand and the organization will typically be able to go deeper into the matter. If white-collar crime is detected by general or local news organizations, the procedure involved will more often be the same as for a general news story, with the same sort of resource balance considerations. It can also be shown that white-collar crime is more often detected by journalists if it is based on a tip from readers or if it is reported as fraud. Underlying all this are the internal news preferences and editorial guidance that are part of the policies of the news medium.

Finally, the most obvious reason for the high detection fraction by journalists is the fact that one of the criteria for our sample is newspaper coverage of the case. Naturally, this will lead to a bias towards journalist detection.

## Auditing role in crime detection

The role of auditing in the detection of white-collar crime is an interesting topic, as it is not certain that auditors are able to detect crime. This might have to do with the responsibilities of auditing functions as well as the procedures and practices followed by auditors in their work (Warhuus, 2011). For example, Beasley (2003) is concerned with the fact that auditors seem to struggle with reducing occurrences of material misstatements due to fraud, even in the light of new standards for auditing. The focus of new standards continues to be fraudulent activities that lead to intentional material misstatements due to fraud, and they expand both the

the guidance and the procedures to be performed in every audit. The expanded guidance will hopefully lead to improvements in auditor detection of material misstatements due to fraud, by strengthening the auditor's response to identified high fraud risks.

One of the surprising results of this research is the lack of crime detection by auditors: only 18 (5 percent) of the 369 criminals in our sample were detected by auditors. Moyes and Baker (2003) asked external, internal and governmental auditors to evaluate the effectiveness of various standard audit procedures in detecting fraud. Although external and internal auditors differed in the types of audit procedures they recommended, the authors conclude that "the audit procedures judged more effective in detecting fraud were those which provided evidence about the existence of internal controls and those which evaluated the strength of internal controls", and that "strategic use of standard audit procedures may help auditors fulfill their responsibilities under SAS No. 99" (Moyes and Baker, 2003: 199). Furthermore,

> the results of this study indicate that fraud detection might be improved through the strategic use of standard audit procedures earlier in the audit examination. ... If these audit procedures were applied during the preliminary stages of the audit, they would be more likely to indicate the potential existence of fraud, in which case the auditor would have more time to revise the audit plan and conduct other necessary investigations.
>
> *(Moyes and Baker, 2003: 216)*

Similarly, Albrecht et al. (2001) reviewed fraud detection aspects of current auditing standards and the empirical and other research that has been conducted on fraud detection. They concluded that

> even though the red flag approach to detecting fraud has been endorsed by policy makers and written about widely by researchers, there is little empirical evidence that shows the red flag approach is an effective way to detect fraud, especially for fraud that has yet to be discovered.
>
> *(Albrecht et al., 2001: 4)*

Their research review reveals that one of the major conclusions of previous studies included the fact that only 18–20 percent of frauds appear to be detected by internal and external auditors, and further that only about half of the perpetrators of fraud detected are duly prosecuted. The article also calls for further fraud detection research. These detection rates are loosely corroborated by Silverstone and Sheetz (2003), who estimate that approximately 12 percent of initial fraud detection is through external audit and approximately 19 percent arises from internal audit. (Both of these estimations apply to the American context.)

An article dealing with the responsibility for prevention and detection of white-collar crime refers to a study undertaken to map how members of the accounting profession viewed the changing role of the external auditor following the introduction of SAS No. 82 (Farrell and Healy, 2000: 25):

> Most of those answering the questionnaire disagreed that they should be responsible for searching for fraud. ... Clearly, this notion concerning the auditor's responsibility is not widely held by the public at large. ... The general public and Congress certainly sided against the CPAs and was the reason for this legislation.

As to the question of whether the certified public accountants (CPAs) should act as police or detectives when performing the audit, the response was a resounding no (Farrell and Healy, 2000: 25):

> This may also indicate that changes brought about with the implementation of the SAS No. 82 requiring a policing component clearly require added responsibility and may necessitate additional training and changes to job description requirements. Again, although the general public may believe policing is within the auditors' duties, even SAS No. 82 does not require this.

Similarly, an investigation into fraud prevention and detection in the United States revealed that the majority of CPAs that responded to the study believed the external auditor's responsibility for fraud detection extends only to assessing the probability of fraud and planning the audit accordingly. They ranked internal auditors as the group most effective in detecting fraud, followed by fraud examiners and client management (Johnson and Rudesill, 2001).

Jones (2004: 12–13) presents a slightly more balanced view of the auditor role in crime detection:

> A persistent debate has dogged relationships between auditors and managers. This debate revolves around the precise roles and duties of each party in relation to fraud and corruption, and particularly who should take responsibility for investigation. Current legal and professional precedents leave little doubt that management bears the main responsibility for ensuring that reasonable measures are taken to prevent fraud and corruption. In any event it is common practice for managers to request assistance and advice from auditors upon suspicion or discovery of fraud. The final responsibility must lie with managers unless the auditor has given specific assurance regarding particular controls or the absence of error or fraud.

In a Norwegian study, Warhuus (2011) found that 11 percent of her cases of white-collar crime were detected by auditing functions; this is lower than the 4 percent (according to our sample) reported above, and also significantly lower than the results presented by Albrecht et al. (2001), Moyes and Baker (2003) and Silverstone and Sheetz (2003). The figures of 4 percent and 11 percent in Norway indicate that Norwegian auditing has an even less pronounced role in detection of white-collar crime than the measurements performed in the U.S., for example.

Iver and Samociuk (2006) argue that fraud risks need to be recorded, monitored and reported. Such recording includes the nature of each risk, likelihood and consequences, current and suggested controls, and the owner of the risk for follow-up action.

Within the extant accounting and auditing research, a great deal of attention is devoted to how the external auditor is a primary figure in the detection of irregularities and corruption, and government and standard setters also stress the importance of the auditing community in this respect. However, there seems to be limited evidence for such views: in only a very few cases does auditing in some form seem to be responsible for the detection, unraveling and exposure of the offense. This opinion is backed up by the work of Drage and Olstad (2008), who analyzed the role of the auditing function in relation to both preventing and detecting white-collar crime. Although their study included a look at the perceived preventative power of the auditing function as well as actual detection of criminal offenses, their findings were consistent with the abovementioned hypothesis: many of their interviewees were skeptical of the auditing function having a central role in the detection of white-collar crime.

Olsen (2007) reminds us that the auditing standards that external auditors must act in compliance with also require them to uncover irregularities should they be present. However, the primary concern of the external auditor is to reduce the auditing risk (i.e. the risk that the financial statements may still contain material misstatements even after the auditor has given a positive auditor's report), not the risk of irregularities. In spite of external auditors rarely being credited for the detection of financial crime, Olsen (2007) still believes that the auditing function contributes significantly to the prevention of such crime by reducing temptations and opportunities, thus corroborating the findings of Drage and Olstad (2008) on prevention.

Rendal and Westerby (2010) examined Norwegian auditors' expectations regarding their own ability to detect and prevent irregularities and compared these with the expectations of other users of financial information on this same issue. Their findings indicate certain gaps in terms of how the auditor is expected to perform. Auditors themselves answer that they sometimes do not act in accordance with laws and regulations, and both auditors and users of financial information feel that the auditing function should include more than what is required today by standards and regulations – for example, pertaining to companies' internal guidelines. They also uncover unrealistic expectations regarding the extent to which the auditing function is capable of uncovering irregularities. They conclude that, to a certain extent, auditors are too reserved and aloof when it comes to their responsibility for the prevention and detection of irregularities, and they call for improvements.

## Crime signal detection theory

In the sample of 405 white-collar crime convicts in Norway, Gottschalk (2017) identified the sources of detection as follows: journalists, 25 percent; victims, 13 percent; bankruptcy auditors, 11 percent; internal auditors, 11 percent; internal revenue employees at the Norwegian Tax Administration, 6 percent; bank clerks, 4 percent; external auditors, 4 percent; police officers, 2 percent; stock exchange employees, 1 percent; and others, 23 percent. Crime signal detection theory can shed light on why relatively many are detected by journalists and relatively few are detected by internal revenue employees and others further down the list.

Fraud examiners are faced with the challenge of detecting signals and discriminating event signals from non-event signals. According to signal detection theory, a number of barriers and enablers influence the extent to which fraud examiners succeed. A personal barrier can be found among some fraud examiners who are not in the physical and psychological state of a detector. They are neither curious nor listening. They have a low perceptual sensitivity and are simply not alert (Szalma and Hancock, 2013). Other barriers include noise and lack of pattern. Noise is signals without any relevant information, while lack of pattern occurs when pieces of information emerge randomly. An enabler can be found in the intensity of the stimulus, e.g. how loud a whistleblower is signalling a concern. Other enablers include personal experience, pattern recognition ability, ability to discern between information-bearing signals and noise.

In addition to challenges in detecting and discriminating signals, there is a challenge of perceiving signals as negative or positive messages. Liu et al. (2014) studied signal detection theory, and they found respondents tend to notice negative messages more often than positive messages. Furthermore, respondents tended to interpret messages more negatively than the contents deserved. Also, respondents claimed to identify negative words, even when such words were not present. The studied concluded that people have lax decision criteria for negative words.

According to signal detection theory, there are a number of determinants in the form of enablers and barriers that influence whether and how a fraud examiner will detect a relevant signal. Changes in correct or false recognition of signals are influenced by both monitoring intensity and memory capability (Huff and Bodner, 2013).

Signal intensity, signal alertness, pattern recognition and personal experience in terms of competence are the basic elements in signal detection theory. Competence is defined as the combination of knowledge, skills, abilities, attitudes, and expectations. High levels of alertness and expectations will lead to a low threshold level for detecting signals. Experience and competence will improve discriminating abilities when faced with various signals.

While police detectives are trained formally and professionally, there are no requirements to private examiners who claim to be internal investigators. Police investigators such as special agents in law enforcement agencies receive classroom teaching and practical training, and it often takes years before they can call themselves senior investigating officers (Gill and Hart, 1997).

Signal detection theory implies that persons make decisions under conditions of uncertainty. The theory assumes that the decision-maker is not a passive receiver of information but is actively making difficult perceptual judgments under conditions of uncertainty. Whether a stimulus is present or absent, whether a stimulus is perceived or not perceived, whether a perceived stimulus is ignored or not will influence the decision in terms of detecting or not detecting white-collar crime.

Gomulya and Mishina (2017: 557) introduce the term signal susceptibility because signals may be differently susceptible to potential errors and manipulation:

> This could be due to a variety of possible reasons, including whether the signal is self- or other-reported, whether it is verifiable, or whether it is a "stock" or a "flow" signal. Self-reported signals should on average be more susceptible to manipulations by the focal signaler (i.e., the one who can benefit from a positive signal) compared to signals reported by third parties.

Given this definition, signal susceptibility can be seen as an aspect of signal intensity, where signal intensity deteriorates as suspicion of errors and manipulation increases. Similarly, noise in general will reduce signal intensity. Gomulya and Mishina (2017: 555) distinguish between two sources of noise during signaling – noise from the signal itself and noise from the behavior of the signaler.

Another term introduced by Gomulya and Mishina (2017: 556) is signal reliance, where reliance on different types of signals is based on the credibility of the signaler, so that "a similar signal is likely to have different effects for credible versus less credible" signalers. Given this perspective, signal reliance can be included as an aspect of signal alertness, where less credible signalers cause lower alertness to the signal.

Gomulya and Mishina (2017) discuss pattern recognition in terms of screening theory, where the receiver prioritizes from among possible types of signal. The focus is on how receivers place differential value on signals irrespective of whether they derive from, for example, documents, accounts or individuals. Screening theory posits that receivers screen by focusing on signals that they believe are highly correlated with unobservable characteristics of interest.

Signal detection theory characterizes the activity of an individual's discrimination as well as psychological factors that bias his or her judgment. The theory is concerned with the individual's discriminative capacity or sensitivity that is independent of the judgmental bias or decision criterion the individual may have had when the discrimination was made.

In Table 4.4, an attempt is made to describe the signal detection features of observers who have noticed/discover white-collar crime. Signal intensity, signal alertness, pattern recognition and personal experience are derived from signal detection theory as characteristics of detection ability.

Pattern recognition is a matter of sensemaking and contextualization. Contextualization captures the ongoing process of understanding and explaining relationships between information elements.

We argue that signal intensity for tips to journalists is normally high, as whistleblowers tend to be upset and want to get attention. Furthermore, we suggest that signal alertness is high among journalists, as they are dependent on tips in their daily work to cover news stories. The issue of pattern recognition is not obvious for journalists, since they often present fragments for publication, rather than a complete and consistent story of events. Personal experience will vary among journalists, who may or may not have already written about white-collar crime, depending on the extent of specialization among the newspaper's journalists.

The idea of Table 4.4 is to apply four characteristics of signal detection theory to detection of white-collar crime. At this stage, the items and values represent exploratory research that need further study to be trustworthy. Both selection of characteristics and judgment regarding these characteristics for each crime detection source need multiple raters to enable inter-rater reliability to be computed.

However, it is an interesting personal experiment. For example, the police in Norway are a passive receiver of signals. The Norwegian police are not undercover in financial markets and have no informants in business corporations. Therefore, police opportunity to receive signals is very limited.

Based on a sample of 369 convicted white-collar criminals in Norway from 2009 to 2015, where 97 offenders were detected by journalists and 272 were detected by others, we found some interesting differences between the two groups. In statistical terms, significant differences can be found regarding the sum of money involved in crime and personal finances as registered by the internal revenue service.

One reason for the high signal alertness among journalists is their complete dependence on external tips for their news stories. Journalists always need sources and have no access unless the sources cooperate with the media. By being polite and receptive, journalists increase the likelihood that whistleblowers and others will contact the media when they learn of potential misconduct and crime.

**TABLE 4.4** Characteristics of stimulus in detection of white-collar crime

| Rank | Crime detection source | Signal intensity | Signal alertness | Pattern recognition | Personal experience | Total score |
|---|---|---|---|---|---|---|
| 1 | Journalists | High | High | Low | Medium | 9 |
| 2 | Crime victims | High | Low | Medium | Low | 7 |
| 3 | Bankruptcy lawyers | Low | Low | Medium | Medium | 6 |
| 4 | Internal control | Low | Medium | Medium | Medium | 7 |
| 5 | Tax authorities | Low | Medium | Low | Medium | 6 |
| 6 | Commercial bank | Low | Medium | Low | Low | 5 |
| 7 | Accounting auditors | Low | Medium | Medium | Low | 6 |
| 8 | Police investigations | Low | Medium | High | Low | 7 |
| 9 | Stock exchange | Low | Low | Medium | Low | 5 |
| 10 | Other sources | - | - | - | - | - |

There seems to be a lot to learn from investigative media and their journalists. Rather than formal procedures often applied on a routine basis by auditors and internal controllers, information sources in the form of persons in networks might be a more fruitful approach to detecting white-collar crime.

Szalma and Hancock (2013: 1741) argue that signal detection theory has provided perhaps the most useful analytical tool for evaluating human performance in detection domains:

> The theory permits the independent evaluation of perceptual sensitivity and response bias. Perceptual sensitivity depends upon the perceptual ability of the observer to detect a signal or target or to discriminate signal from no signal events. Response bias represents the operator's decision criterion as to their propensity to say yes or no given the evidence to be evaluated.

If there is a signal and a response, then the observer makes a hit. If there is no signal, but nevertheless a response, then the oberserver creates a false alarm. If there is a signal but no response, then the observer makes a miss. If there is no signal and no response, then the observer creates a correct rejection. However, this absolute division may not always represent an accurate depiction of the true state of the world (Szalma and Hancock, 2013: 1741):

> In many instances, events are sufficiently complex and/or perceptually ambiguous that they possess ongoing properties of both signal and nonsignal to varying degrees. It is important to note that this complexity does not result from low versus high signal strength (i.e., changes in the magnitude of the evidence variable) but rather a change in the nature of the evidence variable itself. That is, until absolute categorical identification has occurred (often after the fact), the signal itself may retain various nonsignal properties and vice versa. Indeed, it is such categorical (and often multidimensional) blending that induces at least some of the inherent stimulus-based uncertainty in decision-making in the first place. This circumstance is especially true of real-world operational settings.

In our context of crime detection, there can be a signal of crime or no signal of crime from an event or a stimulus. However, an event or a stimulus can send both a signal of crime and a signal of no crime. The signal of crime can be stronger or weaker than the no signal. A possible range for an event or a stimulus dimension might be from zero (100 percent membership in the no signal category) to one (100 percent membership in the signal category). These endpoints correspond to the dichotomous signal detection theory. Values between zero and one reflect different degrees of membership in the two categories (Szalma and Hancock, 2013: 1742):

> A signal value of .5 represents maximal uncertainty in the category membership status of the stimulus itself because a stimulus with a signal value of .5

has properties of both a non signal and a signal to an equal degree. Implicit in this model is the assumption that signal uncertainty exists not only within the observer but also in the state-of-the-world itself.

Szalma and Hancock (2013) suggest a fuzzy signal detection theory where stimuli do not fall into discrete, mutually exclusive categories. The fuzzy theory allows events simultaneously to be in more than one state category – for example, both signal and non-signal. In our context of crime detection, stimuli may be perceived in terms of signal probability, where a stimulus can be perceived as probably a signal or probably not a signal.

Crime signal detection is not only an individual issue. Team cognition may influence individual signal detection. Team cognition, defined as the cognitive activity that occurs within a team, is one of the key factors enhancing team performance (Wildman et al., 2014). When team members hold convergent perspectives and knowledge, developing team cognition can be a success. On the other hand, breakdown of team cognition concerning the situation can lead to failures in coordination and lack of signal detection.

Crime signal detection ability and skill link to general investigative professionalism that includes the ability to collect and evaluate information, the ability to analyze, having specific knowledge of the field, being careful and meticulous, the ability to look at different angles, intelligence and the use of intelligence, and the ability to perform a professional inquiry.

Bond (2008) studied signal detection in deception. He carried out experiments where experts were asked to discriminate between offenders and not offenders. The study specifically investigated law enforcement practitioners' expertise in detecting deception by paroled felons. In signal detection analysis, experts showed high discrimination and did not evidence biased responding. The experts exploited non-verbal cues to make fast, accurate decisions.

## Lack of crime signal detection

Signal detection theory provides a general framework for describing and studying decisions that are made in uncertain and ambiguous situations. Without sufficient information in a noisy environment with many impressions not linked to any particular signal, it is indeed difficult to detect a crime signal (Wickens, 2001).

Accounting auditors receive an average score of six in Table 4.4. The signal intensity is often low, auditors' signal alertness is medium, auditors' pattern recognition is medium, and their personal experience is often low.

Hestnes (2017) studied a case in Norway in order to examine the lack of crime signal detection by auditors. The case concerned a company where the CFO was given a prison sentence for embezzlement. The auditor never detected the embezzlement, although it went on for several years. The case is described twice in the book, since the detection of embezzlement by others caused an internal investigation. The CFO is discussed here as an entrepreneur in white-collar crime, and also referred to with regard to the crime investigation at Hadeland Broadband Network.

Hestnes (2017) conducted semi-structured interviews with a number of people who knew the embezzlement case very well. The results of the case study correspond to crime signal detection theory due to the fact that embezzlement in the company was not detected. Lack of detection was due to the auditor's low score on the four factors in the theory. The findings indicate that the auditor's lack of signal alertness combined with low signal intensity from the audit context was the main reason why the crime was not revealed. Low signal intensity seems to be a result of the financial manager's independent position and the company's ineffective control environment.

In order to be able to detect fraud, the revealing party must be able both physically and mentally to detect signals of misconduct. Signal alertness is a unique readiness to recognize misconduct opportunities when they exist. Auditors are obliged to be aware that fraud may occur, while audit assignments may not necessarily be specifically aimed at detecting fraud unless there are incidents creating suspicion during the auditing process. International auditing standards place great emphasis on the auditor being professionally a skeptic. The auditing standard ISA 200, paragraph A20, states that professional skepticism increases the auditor's vigilance with regard to identifying contradictory audit evidence, "unreliable documentation and responses to requests", "circumstances that may indicate fraud", and other circumstances that require "audit procedures beyond those required of the ISAs". Lack of professional skepticism makes the auditor less aware of abnormal conditions and can cause the auditor to "make false assumptions" for the selection of "audit procedures and evaluation of their results".

However, the auditor will not normally be the receiver of direct signals concerning occurrence of fraud. White-collar offenders strive to conceal their actions, and most fraud will be well hidden and difficult to detect. In the CFO case, the problem is even greater for the auditor, since it is the CFO that typically gives the auditor access to accounting figures. Therefore, the auditor's signal alertness will be a result of how much their focus is on risk assessment actions associated with the audit, as well as what risk signals the auditor receives through documentation from and communication with a company's board, management and employees.

A distinction in auditing has been made between alert and non-alert individuals. An alert individual is defined as a person who is able to perceive that characteristics in the environment change and that the appropriate action must be adapted to the actual situation. A non-alert person fails to perceive or ignores altered signals from the environment, which means that their actions will no longer be as appropriate and effective as they used to be.

It seems that an audit becomes less effective in situations where the same auditor has been used for several consecutive years. Alertness deteriorates as no deviance occurs. By applying the theory of entrepreneurial alertness to the role of the auditor in such situations, it may be argued that the auditor will gradually become over time a non-alert individual. This conception is supported by previous research that looks at why the auditor does not detect fraud (Short et al., 2016).

A distinction can also be made between formal audit and substance audit. Formalities and systems are checked in a formal audit, while transactions and actors are checked in a substance audit. An argument that the auditor is trained to conduct formal audits is that their main objective is to be able to confirm that the accounts are properly prepared. The auditor develops an opinion regarding the accuracy of the accounts and at a fairly low level then looks for errors. This approach may limit and even exclude substance control. The auditor may fall into the confirmation trap by simply checking that the accounts are in accordance with laws and regulations. The auditor neglects to carry out sufficiently detailed tests for factors that may cause red flags to appear. One reason for this neglect might be an auditor's limited cognitive capacity, which is dependent on intelligence and imagination, to detect new signals.

Tax authorities receive an average score of six in Table 4.4. The signal intensity for tax evasion is often low, tax clerks' signal alertness is medium, their pattern recognition is low, and their personal experience with crime is medium.

Brodahl (2016) studied the tax authority in Norway to discuss the lack of crime signal detection when tax evasion occurs. The study focused in particular on corruption. Study results support the hypothesis concerning lack of signal detection. One reason for the lack of detection seems to be that controllers from the internal revenue service no longer visit companies to go through their accounts and talk to people.

Brodahl (2016) interviewed a number of tax auditors in the Norwegian internal revenue service. Interviewees reported that more substantial tax evasion cases because of corruption are often linked to accounts in tax havens where no information is available.

## Characteristics of whistleblowers

The focus on organizational members who speak out about perceived wrongdoing, also known as whistleblowers, has increased in recent years. Whistleblowing has gained recognition as an organizational social control instrument because it can terminate wrongdoing and bring offenders to justice (Bjørkelo et al., 2011).

Johnson (2005) has the following definition of whistleblowing:

> Whistleblowing is a distinct form of dissent consisting of four elements: (1) the person acting must be a member or former member of the organization at issue; (2) his or her information must be about nontrivial wrongdoing in that organization; (3) he or she must intend to expose the wrongdoing, and (4) he or she must act in a way that makes the information public.

Vadera et al. (2009) has the following definition of whistleblowing:

> Whistleblowing is the disclosure by organizational members (former or current) of illegal, immoral, or illegitimate practices under the control of their employers, to persons or organizations that may be able to effect action.

Atwater (2006) defines whistleblowing as an act by which an individual reveals wrongdoing within an organization to those in positions of authority or to the public, with hopes of rectifying the situation. Bjørkelo et al. (2011: 208) argue that the most widely applied definition in research is "the disclosure by organization members (former or current) of illegal, immoral or illegitimate practices under the control of their employers, to persons or organizations that may be able to effect action".

Vadera et al. (2009) identified the following characteristics of whistleblowers and whistleblowing:

- Federal whistleblowers were motivated by concern for public interest, were high performers, reported high levels of job security, job achievement, job commitment and job satisfaction, and worked in high-performing work groups and organizations.
- Anger at wrongful activities drove individuals to make internal reports to management. Retaliation by management shifted individuals' focus away from helping their organizations or victims and towards attaining retribution.
- Whistleblowing was more likely when observers of wrongdoing held professional positions, had more positive reactions to their work, had longer service, were recently recognized for good performance, were male, were members of larger work groups and were employed by organizations perceived by others to be responsive to complaints.
- Whistleblowing was more frequent in the public sector than the private sector.
- Whistleblowing was strongly related to situational variables with seriousness of the offense and supportiveness of the organizational climate being the strongest determinants.
- Inclination to report a peer for theft was associated with role responsibility, the interests of group members, and procedural perceptions.

Zipparo (1999) identified two main factors that deter public officials from reporting corruption:

- concern about not having enough proof;
- absence of legal protection from negative consequences.

One of the more successful whistleblowers is Michael Lissack. He worked as a banker at the Smith Barney brokerage. In 1995 he blew the whistle on a fraudulent scheme known in municipal financing as "yield burning". Dr. Lissack filed a whistleblower lawsuit against more than a dozen Wall Street firms under the False Claims Act. In April 2000, 17 investment banks agreed to pay approximately $140 million dollars to settle charges that they defrauded the federal government by overpricing securities sold in connection with certain municipal bond transactions. The U.S. Government has recovered more than $250 million as a result of Dr. Lissack's whistleblower action. His allegations have brought on more than a dozen civil and criminal investigations by the SEC, IRS and the U.S. Department of Justice. Dr. Lissack has written editorials about whistleblowing for the *New York Times* and *Los Angeles Times* and been profiled in many international publications, including the *Wall Street Journal*, the *Financial Times, Fortune, Business Week, The Economist* and *USA Today* (www.whistleblowerdirectory.com).

In 2001, Sherron Watkins, an employee in the American energy company Enron, notified her chief executive officer Kenneth Lay about a perceived accounting scandal. Watkins did so in the hope that Lay would act. He did not and, because she blew the whistle, was later arrested due to his involvement in the wrongdoing (Bendiktsson, 2010).

The negative consequences suffered by some whistleblowers following their whistleblowing are labeled retaliation. Retaliation can thus be defined as taking adverse action against an employee for opposing an unlawful employment practice or participating in any investigation, proceeding or hearing related to such a practice (Bjørkelo and Matthiesen, 2011).

The National Whistleblowers Center (NWC) in the United States lists a number of whistleblowers (www.whistleblowers.org). A few of them blew the whistle because of corruption in public procurement. One example is Bunnatine Greenhouse, who stood alone in opposing the approval of a highly improper multi-billion dollar no-bid contract to Halliburton for the reconstruction of Iraq. In retaliation for her courageous act she was removed from her position as the highest-ranking civilian contracting official of the Army Corps of Engineers. On June 27, 2005, she testified to a congressional panel, alleging specific instances of waste, fraud and other abuses and irregularities by Halliburton with regard to its operation in Iraq since the 2003 invasion. Vice President Dick Cheney had been CEO of Halliburton. Criminal investigations into Halliburton were opened by the U.S. Justice Department, the Federal Bureau of Investigation and the Pentagon's inspector general. These investigations found no wrongdoing within the contract award and execution process. On July 25, 2011, the U.S. District Court in Washington, DC, approved awarding Greenhouse $970,000 in full restitution of lost wages, compensatory damages and attorney fees.

The Whistleblower Directory (www.whistleblowerdirectory.com) is a comprehensive database showcasing individuals who have reported financial crime. An example is Jim Alderson, who worked as an accountant for Quorum Health Services in Montana and was chief financial officer at the Whitefish hospital. In 1992 he blew the whistle on the hospital's fraudulent bookkeeping practices, wherein reimbursements were routinely sought after filing fraudulent cost reports with Medicare. In retaliation for his whistleblowing disclosure, Alderson was fired. He filed a whistleblower lawsuit against his former employer, Quorum Health Services, and its former owner, Hospital Corporation of America. Five years after Alderson filed the lawsuit, the federal government joined the case. In October 2000, Quorum settled the case. Under the False Claims law, Alderson received $11.6 million dollars and Quorum paid a fine of $77.5 million dollars.

Janet A. Garrison and Herb F. Hyman were procurement professionals who blew the whistle. During the course of their employment with public entities in Florida, they uncovered unethical procurement practices. They then became whistleblowers. In their jobs as government purchasers, both Garrison and Hyman believe that they are entrusted by the public to spend taxpayer dollars wisely and fairly. Each individual also notes that codes of ethics govern their membership in professional procurement associations, as well as their certifications: Garrison and Hyman thus felt it was their public and professional duty to report ethics breaches that clearly violated the nation's laws and/or specific procurement statutes. However, their efforts to "do the right thing" met with unanticipated outcomes, ranging from the mixed reactions of others to a complex maze of ongoing legal proceedings (Atwater, 2006).

Janet A. Garrison's whistleblowing experience occurred when she worked as a purchasing analyst for the Florida Department of Education (DOE). Back in 2003 she was asked to help develop a solicitation for privatizing some 174 jobs in DOE's Office of Student Financial Assistance (Atwater, 2006).

For Herb F. Hyman, procurement manager with the Town of Davie, FL, his whistleblowing experience related to the purchasing practices of the town administrator, Christopher J. Kovanes. Hired by the town council as a contract employee, Kovanes was the town's top leader. Thus, Kovanes was Hyman's boss (Atwater, 2006).

Another whistleblower can be found at the office of information technology in Washington, in a case involving white-collar corruption in public procurement. The subject of the investigation, Yusuf Acar, was unveiled by means of whistleblowing from the office of the chief technology officer (Sidley, 2010: 28): "It was instead the cooperation of a confidential informant that led to the discovery of the fraud".

Miceli et al. (2009) suggest that employees can be encouraged to report wrongdoing both before concerns are expressed and once concerns are expressed. Before concerns are expressed, employees can be encouraged via the development of moral identity and moral agency, the creation of a tough anti-retaliation policy that permits disciplining or dismissing employees who act against whistleblowers, and the dissemination of the policy through the intranet, in orientation materials and elsewhere. After concerns are expressed, employees can be encouraged to focus on the wrongdoing alleged in the complaint and not on the complainant, to investigate reports fully and fairly, and to take swift action when the complaint is well founded.

In a study of corruption in public procurement in the European Union, Wensink and Vet (2013) found that approximately 40 percent of fraudulent activities are detected by a whistleblower alert. They recommend furthering investment in good, well-functioning systems for whistleblowers, including proper protection of whistleblowers. Legislation on whistleblowing as well as the protection of whistleblowers is not yet well developed.

Some potential whistleblowers are reluctant to blow the whistle because they adhere to the loyalty paradox. They consider whistleblowing an act of treachery against the organization. This paradox leads to pro-organizational behavior defined by dedication to the in-group and reflects such values as patriotism, self-sacrifice and allegiance. In the name of loyalty, individuals will sacrifice themselves to save their group members (Fehr et al., 2015).

## Crime signal sources

As illustrated in Table 4.4, crime signal detection theory is based on four characteristics: signal intensity, signal alertness, pattern recognition and personal experience. These characteristics are a mixture of the signal (signal intensity) and the receiver of the signal (signal alertness, pattern recognition and personal experience). Thus, crime signal detection theory mainly emphasizes characteristics of the potential receiver of a signal. In communications, the sender is also of interest. Depending on the trustworthiness of the sender as a source, a signal will or will not be taken seriously by a receiver.

Lack of formal powers requires private fraud investigators to rely on information sources that are voluntarily available to them. As whistleblowing may imply going against formal power structures, this kind of behavior may be regarded as deviant and an aggressive form of communication (Bjørkelo et at., 2011). Because of the special characteristics of a whistleblower and whistleblowing situations, receivers of complaints and reports have two issues to consider when dealing with whistleblowers as an information source. First, not all that is said and not all accusations from a whistleblower are necessarily true. Therefore, information from a whistleblower has to be carefully checked and verified. Second, a whistleblower may be in danger of retaliation, making it a requirement for receivers to protect the whistleblower. Report receivers have to make sure that a whistleblower contributing to an investigation does not experience negative consequences.

To evaluate sources of information and pieces of information, a framework combining sources and pieces can be helpful. The framework can consist of a matrix of, for example, 4 by 4 or 6 by 6. We choose a matrix of 6 by 6 for sources and pieces, and define first a set of six levels for information sources (Police, 2014):

A   *Completely reliable source.* Tested and trusted, no doubt of authenticity, trustworthiness and competence, has always provided accurate information.
B   *Usually reliable source.* Minimal uncertainty about authenticity, reliability and expertise, mostly supplied correct information previously.
C   *Quite reliable source.* Some uncertainty about the authenticity, trustworthiness and competence, but has delivered correct information in the past.
D   *Usually not reliable source.* Considerable uncertainty about the authenticity, trustworthiness and competence, but has in certain situations provided accurate information in the past.
E   *Not reliable source.* Absence of authenticity, reliability and competence; historically supplied information that is not correct; proven unworthy of any confidence.
F   *Reliability cannot be assessed.* Not sufficient basis to evaluate the source's reliability.

It is interesting to note that a not reliable source (5) is considered better than a source where reliability cannot be assessed (6). An explanation for this classification might be that it is better to have some negative insight into a source than no insight into the source at all.

We now define a set of six levels for information pieces (Police, 2014):

1. *Confirmed by other sources*. Verified by other independent sources; logical; corresponds with other information on the same topic.
2. *Probably correct information*. Not confirmed by other independent sources, but seems logical; largely corresponds with other information on the same topic.
3. *Possibly correct information*. Not confirmed by other independent sources, but seems reasonably logical; corresponds to some other information on the same topic; not in conflict with established pattern/trend.
4. *Questionable information piece*. Not confirmed by other independent sources; possible but not logical; no other information on the same subject; information tends to be in conflict with established pattern/trend.
5. *Unlikely information piece*. Not confirmed by other independent sources; not logical; conflicts with other information on the same topic; clearly in conflict with established pattern/trend.
6. *Accuracy cannot be assessed*. Inadequate basis for evaluating the accuracy of information.

Information sources and information pieces are combined in Table 4.5, where A1 is very good and F6 is very bad.

**TABLE 4.5** Quality of information sources and information pieces

|  | Confirmed by other sources | Probably correct information | Possibly correct information | Questionable information piece | Unlikely information piece | Accuracy cannot be assessed |
|---|---|---|---|---|---|---|
| Completely reliable source | *Very good* | *A2* | *A3* | *A4* | *A5* | *A6* |
| Usually reliable source | *B1* | *B2* | *B3* | *B4* | *B5* | *B6* |
| Quite reliable source | *C1* | *C2* | *C3* | *C4* | *C5* | *C6* |
| Usually not reliable source | *D1* | *D2* | *D3* | *D4* | *D5* | *D6* |
| Not reliable source | *E1* | *E2* | *E3* | *E4* | *E5* | *E6* |
| Reliability cannot be assessed | *F1* | *F2* | *F3* | *F4* | *F5* | *Very bad* |

# 5
# INVESTIGATION REPORTS

The purpose of an internal investigation by fraud examiners is to reconstruct the past. The past may be an event or a series of events where, for example, someone did something to somebody. Previous events are typically negative and have caused some damage. The goal of an investigation is to uncover the facts in a particular situation. In doing so, the truth about the situation is the ultimate goal. A private investigation is mainly after the facts, with the goal of determining how a negative event occurred or whether the suspected action occurred at all. The goal may also be to prevent a situation from occurring in the first place or to prevent it from happening again.

Private fraud investigators are not in the business of law enforcement. They are not there to find private settlements when penal laws are violated (Schneider, 2006). Their task is to reconstruct the past as objectively and completely as possible. They should not be in the blame game business.

Internal private investigations examine facts, the sequence of events and the cause of negative events, as well as who may be responsible for such events. Depending on what hiring parties ask for, private investigators can either look generally for possible corrupt or otherwise criminal activities within an agency or a company or more specifically for those who may possibly be committing white-collar crime. In other situations, it is the job of the private investigator to look into potential opportunities for financial crime to occur, so that the agency or company can fix those problems in order to avoid misconduct down the road.

Internal investigations include fact-finding, causality studies, change proposals, suspect identification and assessment of financial irregularities. The form of inquiry aims to uncover unrestricted opportunities, failing internal controls, abuse of position and financial misconduct such as corruption, fraud, embezzlement, theft, manipulation, tax evasion and other forms of economic crime.

Characteristics of a private investigation situation include a serious and unusual event, an extraordinary examination to find out what happened or why something did not happen, the development of explanations, and suggested actions towards individuals and changes in systems and practices. A private investigator is someone hired by individuals or organizations to undertake investigatory services. A private investigator may also go under the title of private eye, private detective, inquiry agent, fraud examiner, private examiner, financial crime specialist or PI (private investigator) for short. A private investigator does the detailed work to find the answers to misconduct and crime without playing the role of a prosecutor or judge. The PI stops the investigation before passing any judgment on criminal liability.

An internal investigation is a goal-oriented procedure for reconstructing past events. It is a process of creating an account of what has happened, how it happened, why it happened, and who did what to make or let it happen. An internal investigation is a reconstruction of past events and the sequence of events by collecting information, developing knowledge and presenting evidence (Osterburg and Ward, 2014).

Internal private investigations typically have the following characteristics (Brooks and Button, 2011; Button and Gee, 2013):

- Extraordinary examination of suspicion of misconduct and crime
- Goal-oriented data collection
- Mandate defined by and with the client
- Clarification of facts, analysis of events, identification of reasons for incidents
- Evaluation of systems failure and personal misconduct
- Independent, careful and transparent work
- Client responsible for implementation of recommendations.

White-collar crime investigations are a specialized knowledge industry. Williams (2005) refers to it as the forensic accounting and criminal investigation industry. It is a unique industry, set apart from law enforcement due to its ability to provide "direct and immediate responsiveness to client objectives, needs and interests, unlike police who are bound to one specific legal regime" (Williams, 2005: 194). The industry provides flexibility and a customized plan of attack according to client needs.

Investigations take many forms and have many purposes. Carson (2013) argues that the core feature of every investigation involves what we reliably know. The field of evidence is no other than the field of knowledge. There is an issue of whether we can have confidence in knowledge. Confidence in knowledge occurs when knowledge emerges in terms of evidence. A private investigator accumulates knowledge about what happened.

When there are rumors, suspicions or accusations of misconduct and financial crime based on media reports, whistleblowing (Liu and Ren, 2017) or other sources, the affected organization has to react in some way. If management decides to report incidents to the police, then the affected organization may lose any control of the case as it evolves (Gottschalk and Tcherni-Buzzeo, 2017). For this reason, many organizations prefer to hire private detectives to reconstruct past events and sequence of events (Brooks and Button, 2011; Gottschalk, 2016a).

The business of private internal investigations by fraud examiners has grown remarkably in recent decades. Law firms and auditing firms are hired by private and public organizations to reconstruct the past when there is suspicion of misconduct and possible financial crime. A criminal investigation is initiated when there is a need to study negative incidents and events that happened in the past. Unlike the police, regulators and other investigative agencies, private financial detectives practice legal flexibility (Button and Gee, 2013; Button et al., 2007a, b).

Examples of private internal investigations include Valukas' (2010) investigation into the bankruptcy at Lehman Brothers, Valukas' (2010) investigation into fraud related to the ignition switch failure at General Motors, BDO's (2014a) investigation into fraud in the Coatesville Area School District, Powers et al.'s (2002) investigation at Enron, and Gray and Evans' (2008) investigation into theft of District of Columbia funds.

## Investigation characteristics

An internal investigation is an inquiry conducted by, or on behalf of, an organization in an effort to discover facts relating to possible improper acts or omissions that may have occurred in the organization. An internal investigation can be a critical means for an organization to uncover and address misconduct that poses a risk to its ethical standards and reputation or may expose it to civil or criminal liability (Lomas and Kramer, 2013).

Investigating white-collar crime is like any other investigation concerned with the past. Investigating is to find out what happened in the past. A negative event or sequence of negative events can be at the core of an investigation. If there is no certainty about events, then finding out whether or not something has occurred can be at the core of an investigation. An investigation is a reconstruction of the past where events have occurred or not occurred. Knowledge is applied to collected information to make sense for a reconstruction of events and sequences of events.

What happened or did not happen? Investigators first develop their know-what in terms of events or absence of events. It might be a bribe that was paid, money that was embezzled, tax that was not paid or a bank that was defrauded. An investigation typically starts by finding facts about what happened.

How did it happen or not happen? Investigators develop a hypothesis about the path for what happened. They identify information sources that support or disapprove the hypothesis. If the hypothesis is discarded, then a new path for what happened is identified.

Why did it happen? Investigators try to establish causality in terms of cause and effect. The cause may be a motive, another event or something else. Causality is easily assumed but very difficult to prove in terms of evidence in an investigation.

Who did what to make it happen or not happen? This is where investigators have to be very careful, especially when it comes to suspects of misconduct and crime. Investigators should work just as hard to prove innocence as to prove guilt. Investigators should give suspects the benefit of the doubt. Suspects must be given the right of contradiction, where they can disagree with what investigators claim to have found out about them.

Investigators should not involve themselves in either prosecution or sentencing. Investigators should leave it to public prosecutors to decide whether or not a person or persons should be prosecuted. If the evidence is not convincing and compelling, then charges should not be pressed. If the prosecutor fails to convince the judge in the question of guilt, then the defendant is to be acquitted. Defendants are to be given the benefit of the doubt.

Investigators collect information from a number of sources and apply a variety of knowledge categories. Information collection involves sources such as interviews with witnesses and suspects, searches in documents and emails and observation of actors. Knowledge categories include organizational behavior, management decision-making, business practices, market structures, accounting principles, deviant behaviors, personal motives, violation of laws and past verdicts.

While being like any other investigation concerned with the past, investigating white-collar crime has its specific aspects and challenges. For example, while street criminals typically hide themselves, white-collar criminals hide their crime. Burglars leave traces of the crime and disappear from the scene. White-collar criminals do not disappear from the scene. Instead, they conceal illegal actions in seemingly legal activities. Bribed individuals stay in their jobs, bribing individuals stay in their jobs, embezzling individuals stay in their jobs and those who commit bank fraud stay in their jobs. They hide their criminal acts among legitimate acts, and they delete their tracks. They create an atmosphere at work where nobody questions their deviant behavior.

Another challenge for white-collar crime investigations is the lack of obvious victims. With burglary, murder or rape, there are obvious and visible victims. In the case of tax evasion, nobody notices any harm or damage. In the case of subsidy fraud, when a ferry company reports lower passenger numbers, the local government does not notice it has been deceived. Victims of white-collar crime are typically banks, the revenue service, customers and suppliers. The most frequent victim is the employer, who does not notice embezzlement or theft by employees.

A third challenge for white-collar crime investigations are the resources available to suspects. While a street criminal tends to be happy – or at least satisfied – with a mediocre defense lawyer, white-collar criminals hire famous attorneys to help them with their cases. While a street crime lawyer only works on the case when it ends up in court, white-collar lawyers involve themselves in preventing the case from ending up in court. A white-collar lawyer tries to disturb the investigation by supplying material in favor of the client while preventing investigators from examining material that is unfavorable for the client. This is information control, which aims at preventing investigators from getting the complete picture or helping investigators to get a distorted picture of past events. In addition, white-collar lawyers engage in symbolic defense, where they use the media and other channels to present the client as a victim rather than potential offender.

White-collar crime investigations are carried out by a variety of professionals in different organizations. Detectives in law enforcement agencies are the most typical crime investigators. All nations in the world have police investigators who reconstruct the past when an offense has occurred. Possibly the best-known agency is the Federal Bureau of Investigation (FBI) in the United States. The FBI has the authority and is required to investigate specific crimes assigned to it and to provide other law enforcement agencies with cooperative services, such as fingerprint identification, laboratory examinations and training. The FBI also gathers, shares and analyzes intelligence, to support both its own investigations and those of its partners. The FBI is the principal investigative arm of the U.S. Department of Justice (Kessler, 2012). In its white-collar crime program, the FBI focuses on identifying and disrupting public corruption, money laundering, corporate fraud, securities and commodities fraud, mortgage fraud, financial institution fraud, bank fraud and embezzlement, health care fraud, and other kinds of financial crime.

Other countries have similar bureaus. In Norway, for example, the Norwegian National Authority for Investigation and Prosecution of Economic and Environmental Crime (Økokrim) is the central unit for financial crime investigations. Økokrim is both a police specialist agency and a public prosecutors' office with national authority. Both the FBI and Økokrim focus on complex investigations that are international or national in scope and where the agencies can bring to bear unique expertise or capabilities that increase the likelihood of successful white-collar crime investigations.

Outside regular law enforcement we find other investigating agencies within the public sector. An example is the IRS criminal investigation division in the United States. The division investigates potential criminal violations of the U.S. internal revenue code and related financial crime in a manner intended to foster confidence in the tax system and deter violations of tax law.

Outside governments' criminal justice systems, private investigators can be found internally in organizations and externally. Internal investigators include fraud examiners in insurance companies who investigate insurance customers' claims. Norwegian insurance firms suggest that 10 percent of what they pay out to customers is based on false claims.

Another example is internal investigators in banks who investigate suspicions of fraud and money laundering. A final example is internal auditors and compliance officers who investigate suspicions of financial crime.

External investigators are fraud examiners who are hired by clients to perform investigations in the clients' organizations. While the investigators are employed by law firms, accountancy firms and consultancy firms, they are hired by business and government organizations to carry out internal investigations. Their backgrounds are in areas such as forensic accountancy, police detective work, business law, organizational psychology and executive management.

## Reasons for private investigations

Criminal investigation is initiated when there is a need to study negative incidents and events that happened in the past. Unlike the police, regulators and other investigative agencies and forensic accounting and corporate investigation firms are able to conduct their investigations under a cloak of secrecy, providing resolutions that are largely private in nature and which help to safeguard the client from embarrassment and unwanted publicity. Many companies want to deal with misconduct internally by resolving the matter by themselves. They want no publicity. They want to avoid courts because, for example, they do not want their shareholders, customers or suppliers to see that misconduct and crime has occurred. Cases are resolved through informal means such as negotiated settlements and the dismissal of an offending employee (Williams, 2014).

Corporations and other organizations value the possibility of secrecy, discretion and control that private specialists bring to investigations. Openness could lead to problems such as reputational loss, which can have economic repercussions. While private investigations can consider secrecy, openness is a key characteristic of public criminal justice procedures. Meerts (2014) argues that the reluctance of victim companies to report crime to the police because of fear of reputational damage is a well-researched subject. Reputational damage provides a motivation for a company to avoid publicity (Dupont, 2014: 272):

> The reputation of a company represents a valuable asset that can quickly become a liability when the erosion of customers' and suppliers' trust provokes a loss of competitiveness. Shareholders are also very receptive to such signals and several security managers explained how their performance was indirectly tied to their company's public valuation. The ambiguity that characterizes this risk category explains why contract security firms providing investigative and consulting services of all sorts are routinely called in before the police – when the police are involved at all – in order to minimize external scrutiny and to maximize procedural control.

An important advantage of private investigations is legal flexibility. Following an internal investigation, the client can choose from an array of legal alternatives and decide which is best for the current case. Law enforcement, however, is more limited, generally working towards a criminal prosecution or taking no further action by dismissing the case. Minimizing and repairing damage is often the focus of private investigations, which makes legal possibilities other than those provided by criminal law more attractive. Employers often have nothing to gain by triggering a criminal justice procedure (Meerts, 2014).

Another advantage of private investigations is private examiners' role in the deterrence of fraud. The principle of deterrence is important in the perspective of convenience theory, as described below. However, poor investigations do not deter people from committing fraud.

Private sector investigative consultants conduct inquiries for their clients in cases of suspected corporate crime. Recent developments internationally when it comes to corporate criminal liability have led many business and government organizations to recruit consultants to develop internal compliance systems because the function of such systems is increasingly taken into account by prosecution authorities.

While public police are bound by the legal definitions of criminal conduct, corporate security is more flexible and can adapt to the definitions provided by their clients. Private investigators can focus exclusively on the occurrences pointed out as problematic by their clients. This means that private investigators can examine behavior harmful to their clients that is not criminal; and, conversely, that they can ignore behavior that is criminal but not damaging to their client (Meerts, 2014).

Internal investigations in private and public organizations have an important function in society. They allow entities to discover misbehavior within management, make corrections and define future conduct to assure compliance with laws, regulations, policies and guidelines. Private investigations offer organizational solutions to organizational problems, while providing an incentive to corporations and public authorities to unmask misconduct. Internal investigations also allow corporations as well as other organizations to quietly examine allegations that may later prove to be wrong, without fear that disclosure will hurt the organization's or an individual's reputation (Green and Podgor, 2013).

Another reason for private internal investigations is that white-collar crime is often a difficult crime for police to handle. Police force resources are frequently stretched thin and mainly focused on potential terrorism, physical violence and threats to the welfare of citizens. Successful prosecutions of white-collar crime are frequently knowledge and labor intensive, and a decision has to be made as to where people and man-hours are best allocated (Brooks and Button, 2011).

The main purpose of an investigation is to establish if, how, where, when, why and by whom misconduct or crime was committed. To do this, detectives must discover, collect, check and consider clues from various sources of information and try to construct a coherent account of the event. In some cases this is straightforward, but in others the challenge is considerable (Fahsing, 2016). An inquiry is a process that has the aim of augmenting knowledge, resolving doubts or solving a problem.

According to Fahsing (2016) an investigation can be perceived as sensemaking and abductive logic or as hypothesis testing. In abductive reasoning, an investigator tries to presume potential facts by using supporting facts. In hypothesis testing, an investigator tries to collect evidence that can both favor and disfavor a hypothesis.

## Private fraud examinations

Fraud investigations into individuals and organizations by private investigators have increased in intensity. No amount of legislation can protect against dishonesty (Coburn, 2006). When an organization wants to investigate facts, causes and responsibility for an incident, the investigation can be carried out by financial crime specialists and fraud examiners. Fraud examination has elements of intelligence and investigation as well as analysis, as in police work. Elements of inquiries where the term fraud examination is used include fact-finding, causality study, change proposals and suspect identification.

Fraud examination as intelligence emphasizes the systematic and goal-oriented collection of information that is transformed and analyzed according to a rigid procedure to detect suspects' capacity, dispositions and intentions. The purpose is to improve both prevention and detection of crime. Risk-based techniques can be applied to survey environments and persons in order to collect information on their moves. Intelligence can also be defined as the result of information collection about possible offenses and potential suspects to arrive at conclusions about threats, point out problems and identify criminal activity with the intention of following the case.

Fraud examination as investigation is the systematic and goal-oriented collection of information to confirm or disconfirm that an action is a crime and the actor is a criminal. Investigation is to prepare evidence for court proceedings. An investigation only occurs when something wrong has happened; intelligence occurs when something wrong might happen.

Fraud examination as analysis is the process of breaking down a complex material or subject into smaller pieces to improve understanding and insight into the case. Analysis is to create meaning based on data by manipulating, interpreting and reorganizing the structure of collected evidence. To analyze is to ask questions such as what, where, how, who, when and why. What happened? How did it happen? Why did it happen? Elements of know-what, know-how and know-why are created through analysis.

While fraud examination has elements of intelligence, investigation and analysis as in police work, it is also different. For intelligence, something might happen. For investigation, something has happened. For analysis, evidence is to be produced. In fraud examinations, something might happen or something has happened. Fraud examiners do not know when they start their work.

Wikipedia has the following definition of a private investigator:

> A private investigator (often abbreviated to PI and informally called a private eye), a private detective or inquiry agent, is a person who can be hired by individuals or groups to undertake investigatory law services. Private detectives/investigators often work for attorneys in civil cases. A handful of very skilled private detectives/investigators work with defense attorneys on capital punishment and criminal defense cases. Many work for insurance companies to investigate suspicious claims. Before the advent of no-fault divorce, many private investigators were hired to search out evidence of adultery or other conduct within marriage to establish grounds for a divorce. Despite the lack of legal necessity for such evidence in many jurisdictions, according to press reports collecting evidence of adultery or other "bad behavior" by spouses and partners is still one of the most profitable activities investigators

undertake, as the stakes being fought over now are child custody, alimony, or marital property disputes.

Private investigators can also be used to perform due diligence for an investor who may be considering investing money with an investment group, fund manager or other high-risk business or investment venture. This could serve to help the prospective investor avoid being the victim of a fraud or Ponzi scheme. By hiring a licensed and experienced investigator, they could unearth information that the investment is risky and or that the investor has suspicious red flags in his or her background. This is called investigative due diligence, and is becoming much more prevalent in the 21st century with the public reports of large-scale Ponzi schemes and fraudulent investment vehicles such as Madoff, Stanford, Petters, Rothstein and the hundreds of others reported by the SEC and other law-enforcement agencies.

Wells (2003) argues that becoming a fraud examiner – a kind of a financial detective – is not for everyone. Detectives – either in law enforcement or in the private sector – typically have distinct personality traits. They need to be as good with people as they are with numbers, and they need to be inclined to be aggressive rather than shy and retiring.

Gill and Hart (1997) found that the market for private fraud examinations is growing because client companies are rarely keen to involve the police in fraud investigations since a prosecution may expose them to speculation about their internal procedures. Corporate clients tend to take great care to ensure the confidentiality of the investigations they commission. Private investigators receive instructions to examine various kinds of fraud.

## Financial crime specialists

The Association of Certified Financial Crime Specialists (ACFCS) was created to respond to a growing need for documented, verifiable and certifiable knowledge and skill in the financial crime field and to meet the career development needs of the diverse and growing number of specialists in the private and public sectors who work in this field (CFCS, 2013).

ACFCS is a member organization that provides training, news, analysis and networking to a worldwide membership of professionals in the financial crime field. ACFCS awards the Certified Financial Crime Specialist (CFCS) certification to persons who meet certain qualifications and pass a rigorous examination offered at 700 authorized testing centers worldwide. It is a credential that tests competence and skill across the financial crime spectrum, including money laundering, corruption, tax evasion, compliance and investigations.

A private investigation is conducted by a variety of private sector financial crime specialists who can be investigators, forensic accountants or lawyers, all of whom may be supported by investigative analysts, who the government usually calls intelligence analysts.

ACFCS stresses the importance of the following topics for financial crime specialists:

1. The challenge of financial crime
2. Financial crime overview, commonalities and convergence
3. Money laundering
4. Understanding and preventing fraud
5. Global anti-corruption compliance and enforcement
6. Tax evasion and enforcement
7. Asset recovery
8. Financial crime investigations
9. Interpreting financial documents
10. Money and commodities flow
11. Compliance programs and controls
12. Data security and privacy
13. Ethical responsibility and best practices
14. International agreements and standards

In the UK it is expected that companies contribute to the detection of law violations in the form of self-reports. For a self-report to be taken into account as a public interest factor tending against prosecution it must form part of a genuinely proactive approach adopted by the corporate management team. Prosecutors will consider whether it has provided sufficient information, including making witnesses available and disclosing the details of any internal investigation, about the operation of the corporate body in its entirety. This is in accordance with the UK serious fraud office guidance on corporate prosecutions, which is outlined below:

1. Initial contact, and all subsequent communication, must be made through the SFO's Intelligence Unit. The Intelligence Unit is the only business area within the SFO authorized to handle self-reports.
2. Hard copy reports setting out the nature and scope of any internal investigation must be provided to the SFO's Intelligence Unit as part of the self-reporting process.
3. All supporting evidence including, but not limited to, emails, banking evidence and witness accounts, must be provided to the SFO's Intelligence Unit as part of the self-reporting process.
4. Further supporting evidence may be provided during the course of any ongoing internal investigation.

ACFCS – www.acfcs.org – offers the CFCS certification exam from its headquarters in Miami, Florida. This is the CFCS examination outline:

- Understanding financial crime: financial crime commonalities, money laundering controls and investigation, ethical responsibility and best practices.

- Investigating financial crime: financial crime investigation, fraud detection and investigation, money and commodities flow.
- Enforcement actions and mechanisms: tax evasion and enforcement, asset recovery.
- Compliance: programs and controls, global anti-corruption compliance and enforcement, international regulations and standards, data security and privacy.

The University of New Haven and the Association of Certified Financial Crime Specialists (ACFCS.org) announced in 2013 that the Department of Criminal Justice at the University of New Haven was the first to offer a course leading to ACFCS certification. Students enrolled in the course on Investigating Financial Crimes were to learn the legal, ethical and practical aptitudes necessary to become financial crime specialists. The course was to use the 340-page CFCS Certification Exam Study Manual and online preparatory course resources from ACFCS as its educational materials (www.newhaven.edu).

## Certified fraud examiners

The Association of Certified Fraud Examiners (ACFE) was created for the same sort of reasons as the ACFCS. Becoming a certified fraud examiner requires documented academic and professional qualifications. Formal education in the fraud examination field is new and limited (Wells, 2003). The ACFE website (www.acfe.com) addresses the needs of ACFE members and also provides free resources to the general public (Anders, 2006). Certified fraud examiners have ample career opportunities, since the CFE certification was created in response to the demand for expertise in fraud prevention and detection (Morgan and Nix, 2003).

Perhaps Debbie Cutler was born to be a fraud examiner (Wells, 2003: 77):

> "When I was young, my family referred to me as Perry Mason," she said. "I was a very inquisitive child who wouldn't give up until I got the answers." It was happenstance that led her to combine her natural talents with her accounting degree. "I'd spent 10 years in public accounting performing traditional audit work," Cutler said. "One day a partner invited me to help investigate an accounting malpractice case that included fraud allegations against a U.S. senator. I jumped at the chance, and as it turned out, I loved the work."

As in other countries, investigators in the United States have a variety of backgrounds. It is not only lawyers, accountants and business consultants who are investigators. Sociologists and criminologists may also undertake tasks relating to the investigation. Examples are mentioned by Kennedy (2013), who writes about forensic sociology and criminology. Investigation by sociologists and criminologists might be concerned about people who have neglected their responsibilities, people who have abused their positions, or organizations where training and guidelines have been missing.

Thus, fraud examiners encompass a wide array of professions, including auditors, accountants, fraud investigators, loss prevention specialists, attorneys, educators, sociologists and criminologists. While fraud examiners in the United States can work independently, many are also member of the ACFE. Fraud examiners provide a broad range of services to businesses and governmental agencies as either employees or independent consultants (ACFE, 2008). A fraud examiner may assist in a fraud investigation by procuring evidence, taking statements and writing reports (Machen and Richards, 2004).

When hiring a fraud examiner, a company should seek an evaluation that is both disinterested and reliable (Machen and Richards, 2004: 68):

> These objectives, however, can occasionally conflict. Where employees within the organization conduct the fraud investigation, the results of such an investigation may be considered suspect because they are obtained by parties who are or at least appear to be biased. Thus, while the company may prefer to use examiners with historical knowledge and details about the company, personnel, and accounting systems, their retention may raise issues of credibility. On the other hand, while the investigation of a fraud examiner who has no prior connection with the company may be unbiased, the resulting evaluation may also exhibit the examiner's inexperience with the particular organization and its business practices.

In balancing the twin goals of disinterestedness and reliability, Machen and Richards (2004) suggest that a company should consider the purpose of the investigation. Where the results are to be used in-house or where the company is simply establishing a fraud prevention system, there is less concern regarding credibility. Thus, a fraud examiner who has knowledge of the business may be a smarter choice in that instance because of their familiarity with the company. In contrast, where information from the fraud investigation may be subject to scrutiny by those outside the company, the appearance of disinterestedness becomes more critical and the company should consider hiring an independent fraud examiner.

Within the broad category of fraud examiners are forensic accountants who specialize in a unique brand of accounting that departs from the traditional methods employed in the accounting field (Machen and Richards, 2004).

Similar to the situation in the UK, where companies are expected to contribute to the detection of law violations via their self-reports, companies in the U.S. are expected to make disclosures. Prosecutors in the U.S. consider whether the company made a voluntary and timely disclosure as well as the company's willingness to provide relevant information and evidence and identify relevant actors inside and outside the company, including senior executives. This is according to a resource guide to the U.S. foreign corrupt practices act.

In their report to the nation on occupational fraud and abuse, ACFE (2014) analyze more than a thousand cases of occupational fraud. The majority of cases reported (61 percent) were referred to law enforcement for criminal prosecution.

The median loss for cases referred to prosecution was $200,000, while cases that were not referred had a median loss of $75,000.

The Association of Certified Fraud Examiners is not a U.S.-only organization. The CFE designation is an international designation and the ACFE has reported that approximately 40 percent of its membership is outside the United States. They are all fraud fighters. It is rumored that there are at least 16 CFEs in Norway. Some of these individuals work at the large accounting firms.

## Police versus internal investigations

An investigation is an investigation, regardless of whether the investigator belongs to a police agency or a private firm. The goal is to uncover the facts in a particular situation. In doing so, the truth of the situation is the ultimate objective. However, an investigation by the police starts with a crime, or suspected crime, and the end goal is to arrest and successfully prosecute the guilty person(s), or alternatively, dismiss the case because of innocence or lack of evidence. A private internal investigation always has the goal of determining how and why a negative event or negative events occurred. It is after the facts to produce a statement of facts that all involved can agree upon. Also, a private investigation may have the goal of preventing it from happening again. Of course, if there was no event, there is nothing to investigate. Fraud awareness as prevention and fraud investigations can be carried out separately and have different objectives.

The purpose of an internal investigation is to define the points to prove and then collect documentary, interview-based and other evidence, which either confirms these points or finds there is no case to answer. These conclusions, and the evidence on which they are based, are set out in a report, which should then be considered by a person or people external to, and independent of, the investigation process.

Police investigations differ from private investigations because they aim to convict a person of a crime or dismiss a person from the case, while internal investigations are used more to evaluate the potential for economic crime to occur and to deal with the issue internally rather than through the involvement of the police.

Private investigators tend to be offense focused, while police investigators tend to be suspect focused. However, despite these differences there is sufficient commonality between the two types of investigation for cooperation and joint working to be possible. For example, they each gather intelligence on accepted cases, interview suspects in accordance with defined procedures and preserve evidential continuity. In addition, both separate intelligence from investigation, employ trained and qualified staff, use credit reference and other publically available data, record their investigations on a computerized case management system, and utilize interview rooms and evidence storage.

The roles of police officers and private investigators differ in that they do not have the same powers. Police officers have strict rules that they have to follow as part of their remit. They are responsible for following the rules and guidelines set out by their law enforcement unit. Private investigators have more freedom to explore and conduct inquiries into suspected crime and criminals. However, police officers have the advantage of being able to seize documents and subpoena the guilty party. The police have formal power as law enforcement officers on behalf of society. While private police have less power in their work, they enjoy more freedom in how they do their work. Private investigators do not have the same powers as the police, but nor do they have to work according to the same strict guidelines.

The government allows the police to conduct special investigation activities such as intrusive inquiry, covert human operations, infiltration, surveillance and covert recording of communications. The police may set up undercover enterprises, institutions, organizations and units. During undercover questioning, law enforcement officers can mask their identity or the purpose of the questioning.

The criticism that arises in relation to white-collar crime is the cost of policing fraud. When dealing with small internal frauds, the "police would be called but often they did not offer help" (Brooks and Button, 2011: 307). The lack of or limited nature of resources has constrained the police force in the area of fraud. The private sector has criticized the police for being unwilling to tackle fraud investigations, but it is sometimes simply a matter of resources not being available for confronting the issue. There may also sometimes be a question mark over whether the police view fraud as a serious crime – or have the capabilities in education and training to tackle economic crime (Button et al., 2007a, b).

Organizations may feel that the police lack commitment to cases of this sort and so do not report them. Instead, they may report them to the private investigation sector. The problem with this is that fraud may be seen as a private matter, which "can downgrade the seriousness of the offence as it does not require a public 'state' sanction, censure and condemnation and is hidden, and dealt with in-house in a secretive manner" (Brooks and Button, 2011: 310). People go to private investigators when they feel that the police will not take their concerns seriously. However, the police still hold power when it comes to preparing an arrest and deciding whether or not a place may be searched for evidence. The police must be present when an unwanted search occurs on business premises or homes.

Gill and Hart (1997) argue that distinctions between public and private forms of policing are becoming increasingly blurred, and a number of hybrid organizations have materialized as part of "gray" policing. The two sectors overlap in different ways. Although the public police have traditionally expressed skepticism about the caliber of their private sector counterparts, there are a number of examples of effective cooperation. In some instances the public police have benefited from an additional source of relevant information.

Private investigators have been criticized for possible bias in favor of the client that hires them to investigate an organization. They are usually paid by the client to find something out of the ordinary. This can lead to bias when conducting their research. Thus, the investigator might not want to go against the client that is paying for their service. This will have a negative impact on the other parties involved. Clients "may themselves attempt to influence investigations in order to limit lines of responsibility and produce narrow interpretations of incidents" (Williams, 2005: 199). There can thus be "a constant tension between commercial imperatives and professional standards" in white-collar crime investigations (Williams, 2005: 199).

A private investigator can potentially challenge the rule of law by acting in effect as a police investigator, public prosecutor and court judge. This kind of privatization of law enforcement can represent a threat to the criminal justice system in democratic societies (Gottschalk, 2017).

Private investigators may work alongside police detectives in order to collect evidence. Direct evidence such as forensic samples such as hair, clothing fibers or computer documents is physical proof of an illegal act. Indirect evidence is collected through interviewing witnesses or potential accomplices or through someone identifying the offender, for example from a photograph (Carson, 2013).

Witness intimidation should be minimized or completely avoided in interviews. Certain witnesses to an investigation might feel intimidated by the alleged wrongdoer, even by the simple fact that the alleged wrongdoer is in the workplace. Even worse, the alleged wrongdoer (and even the complainant) might intimidate, harass or retaliate against witnesses in an attempt to influence the outcome of an investigation. Extreme circumstances might require removing the suspect, the complainant or witnesses from the workplace via paid suspension.

## Implications from convenience

Convenience theory has implications for investigations of white-collar crime. Convenience theory suggests that white-collar crime can be explained by economic motive, organizational opportunity and deviant behavior. Economic motives include both personal profit from occupational crime and organizational profit from corporate crime. Investigating illegal personal profit will typically be concerned with embezzlement from employers, receipt of bribes from suppliers or any other activity where an individual abuses his or her position for personal gain. The investigation will focus on transactions initiated by suspected individuals. Investigating illegal corporate profit will typically be concerned with financial manipulation, provision of bribes to customers or any other activity where a corporate executive abuses his or her position to improve business performance. The investigation will focus on activities related to reaching business goals.

Organizational opportunity can be found in the power and influence that individuals enjoy in inter-organizational relationships as well as intra-organizational relationships. Investigating organizational opportunities will typically be concerned with power structures as well as formal and informal decision-making in the business. Degrees of freedom for top executives should be examined to determine the extent to which their activities are monitored by others in the organization. Goal achievements should be studied in terms of the means that were applied.

Deviant behavior can be found in cultures where individuals are allowed to determine for themselves how they do their job, while others determine what they should achieve. Key personnel are given a description of what performance outcomes should be; how these outcomes are achieved is left to their discretion. If traditional as well as non-traditional behaviors are allowed so long as outcomes match goals, and if transparency is lacking, then investigations should focus on incidents of deviant behavior reported by whistleblowers and other sources of information.

Lee and Fargher (2013) studied variation in the extent of whistleblowing disclosures. As a measure of whistleblowing implementation, they examined the provision of a hotline channel. Their results suggest that the extent of whistleblowing disclosures is positively associated with the permissibility of anonymous reporting and organizational support for whistleblowing, the number of external directors on the audit committee and the existence of concentrated shareholdings. The findings also indicate a greater likelihood of hotline provision when companies are larger in size, have a higher level of current inventory and permit anonymous reporting. A standard reporting policy may lack credibility. Mere disclosures within a whistleblowing policy do not guarantee that a good whistleblowing system is in place. Therefore, reporting hotlines seem more effective in detecting fraud.

# 6
# CRIME INVESTIGATIONS IN NORWAY

Most reports from private internal investigations are not available to the public because of secrecy. This is related to business secrets and other confidential information, data protection of sensitive information about identified individuals, and general wish to avoid public attention (Gottschalk and Tcherni-Buzzeo, 2017).

In Norway, we were able to obtain 60 private investigation reports written for their clients by law firms, consulting firms and global auditing firms such as BDO, Ernst & Young, KPMG and PwC. All reports are the property of client organizations, and it is up to clients to make reports publicly available.

For our empirical study we have selected seven reports of investigations out of 60 examinations. Our sample consists of cases where all suspects received prison sentences after the private internal investigations were completed. While information from the private internal investigations did not necessarily cause convictions, the cases all involved public investigation in the form of police investigation in addition to private internal investigation, as well as public prosecution and, finally, conviction in Norwegian courts. Table 6.1 lists the seven cases.

In this chapter we first present the total sample of 60 internal investigations. We then discuss the findings of each of the seven investigation reports listed in Table 6.1 as they relate to the suspected white-collar criminal who ended up in prison. The three dimensions of convenience theory are discussed for each of the seven convicted white-collar offenders.

## Sixty investigation reports

A sample of 60 private internal investigation reports from Norway is presented in Table 6.2. They can be described in terms of their start, process, result and impact. Quality can be determined by the mandate and motivation for the examination, the professional examination process and the investigation results, as well as the

**TABLE 6.1** Summary of convenience findings in reports of internal investigations

| White-collar criminal | White-collar crime | Economic dimension (motive) | Organizational dimension (opportunity) | Behavioral dimension (deviance) |
|---|---|---|---|---|
| Are Blomhoff CEO Priest 52 years old | Embezzlement Betanien Foundation 3 years prison | Greed for private apartment and expensive parties | Exclusive responsibility for money transfers | Different behavior in Spain and Norway |
| Leif Walle Chairman 61 years old | Misappropriation of funds Building society 3 years prison | Desire to expand own construction enterprise | Chairman position in customer organization | Defined it as a win-win situation |
| Lars Brorson CFO 40 years old | Embezzlement Hadeland Broadband 4.5 years prison | Greed for expensive property and consumer goods | Exclusive responsibility for money transfers | Blamed lack of control mechanisms for his fraud |
| Johannes Lunde CEO 23 years old | Tax evasion Lunde Group 6 years prison | As the founder he wanted to rescue his enterprise | Accounting manipulated by trusted executives | Intended to pay back after corporate recovery |
| Ivar Henriksen CEO 65 years | Fraud Public Water 8 years prison | Desire for power and influence in the local community | Double-bind leadership with frightened employees | No harm or damage, only business success |
| Frank Murud Property manager 48 years old | Fraud School buildings 7 years prison | Greed to buy boats, cars and houses | Procurement of goods and services to school buildings | Lack of control when violation of powers |
| Helge Leite CEO 51 years old | Corruption Unibuss transport 3.5 years prison | Desire to expand personal property and home | Offer of bribe by vendor | Everyone else in the procurement business does it |

consequences of the investigation. We focus on the reports by describing how key issues in private investigations were dealt with by financial crime specialists in the 60 investigations. Our four key issues are privatization of law enforcement, disclosure of investigation reports to the police, competence of private investigators and limits imposed by investigation mandates.

The column for disclosure in Table 6.2 lists how investigation reports were obtained for this research. It is important to keep in mind that these were the only ones we were able to obtain. We were denied access to a number of other reports. In addition, there is probably a much larger number of private investigation reports that we as researchers do not know about (Gottschalk and Tcherni-Buzzeo, 2017).

**TABLE 6.2** Key issues in private investigations

| # | Private investigation case | Privatization of law enforcement | Disclosure of investigation report | Competence of private investigators | Limits by investigation mandate |
|---|---|---|---|---|---|
| 1 | Adecco helse<br>Nursing and cleaning services business<br>Wiersholm (2011) | Violation of labor laws for employees working too long hours | Denied disclosure for research, only summary available | Lawyers without investigative focus | Limited to possible violations of working environment legislation |
| 2 | Ahus hospital<br>Public hospital<br>PwC (2013) | Fraud by vendor, paid back without prosecution | Posted on Ahus hospital website | Forensic accounting with investigative focus | Limited to transactions with vendor |
| 3 | Andebu kommune<br>Municipality<br>BDO (2014) | Corruption in procurement of public property | Posted on municipality website | Mainly legal knowledge | Limited to two local suspects |
| 4 | Betanien stiftelse<br>Nursing homes<br>BDO (2014) | Embezzlement by CEO when in Spain | Pressure from media and whistleblowers | Forensic management accounting | Limited to CEO transactions |
| 5 | Briskeby<br>Football stadium<br>Lynx (2011) | Suspected fraud never investigated | Posted on Hamar municipality website | Lawyers with investigative focus | Mandate revised during investigation |
| 6 | Demokratene parti<br>Political party<br>Partirevisjon (2016) | Illegal subsidies from the government | Posted on website for control committee | Both legal and accounting expertise | Limited to political party obligations |
| 7 | DNB bank<br>Financial institution<br>Hjort (2016) | Money laundering in tax havens | Panama Papers on tax havens | Only formal legal review of documents | Limited to reputation damage |
| 8 | Drammen kommune<br>Municipality<br>Deloitte (2017) | Corruption in building permits | Posted on municipality website | Detective and managerial knowledge | Limited to rules and regulations |
| 9 | Eckbo stiftelse<br>Family foundation<br>Thommessen (2009) | Misconduct in assets, but no crime | Posted on Oslo city website | Lawyers without investigative focus | Limited to asset mis-appropriation |
| 10 | Fadderbarna stiftelse<br>NGO for children<br>BDO (2011) | Individual dismissed, but never prosecuted | Accepted disclosure for research | Auditors with investigative focus | Limited to accusations |
| 11 | Forsvaret militæret<br>Defense army<br>Dalseide (2006) | Individual dismissed, but never prosecuted | Posted on defense ministry website | Auditors with bureaucratic approach | Limited to corruption suspicions |
| 12 | Forsvaret militæret<br>Defense army<br>PwC (2014) | Sale of old navy vessels to terrorists | Posted on government website | Forensic accountants | Limited to transactions by suspect |
| 13 | Forsvars-departementet<br>Ministry of Defense<br>PwC (2015) | Sale of old navy vessels to terrorists | Posted on government website | Lawyers | Limited to rules and regulations |

Crime investigations in Norway 99

| # | Private investigation case | Privatization of law enforcement | Disclosure of investigation report | Competence of private investigators | Limits by investigation mandate |
|---|---|---|---|---|---|
| 14 | Furuheim stiftelse Church foundation Dalane and Olsen (2006) | Two persons convicted to prison | Accepted disclosure for research | Lawyers with investigative approach | Open investigation of management issues |
| 15 | Gassnova institution Carbon capture and storage company BDO (2013) | No misconduct or crime | Accepted disclosure for research | Auditors with formalistic approach | Limited to procurement processes |
| 16 | Grimstad kommune Municipality BDO (2016) | Corruption in public procurement | Posted on municipality website | Legal knowledge | No access to emails for review |
| 17 | Hadeland og Ringerike Bredbånd Communication company PwC (2014) | CFO convicted to prison, CEO and chairman left after massive media pressure | Disclosed after massive media pressure, obtained from local newspaper for research | Auditors with formalistic approach without investigative focus | Limited to facts, legal issues and internal controls |
| 18 | Hadeland Energi Utility company PwC (2014) | CFO convicted to prison, CEO and chairman left after massive media pressure | Disclosed after massive media pressure, obtained from local newspaper for research | Auditors with formalistic approach without investigative focus | Limited to transactions and legal issues |
| 19 | Halden Ishall Sports ice Arena KPMG (2012) | Misconduct without consequences | Obtained from Halden municipality for research | Auditors with passive approach | Limited by small investigation budget |
| 20 | Halden kommune Municipality Gjørv and Lund (2013) | Misconduct without consequences | Obtained from Halden municipality for research | Lawyers with passive approach | Limited to accusations by two whistle-blowers |
| 21 | Hordaland politi Police department Wiersholm (2015) | Misconduct without consequences | Posted on government website | Lawyers with formal approach | Limited to one whistleblower |
| 22 | Kraft & Kultur Power utility company Ernst & Young (2012) | CEO prosecuted by the police | Disclosed after massive media pressure, obtained from newspaper for comments | Auditors with forensic accounting approach | Open investigation of board members' knowledge roles |
| 23 | Kragerø Fjordbåtselskap Shipping company Deloitte (2012) | Dismissed CEO never prosecuted | Posted on Kragerø municipality website | Lawyers without investigative focus | Limited to conflicts between board and management |
| 24 | Kvam Auto Car dealer Wikborg (2015) | Executives' abuse of company assets | Leaked from victim of executives' actions | Formal legal without inquiry | Limited to a few suspects and transactions |

(Continued)

**TABLE 6.2** *Continued*

| # | Private investigation case | Privatization of law enforcement | Disclosure of investigation report | Competence of private investigators | Limits by investigation mandate |
|---|---|---|---|---|---|
| 25 | Leksvik kommune *Municipality* Revisjon Midt (2017) | Lucrative employment contract for councilor | Posted on municipal website | Financial crime specialist | Limited to one person's employment contract |
| 26 | Lindeberg sykehjem *Nursing home* Kommunerevisjon (2013) | Labor laws violated, but no public prosecution | Posted on website by radical party in Oslo municipality | Passive investigation | Limited to control of formal procedures |
| 27 | Lunde Group *Transportation company* Bie (2012) | Public prosecution based on bankruptcy report | Obtained for research from bankruptcy lawyer | Active investigation by bankruptcy lawyer | Complete bankruptcy report, no limitations |
| 28 | Moskvaskolen *Norwegian school in Moscow* Ernst & Young (2013) | Rector dismissed and reported, but case dismissed by the police | Obtained for research from Skedsmo high school | Passive investigation of documents and failed interviews | Limited to consequences for suspected individuals |
| 29 | NAV tjenester *Social security* Wiersholm (2016) | Revealing celebrities for profit | Posted on social security website | Digital search and retrieval | No investigation of possible profits |
| 30 | Nordea Bank *Financial institution* Mannheimer Swartling (2016) | Money laundering in tax havens | Panama Papers on tax havens | Only formal legal review of documents | Limited to subsidiary activities |
| 31 | Norges Fotballforbund *Football association* Lynx (2013) | Misconduct but no crime | Obtained from newspaper asking for comments | Active inquiry prevented by client | Limited access to data |
| 32 | Norsk Tipping *Public betting firm* Deloitte (2010) | Misconduct but no crime | Posted on company website | Passive legal investigation of relationships | Limited to individual financial dispositions |
| 33 | Næringsdepartementet *Ministry of Commerce* PwC (2016) | Corruption in state-owned companies | Posted on government website | Formal legal review | Limited to formal rules and procedures |
| 34 | Omsorgsbygg Oslo *Municipality service* PwC (2008) | Contract terminated, but case dismissed in court | Obtained from City of Oslo for research | Financial crime specialists trusting outside single judgment | Limited to Labor Inspection Authority's accusations |
| 35 | Omsorgsbygg Spania *Municipality service* PwC (2009) | Displaced executive without prosecution | Posted on City of Oslo website | Forensic accounting without investigative interviews | Superficial investigation because of cost constraints |
| 36 | Oslo Renovasjon *Municipality service* Deloitte (2017) | Terminated contract after political pressure | Posted on City of Oslo website | Passive formal review | Focus on bureaucracy rather than results |

Crime investigations in Norway  **101**

| # | Private investigation case | Privatization of law enforcement | Disclosure of investigation report | Competence of private investigators | Limits by investigation mandate |
|---|---|---|---|---|---|
| 37 | Oslo Vei<br>Road construction company<br>Kvale (2013) | Misconduct and crime, but no police investigation | Disclosed by bankruptcy lawyer for research | Bankruptcy lawyers avoided crime focus | Only focusing on bankruptcy issues |
| 38 | Politiets utlending<br>Police department<br>KPMG (2016) | Misconduct by executives revealed by whistleblowers | Denied insight until pressure from students | Management behavior | Criticism of whistleblowers |
| 39 | Rana kommune<br>Cities investing in Terra bonds<br>PwC (2008) | Misconduct but no crime, mayor left | Obtained from city mayor | Financial crime specialists without responsibility focus | Limited to roles in failed investments |
| 40 | Region Syd<br>County<br>Kromann Reumert (2015) | Accusation of misconduct against politician | Published by the government | Legal review without substance | Limited to politician behavior |
| 41 | Romerike Vannverk<br>Public water supply<br>Distriktsrevisjonen (2007) | CEO and others sentenced to prison | Posted on website by Romerike public district | Combined legal and forensic accounting | No limitations |
| 42 | Samferdselsetaten<br>Public transportation<br>PwC (2007) | Removed executive without prosecution | Obtained from City of Oslo for research | Formal investigation procedure | Limited to accusations against named individuals |
| 43 | Sandefjord kommune<br>Municipality<br>Tenden (2017) | Abuse of councilor position | Posted on municipality website | Purely legal consideration | Limited to whistleblowing |
| 44 | Skjervøy kommune<br>Municipality<br>KomRev NORD (2015) | Abuse of mayor position | Retrieved from police records | Facts without conclusions | Limited to documents and selective interviews |
| 45 | Stangeskovene<br>Private forest property<br>Roscher and Berg (2013) | Investigation report failed as evidence in court | Obtained from one shareholder for research | Detailed transaction review without other investigative sources | Limited to shares handled by the board |
| 46 | Stavanger kommune<br>City of Stavanger project for children<br>PwC (2013) | Investigators failed to find out what had happened in Turkey | Obtained from City of Stavanger | Failed to interview main information source | Limited to transactions within a law firm |
| 47 | Sykehuset Innlandet<br>Hospital<br>Davidsen and Sandvik (2011) | Misconduct but no crime, no consequence | Posted on hospital website | Legal assessment without other perspectives | Limited to accusations by whistleblowers |
| 48 | Telenor VimpelCom<br>Telecom licenses<br>Deloitte (2016) | Corruption in VimpelCom | Some obstacles before obtaining | Legal and accounting knowledge | Assumptions about executive behavior |

(*Continued*)

**TABLE 6.2** Continued

| # | Private investigation case | Privatization of law enforcement | Disclosure of investigation report | Competence of private investigators | Limits by investigation mandate |
|---|---|---|---|---|---|
| 49 | Tomter Handel *Property management* Holmen (2014) | Abuse of political power | Some obstacles before obtaining | Management accounting knowledge | Auditing perspective |
| 50 | Troms Kraft *Power supply company* Nergaard (2013) | Misconduct but no crime, board members left | Disclosed after massive media pressure, obtained from journalist asking for comments | Management review rather than inquiry | Unlimited and unfocused inquiry of too many issues |
| 51 | Undervisningsbygg *School maintenance* Kommunerevisjonen (2006) | Some internal and external persons sentenced to prison | Posted on Oslo City website | Failed to detect more crime, that was later revealed by police investigation | Limited to a formal review and audit |
| 52 | Undervisningsbygg *School maintenance* Kommunerevisjonen (2006) | More internal and external persons sentenced to prison | Posted on Oslo City website | Failed to detect more crime, that was later revealed by police investigation | Limited to a formal review and audit |
| 53 | Unibuss *Public transportation* Wiersholm (2012) | Bribes received from vendor | Posted on website by company | Legal knowledge | Mainly documents |
| 54 | Utenriksdepartementet *Foreign Affairs* Duane Morris (2016) | Corruption at embassy housing | Disclosed by request | Legal knowledge | Interviews and documents in Vietnam |
| 55 | Utenriksdepartementet *Foreign Affairs* Sentral kontroll (2016) | Funding to ex-colleagues without tender | Disclosed by request | Foreign affairs knowledge, no detective knowledge | Superficial review of documents and interviews |
| 56 | Utenriksdepartementet *Foreign Affairs* Sentral kontroll (2017) | Misconduct in external funding procedures | Disclosed by request | Foreign affairs knowledge, no detective knowledge | Superficial review of documents and interviews |
| 57 | Utlendingsdirektoratet *Foreign refugees* Deloitte (2016) | Returned refugees to Afghanistan | Disclosed by request | Formal review of rental agreements | Reviewed Afghan documents |
| 58 | Verdibanken *Religious bank* Wiersholm (2012) | Misconduct, but not crime, one executive dismissed | Obtained from executive in the bank | Lawyers without investigative skills | Limited to legal assessment of accusations in the media |
| 59 | Videoforhandlere *Video film distributors and dealers* BDO (2013) | Misconduct, but not crime, no consequences | Obtained from victim of the investigation | Lawyers without investigative skills | Limited to review of subsidy payments and routines |
| 60 | World Ventures *Gambling company* Lotteritilsynet (2014) | Illegal Ponzi scheme | Disclosed by request | Lottery expertise | Comparison of law and firm activities |

Investigation report references:
1. Wiersholm (2011). *Granskingsrapport. Oppsummering. Adecco Norge AS (Investigation Report. Summary. Adecco Norway Inc.)*, law firm Wiersholm, Oslo, Norway, September 23, 23 pages.
2. PwC (2013). *Utvidet revisjon av Akershus universitetssykehus HF (Extended audit at Akershus university hospital)*, auditing firm PwC, Oslo, Norway, May 22, 15 pages.
3. BDO (2014). *Undersøkelse av påstander om inhabilitetsforhold i Andebu commune (Investigation into allegations of biased decision-making in Andebu municipality)*, auditing firm BDO, Oslo, Norway, September 24, 23 pages.
4. BDO (2014). *Stiftelsen Betanien. Sammendrag (Betanien Foundation. Summary)*, auditing firm BDO, Oslo, Norway, June 21, 10 pages.
5. Lynx (2011). *Briskebyrapporten (The Briskeby Report)*, law firm Lynx, Oslo, Norway, August 17, 267 pages.
6. Partirevisjon (2016). *Oppdrag om kontroll av Demokratene i Norge (Assignment concerning control of the Democrats in Norway)*, Partirevisjonsutvalget (Party Auditing Committee), Oslo, Norway, February 29, 5 pages.
7. Hjort (2016). *Rapport til styret i DNB (Report to the DNB board)*, law firm Hjort, Oslo, Norway, September 11, 18 pages.
8. Deloitte (2017). *Gransking. Byggesaksavdelingen. Drammen kommune (Investigation. Building permits department. Drammen municipality)*, auditing firm Deloitte, Oslo, Norway, January 24, 53 pages.
9. Thommessen (2009). *Uavhengig undersøkelse av Eckbos Legater (Independent inquiry into Eckbo's Foundations)*, law firm Thommessen, Oslo, Norway, January, 119 pages.
10. BDO (2011). *Rapport til Lotteri- og stiftelsestilsynet vedrørende gransking av stiftelsen Fadderbarnas Framtid (Report to the Lottery- and Foundation Authority concerning inquiry into Sponsored Childrens' Future)*, auditing firm BDO, Oslo, Norway, December 19, 46 pages.
11. Dalseide (2006). *Rapport fra Granskingsutvalget for IKT-kontrakter i Forsvaret oppnevnt av Kongen i statsråd 6. januar 2006 (Report from the investigation committee for ICT contracts in the Defense appointed by the King in state council January 6, 2006)*, committee leader Nils Dalseide, Oslo, Norway, June 16, 184 pages.
12. PwC (2014). *Forsvarets logistikkorganisasjon. Rapport etter gjennomgang av salg av fartøy (Report after review of vessel sales)*, auditing firm BDO, Oslo, Norway, October 21, 35 pages.
13. PwC (2015). *Forsvarsdepartementet. Undersøkelse av forhold knyttet til Forsvarets avhending av fartøyer (Ministry of Defense. Inquiry into circumstances related to Defense sales of naval vessels)*, auditing firm PwC, Oslo, Norway, March 20, 50 pages.
14. Dalane and Olsen (2006). *Granskingsrapport. Ledelse og styring av Øyestad helselags boligstiftelse Furuheim (Report of investigation. Leadership and management of Øyestad health institution's housing foundation Furuheim)*, law firm Hald, Dalane and Heimvik, Arendal, Norway, December 1, 164 pages.
15. BDO (2013). *Gjennomgang av anskaffelsesprosess, konsulentinnleie og habilitiet i Gassnova (Review of procurement process, consultancy and bias in Gassnova)*, auditing firm BDO, Oslo, Norway, June 25, 27 pages.
16. BDO (2016). *Rapport til kontrollutvalget. Undersøkelse om kjøp av helsetjenester i Grimstad kommune (Inquiry into procurement of health care services in the municipality of Grimstad)*, auditing firm BDO, Oslo, Norway, December 7, 64 pages.
17. PwC (2014). *Hadeland og Ringerike Bredbånd. Rapport – gransking (Hadeland and Ringerike Broadband. Report – investigation)*, auditing firm PwC, Oslo, Norway, June 10, 32 pages.
18. PwC (2014). *Hadeland Energi. Rapport – gransking (Hadeland Energy. Report – investigation)*, auditing firm PwC, Oslo, Norway, June 23, 25 pages.
19. KPMG (2012). *Halden kommune – Granskingsrapport (Municipality of Halden – Report of Investigation)*, auditing firm KPMG, Oslo, Norway, February 1, 121 pages.
20. Hjort (2013). *Gransking i Halden kommune / Enhet for plan, byggesak og geodata (Investigation in the municipality of Halden / Department for planning, building permits and geo data)*, law firm Hjort, Oslo, Norway, October 24, 46 pages.

(*Continued*)

**TABLE 6.2** *Continued*

21. Wiersholm (2015). *Monika-saken. Arbeidsgivers håndtering av Robin Schaefers varsling (The Monika case. Employer's handling of Robin Schaefer's notice)*, law firm Wiersholm, Oslo, Norway, June 25, 111 pages.
22. Ernst & Young (2012). *Troms Kraft AS. Gransking av Kraft & Kultur i Sverige AB (Troms Energy Inc. Investigation into Energy & Culture in Sweden Inc.)*, auditing firm Ernst & Young, Stockholm, Sweden, May 11, 31 pages. (Swedish firm subsidiary of Norwegian energy company.)
23. Deloitte (2012). *Rapport Kragerø Fjordbåtselskap AS – Gransking (Report Kragerø Fjord Boats Inc. – Investigation)*, auditing firm Deloitte, Skien, Norway, March 30, 109 pages.
24. Wikborg (2015). *Granskingsrapport Kvam Auto AS (Investigation Report Kvam Auto Dealer Inc.)*, law firm Wikborg Rein, Bergen, Norway, May 12, 93 pages.
25. Revisjon Midt (2017). *Gransking. Rådmannens arbeidsavtaler. Leksvik kommune (Investigation. Councilor's employment contract. Municipality of Leksvik)*, regional auditing network Revisjon Midt-Norge, January, 36 pages.
26. Kommunerevisjon (2013). *Oslo kommunes saksbehandling i Lindebergsakene (Oslo municipality's handling of the Lindeberg cases)*, municipality auditing authority Kommunerevisjonen, Oslo, Norway, June 11, 92 pages.
27. Bie (2012). *Rapport til Stavanger tingrett. Lunde Gruppen AS, konkursbo med datterselskaper og deleide sleskaper (Report to Stavanger district court. Lunde Group Inc. bankruptcy with subsidiary companies and partially owned companies)*, law firm Vierdal, Stavanger, Norway, 86 pages.
28. Ernst & Young (2013). *Gransking – NRVS (Investigation – NRVS)*, Ernst & Young, Oslo, Norway, October 30, 52 pages.
29. Wiersholm (2016). *Tilgangskontroller i NAV. Gjennomgang, analyse og forslag til forbedringer (Access controls in NAV. Review, analysis and suggestions for improvements)*, law firm Wiersholm, Oslo, Norway, October 31, 41 pages.
30. Mannheimer Swartling (2016). *Report to Nordea Bank AB Governance Review*, law firm Mannheimer Swartling, Stockholm, Sweden, July 19, 42 pages. (Nordea operates in Norway, and Norwegians were paid attention in the Panama Papers.)
31. Lynx (2013). *1192-rapporten. Gransking. Internasjonale spilleroverganger (The 1192 report. Investigation. International player transitions)*, law firm Lynx, Oslo, Norway, 50 pages.
32. Deloitte (2010). *Norsk Tipping – Granskingsrapport (Norwegian Betting – Report of Investigation)*, auditing firm Deloitte, Oslo, Norway, August 16, 61 pages.
33. PwC (2016). *Gjennomgang av korrupsjonsregelverk, antikorrupsjonstiltak og eierstyring (Review of corruption regulations, anti-corruption efforts and owner management)*, auditing firm PwC, Oslo, Norway, September 1, 77 pages.
34. PwC (2008). *Granskingsrapport. Undersøkelser foretatt på oppdrag fra Oslo kommune, Byrådslederens avdeling v/Seksjon for internrevisjon (Investigation report. Inquiries carried out on behalf of the municipality, city council leader department, section for internal audit)*, auditing firm PwC, Oslo, Norway, May 21, 27 pages.
35. PwC (2009). *Gransking av "Spania-prosjektet" Oslo kommune (Investigation of the Spain project in the municipality of Oslo)*, auditing firm PwC, Oslo, Norway, December 17, 92 pages.
36. Deloitte (2017). *Renovasjonsetaten Oslo kommune. Gjennomgang av anskaffelsesprosess og kontraktsoppfølging i Renovasjonsetaten (Renovation service Oslo municipality. Review of procurement process and contract follow-up in the renovation service)*, auditing firm Deloitte, Oslo, Norway, April 25, 93 pages.
37. Kvale (2013). *Innberetning til Oslo byfogdembete i konkursbo Oslo Vei AS (Report to Oslo city bailiff authority in Oslo Road bankruptcy)*, law firm Kvale, Oslo, Norway, December 11, 53 pages.
38. KPMG (2016). *Politiets utlendingsenhet. Faktaundersøkelse og vurdering (Police immigration unit. Factual survey and assessment)*, auditing firm KPMG, Oslo, Norway, 74 pages.
39. PwC (2008). *Granskingsrapport. "Terra-saken i Rana kommune" (Report of investigation. The «Terra case» in Rana municipality)*, auditing firm PwC, Oslo, Norway, June 10, 52 pages.
40. Kromann Reumert (2015). *Undersøgelse af hændelsesforløbet vedrørende tilretning og ændring af fakturatekst fra ekstern leverandør (Investigation of event sequence regarding alignment and change of invoice

*text from external supplier)*, law firm Kromann Reumert, Copenhagen, Denmark, November 21, 27 pages. (Evaluated by student in Norway.)

41. Distriktsrevisjonen (2007). *Rapport etter granskingsoppdrag fra styrene i Nedre Romerike Vannverk og Sentralrenseanlegget (Report following inspection assignment from the boards of Lower Romerike Water Works and Central Drainage Plant)*, regional auditing service Nedre Romerike Distriktsrevisjon, Lillestrøm, Norway, May 30, 555 pages.
42. PwC (2007). *Granskingsrapport Samferdselsetaten. Undersøkelser foretatt på oppdrag fra Oslo kommune – Byrådslederens avdeling v/Seksjon for internrevisjon (Report of investigation. City Transportation Authority. Inquiry carried out on behalf of Oslo Municipality – Council manager's department at Internal Audit Function)*, auditing firm PwC, Oslo, Norway, December 19, 88 pages.
43. Tenden (2017). *Rapport fra undersøkelse varsling Sandefjord kommune (Report from investigation whistleblowing Sandefjord municipality)*, law firm Tenden, Sandefjord, Norway, July 4, 54 pages.
44. KomRev NORD (2015). *Undersøkelse i Skjervøy Fiskeriutvikling (Investigation into Skjervøy Fisheries Development)*, regional auditing service KomRev NORD, Tromsø, Norway, October 2, 138 pages.
45. Roscher and Berg (2013). *Stangeskovene granskingsberetning (Stange forests investigation report)*, auditing firm Ernst & Young and law firm Lynx, Oslo, Norway, January 4, 103 pages.
46. PwC (2013). *Kontrollutvalget i Stavanger kommune v/Rogaland Kontrollutvalgssekretariat. Undersøkelse/ gransking knyttet til Stavanger kommunes utbetaling av a-kontobeløp i forbindelse med den såkalte «Tyrkia-saken» (The control committee in Stavanger municipality by Rogaland control committee secretariat. Investigation/review related to the payment of account amounts by the municipality of Stavanger in connection with the so-called Turkey case)*, auditing firm PwC, Stavanger, Norway, September 11, 14 pages.
47. Davidsen and Sandvik (2011). *Undersøkelse av bekymringsmelding vedrørende psykiatridivisjonen (Inquiry into the concern message regarding the psychiatry division)*, law firm Haavind, Oslo, Norway, June 21, 15 pages.
48. Deloitte (2016). *Review – Ownership VimpelCom. Telenor ASA*, auditing firm Deloitte, Oslo, Norway, April 27, 54 pages.
49. Holmen (2014). *Granskning Tomter Handelsforening AS – Rapport (Investigation Tomter Trade Association Inc. – Report)*, auditing firm Holmen, Halden, Norway, May 2, 16 pages.
50. Nergaard (2013). *Sammendrag av granskingsrapport – Troms Kraft AS. I henhold til Nord-Troms tingretts kjennelse av 4. juli 2012 (Summary of investigation report – Troms Energy Inc. According to North Troms district court's decision of July 4, 2012)*, September 9, 38 pages.
51. Kommunerevisjonen (2006). *Granskingsrapport Undervisningsbygg Oslo (Report of Investigation School Buildings Oslo)*, municipality auditing Kommunerevisjonen, report number 16, Oslo, Norway, August, 30 pages.
52. Kommunerevisjonen (2006). *Granskingsrapport 2 Undervisningsbygg Oslo (Report of Investigation 2 School Buildings Oslo)*, municipality auditing Kommunerevisjonen, report number 27, Oslo, Norway, December, 44 pages.
53. Wiersholm (2012). *Rapport til styret i Unibuss (Report to the board at Unibuss)*, law firm Wiersholm, Oslo, Norway, May 24, 23 pages.
54. Duane Morris (2016). *Project House – report, conclusions and notes from interviews with selected landlords, real estate agents and locally engaged employees of the Royal Norwegian Embassy in Hanoi*, law firm Duane Morris, Hanoi, Vietnam, January 22, 172 pages.
55. Sentral kontroll (2016). *Gjennomgang av Utenriksdepartementets tildeling og forvaltning av tilskudd til ILPI gjennom prosjektet Nuclear Weapons Project (Review of the Ministry of Foreign Affairs' allocation and management of grants to ILPI through the project Nuclear Weapons Project)*, central control unit in the ministry Sentral kontrollenhet, Oslo, Norway, December, 23 pages.
56. Sentral kontroll (2017). *Gjennomgang av Utenriksdepartementets forvaltning av samarbeidet med ILPI 2009–2016 (Review of the Ministry of Foreign Affairs' management of the cooperation with ILPI 2009–2016)*, central control unit in the ministry Sentral kontrollenhet, Oslo, Norway, May, 25 pages.
57. Deloitte (2016). *Report of factual findings on the review of IRRANA program components VTY and HA*, auditing firm Deloitte, Oslo, Norway, February 12, 36 pages.

*(Continued)*

**TABLE 6.2** *Continued*

58. Wiersholm (2012). *Verdibanken ASA (The Value Bank Inc.)*, law firm Wiersholm, Oslo, Norway, November 19, 5 pages.
59. BDO (2013). *Gjennomgang av økonomiske bidrag til NVHF Forlag (Review of financial contributions to NVHF Publishing)*, auditing firm BDO, Oslo, Norway, June 28, 20 pages.
60. Lotteritilsynet (2014). *Lotteritilsynets tilsynsrapport om World Ventures i Norge med varsel om stans av ulovlig pyramidevirksomhet (Lottery Authority's surveillance report on World Ventures in Norway with notification of suspencion of illegal pyramid activities)*, Norwegian authority for lotteries and foundations Lotteri- og stiftelsestilsynet, February 19, 17 pages.

## Betanien Nursing Home

*Are Blomhoff* took advantage of a special assignment where he was the only executive involved in transfers of money from Norway to Spain. The money represented an investment in building a nursing home in Spain for retired Norwegians. Blomhoff was a trusted chief executive officer (CEO) at the religious foundation Betanien which invested in Spain. He is a priest by education and profession. He bought himself an apartment, and he also spent foundation money on parties with prostitutes. The Betanien foundation operates nursing homes, kindergartens, and health institutions. Two whistleblowers in Spain notified the chairman at Betanien in Norway, but they were ignore; the chairman could not believe that a priest would do such a thing. When the whistleblowers threatened to tell Norwegian media about the case, the chairman confronted the CEO with the allegations, and Blomhoff confessed to embezzlement. Fraud examiners from accounting firm BDO (2014b) were hired by the chairman to find out if the CEO had embezzled more money than he had already admitted. The private investigators found evidence of more embezzlement. In terms of convenience theory, we find evidence of all three dimensions:

1. *Motive in the economic dimension: Greed for private apartment and expensive parties in Spain.* While being a priest and CEO in Norway, he had suppressed all his desires for a wild life that could be enabled by money. Finally, he could enjoy life the way he really wanted.
2. *Opportunity in the organizational dimension: Exclusive responsibility for money transfers and no control by others.* He was handling large sums of money for the construction project, and only an invisible fraction of the money was taken by him. He did not really conceal his illegal transactions, but he knew that nobody else had access to the relevant accounts. The abused accounts were not part of either the Betanien Foundation in Norway or the Fundacion Betanien in Spain. Money transfers from Norway were conducted by employees after instructions from the CEO. The transfers were based on fake offers and invoices from Spanish suppliers. Blomhoff got travel and other personal expenses refunded by both Stiftelsen Betanien and Fundacion Betanien. Some of the money transfers occurred via a bank account in Luxembourg.

3. *Deviance in the behavioral dimension: Different behavior in Spain and Norway.* He would never have done it at home. While in Spain, he became a different person and was willing to embezzle money and hire prostitutes for parties with friends. His willingness increased as he did not see any damage or any victims of his crime. Blomhoff had problems with substance abuse, which was noticed by the whistleblowers.

In the report of investigation, fraud examiners at BDO (2014b: 7) write: "According to the assessment of BDO, the Foundations organizational and internal control is characterized by a situation where the chief executive has enjoyed substantial trust among board members and employees of the foundation and thus had wide powers".

Fraud examiners also criticize the board for not reacting timely to whistleblowing and to other information (BDO, 2014b: 10):

> Information has come to our attention about a safe that was removed from the former CEO's house in Spain, in addition to another safe that was allegedly stolen during a burglary. This happened in the days after the former CEO was confronted with the embezzlement claims. It is our opinion that the case could possibly have been far better documented if the board had chosen to contact the police before the former CEO was confronted with the issue.

## Furuheim Housing Foundation

*Leif Walle* was a trusted person in the community. He had been deputy mayor of Øyestad. He admitted infidelity and embezzlement. The police seized assets worth 35 million kroner (US$5 million). Walle had previously been head of the Joint Council of Churches in Arendal. In 2012 he was charged with gross misappropriation of funds and gross embezzlement as chairman and CEO in a housing foundation for seniors. He also misappropriated more than two million NOK from a church, an estate and a woman who was his ward.

Walle had involved a colleague in his fraud scheme. While Walle was sentenced to three years in prison, his colleague Knut Gausi was sentenced to three years and six months. Leif Walle confessed in court; Knut Gausi did not.

Locals found the Walle affair especially ugly. He defrauded his own church, an estate and – as a guardian – a psychiatric patient. He was an ex-deputy mayor and a senior figure within the bank and the church in Arendal. People thought it was absolutely incredible. In terms of convenience theory, we find evidence of all three dimensions:

1. *Motive in the economic dimension: Expansion desire for own construction enterprise.* Walle and Gausi were companions in the jointly owned Natvig Property. They were ambitious on behalf of the company that they were developing.

2. *Opportunity in the organizational dimension*: *Chairman position in the customer organization*. He was able to convince a land owner to sell an extremely attractive property at a low price to the church foundation, since he was the chairman of the board, so that he later could transfer the land to his own Natvig Property. Walle had all the powers necessary.
3. *Deviance in the behavioral dimension: Defined it as a win-win situation*. They claim that they did what was best for both parties (Hald, 2007: 15):

> Walle and Gausi have during the investigation stated that they contacted various developers to see if others might have an interest in taking over the project. However, no evidence was submitted to support this, either in the form of written requests, via advertising or in meetings with relevant interested parties.

## Hadeland Broadband network

*Lars Brorson* took advantage of his role as the only executive involved in transfers of money between companies in the corporation. According to fraud examiners from PwC (2014), Brorson transferred a total of 18 million Norwegian kroner (about US $3 million) to his own accounts and spent the money on housing and luxury goods. Brorson was the chief financial officer (CFO) at Hadeland Broadband, a subsidiary of Hadeland Energy. Since he came from a position at the mother company Hadeland, nobody in the subsidiary tried to question his deviant behavior.

During the same period, the Deloitte auditor wrote that financial statements were prepared in accordance with Norwegian laws and regulations. Auditor Ragnar Nesdal was one of six from Deloitte interviewed by investigator Gunnar Holm Ringen at auditing firm PwC (2014). In the interview, Nesdal felt that the company was so small that there was no requirement for annual meetings between the board and the company's auditors in accordance with Norwegian auditing law. The auditor had not attended board meetings or general assembly meetings. The only communication with the board had therefore been through written auditing statements from Deloitte.

For a long time there were attempts to keep the PwC (2014) report secret from the public. The local newspaper *Hadeland* was active in getting disclosure. The newspaper argued for transparency and wrote in its editorial on July 13, 2014:

> Hadeland has requested access to investigation reports prepared after the embezzlement in Hadeland and Ringerike Broadband (HRB) and Hadeland Energy (HE). The answer has been no, with reference to the Norwegian freedom of information act section 24, which states that documents can be exempted if they deal with offenses.

Finally, the owners agreed to public insight into the report. Soon after, Lars Brorson was convicted in the Norwegian district court to four years and six months in prison. In terms of convenience theory, we find evidence of all three dimensions:

1. *Motive in the economic dimension: Personal finances were a mess.* He wanted to impress his new girlfriend, and he also enjoyed luxury himself. He bought expensive cars, a cabin and a house, and he maintained a high level of consumption of expensive cognacs and other consumer goods.
2. *Opportunity in the organizational dimension: In charge of financial matters between parent and daughter companies.* Since he came from a position in the parent company Hadeland Energy, nobody at the subsidiary Hadeland Broadband dared to question his actions or behavior. They all assumed that Brorson had good contacts at the highest levels in Hadeland Energy, and that people at the highest levels had approved his style of financial management. Brorson had himself introduced formal routines at Hadeland Broadband while at Hadeland Energy, and he followed those routines when he joined Hadeland Broadband.
3. *Deviance in the behavioral dimension: Lack of control by auditor invited him to commit fraud.* He applied the neutralization technique that no damage had occurred as Hadeland Broadband still made a substantial profit. He admitted to lack of self-control when he explained himself in court. The impression in the court room was that Brorson perceived himself as a victim of his own desires and lack of self-control.

The Brorson case was uncovered on March 10, 2014, in connection with police investigations of another firm for tax and accounting offenses in a neighboring police district. Lars Brorson had done some accounting for this firm in addition to his job as CFO at Hadeland Broadband. He was also charged for these offenses, making the total add up to more than 20 million NOK. During the police investigation, it became known that Brorson had been convicted of embezzlement before, in combination with tax evasion, and that he had spent three years behind bars for it. The previous offense was committed while he was management for hire. It turned out that board members at Hadeland Energy were familiar with Brorson's past economic crime when he was hired in 2009.

## Lunde Transportation Group

*Johannes Lunde* was the founder of the Lunde Group, which quickly expanded into various forms of transportation of goods nationally and internationally. After two decades of sensational growth, the company faced possible collapse and bankruptcy. Lunde had worked very hard and did not want his life's work to collapse. He involved some of his trusted executives in a fraudulent scheme whereby they avoided taxes and bank repayments.

While Lunde was sentenced to six years in prison, his accomplices Morten Arnold Berg (CFO) and Ruth Karianne Hinna (accounting manager) were sentenced to four years and half a year respectively.

The Lunde Group finally went bankrupt, despite the acrobatic financial conduct of Lunde, Berg and Hinna. Law firm Vierdal (2012: 10) was hired to conduct an internal investigation:

> Johannes Lunde has had a pivotal role in all the companies and been the main person initiating and implementing or imposing on others to carry out dispositions in the Lunde system. It is currently the view that Johannes Lunde has predisposed everything on behalf of each individual company without regard for individual company interests (...)
>
> Internal transactions in the Lunde system have been very extensive. So far in the bankruptcy investigation it appears that the management in most companies, presumably supported by Johannes Lunde, has used companies' assets and debt obligations across the system, regardless of how well this served each individual company.

In terms of convenience theory, we find evidence of all three dimensions:

1. *Motive in the economic dimension: As the founder he wanted to rescue his enterprise.* Many founders fear the loss of identity and social prestige if they fail and fall. Their social status is tightly connected to positions that they have established after many years of hard work. They want to be perceived as successes and not failures by their environment. They know that many friendships and their participation in privileged networks are related to the enterprise they have created. Fear of falling was evident in the case of Johannes Lunde, when he initiated different fraud schemes.
2. *Opportunity in the organizational dimension: Accounting manipulated by trusted executives.* There being a conglomerate of registered companies, it was difficult if not impossible for outsiders to understand the performance or lack of performance in each company. For example (Vierdal, 2012: 9):

   > Payments totaling MNOK 15 have been posted in the accounting to Johannes Lunde in connection with borrowing from the vessel Time Bandit, via the enterprise Lunde and Haugland Property Inc.
   >
   > Single transactions have been detected where transfer declarations of receivables and liabilities have put third parties in a position of counter-claims by sale of shares.

3. *Deviance in the behavioral dimension: Intended to pay back after corporate recovery.* It is assumed that many white-collar criminals successfully engage in temporary tax evasion and bank fraud, making refunds when the business has recovered. Bankruptcy only occurs when there is no recovery. Following bankruptcy there is sometimes a court-ordered investigation of potential fraud. It seems that Johannes Lunde believed that collapse could be averted by fraud, his group of companies then being in a position to rectify the situation.

## Romerike Water Supply

*Ivar Henriksen* was CEO at the public water works outside Oslo, where he became well known for the good works that the company did for the local community. For example, he got a water fountain built outside a retirement home. For all these good deeds he received the Norwegian king's medal of merit. With company money he bought himself a hunting farm, complete with giraffes and other wild animals, in South Africa. He invited friends and associates to visit the farm. Many people knew about it, but nobody dared blow the whistle. Finally, someone got in touch with a journalist at the largest newspaper in Norway, which started write, with some care, about Henriksen. After a while, Distriktsrevisjonen (2007) was hired to conduct a private internal investigation. At the end of the fraud examination, the case was handed over to the police. Some years later, Henriksen was sentenced to eight years in prison for fraud, embezzlement and corruption.

In terms of convenience theory, we find evidence of all three dimensions:

1. *Motive in the economic dimension: Desire for power and influence in the local community.* Henriksen was labeled "king" in the local community. Using equipment and vehicles from the public waterworks, he found solutions for all kinds of problems. He saw himself as a key community supporter.
2. *Opportunity in the organizational dimension: Double-bind leadership with frightened employees.* Henriksen was charismatic (Distriktsrevisjonen, 2007: 133):

   > Ivar Henriksen has through years of hectic activity for the water works gained a special status in the community. His ability to persuade, to get his thoughts and ideas transferred to practical action, not to mention his contacts and influence in circles where decisions occurred, had given him a reputation for being a man of action with great power and influence.

3. Double-bind leadership belongs to the dark side of leadership. Mixed messages from Henriksen created a double bind for colleagues, subordinates, vendors and customers. Individuals were caught in situations where the criminal leader was expressing two orders of message, one denying the other. Victims of his leadership style found themselves in a position where they were unable to respond to the contradictory messages, since the nature of double-bind leadership makes meta communicative statements an impossibility (Distriktsrevisjonen, 2007: 109):

   > Investigators received a number of independent explanations showing that Henriksen often behaved in an authoritarian manner, especially towards employees, but also towards supplier representatives. This being the way he practiced leadership, he was surrounded by people who

feared him. The fear was based on the risk that you might fall out of favor, not to mention the employment difficulties that Henriksen could create. In addition, Henriksen is described as having changeable moods, which in itself created uncertainty for and distance from employees. Several informants have told investigators that on bad-mood days, it was best to stay away from Henriksen.

4. *Deviance in the behavioral dimension: No harm or damage, only business success.* Henriksen was an expansive chief executive who had a business idea of water works that extended beyond clean water in and used water out. He looked at himself as a business entrepreneur, whose genius entrepreneurship few understood. When he was caught, he applied one neutralization technique in particular, which was to condemn his condemners.

Distriktsrevisjonen (2007: 109) confirm in their report that Henriksen had undoubtedly made substantial efforts and succeeded in building and operating plants that were solid, efficient and very well suited for the future:

> Henriksen had great professional insight and innovative abilities, and he was energetic in his goal of developing the water works companies. The same applies to his interest in searching for new opportunities for the utilization of energy, especially with regard to sludge and wastewater. He set these capabilities into a broader context, and believed them to be of great interest to both the region and society at large. Through conversations with Henriksen, investigators have come to understand that he thinks he has not gained the acceptance he deserves for what he has contributed over many years.

## School buildings administration

*Frank Murud* was property manager for school buildings in the city of Oslo. He hired suppliers of building services and maintenance services. All invoices of amounts greater than 200,000 NOK (25,000 US dollars) were to be approved by two property managers. Murud wanted to challenge the system and approved alone an invoice for a substantially larger amount. The invoice was not stopped and the issuer got paid. Then Murud made an arrangement with certain trusted suppliers that they should send him fake invoices, he would approve them, and then they would share the money. This went on for many years, and Murud and his accomplices were able to get more than 80 million NOK (US$10 million) out of the city treasury.

Murud finally left this job to assume a position in another business. After some time he bought himself an expensive summer house in the southern part of Norway. He withdrew the money from his bank account just before New Year and paid the seller of the summer house. The bank reacted to the large sum and reported the incident to the police as possible tax evasion at year end. When the police looked into the matter, they could find no reason to suspect tax evasion, but there was a question of how Murud could have that much money given his regular income, according to figures from the internal revenue service. The fraud committed against the city of Oslo by the property manager was finally revealed.

Kommunerevisjonen (2006: 30) describe the role of Murud in their investigation report:

> The former property manager was part of senior management of School Buildings and had wide powers. He managed extraordinary actions across the property department without full or disaggregated budgets in place. The property manager was much more directly involved in procurement matters than other property managers.

Frank Murud comes across as a friendly and open-minded person. Even when some people noticed that he had a lot of money while working for the city, nobody suspected him of any wrongdoing. He told his wife that he was very successful in betting games and other kinds of gambling. In terms of convenience theory, we find evidence of all three dimensions:

1. *Motive in the economic dimension: Greed for boats, cars and houses.* He really enjoyed material wealth. When Murud was interviewed in prison, he was asked what the worst aspect was: prison sentence, marriage breakup, media coverage or asset recovery by the government. Murud answered that he had made new friends in prison, so that was OK. His wife had been unfaithful, so breakup was OK. Media coverage was also OK, as he had not noticed it during the trial. The only thing that made him upset was that his assets were taken away from him.
2. *Opportunity in the organizational dimension: Procurement of goods and services for school buildings.* Kommunerevisjonen (2006) found that there was no real management of financial transactions related to the maintenance of school buildings in Oslo. Both planned and ad hoc maintenance activities lacked budgetary controls. Murud found out about the shortcomings and exploited them.
3. *Deviance in the behavioral dimension: Lack of control when powers abused.* When Murud was serving his sentence in prison, he was more than willing to talk to people in the media and others about his experience and reflections. When we visited him in prison, he had prepared documents to show that it was quite common for fraud to be committed in the school buildings organization. He named a number of his former colleagues in that regard. Furthermore, he had prepared documents to show why controls had failed while he was implementing his fraud scheme. Murud blamed failing controls on the incompetence of internal auditors and accountants. Murud was upset that the city would not hire him as a consultant to review control procedures in all branches of city business.

Twelve accomplices were sentenced to prison in the same court case as Frank Murud. They had all been involved in fraud schemes at the Oslo school buildings department headed by former property manager Murud and a project manager.

## Unibuss public transportation

*Helge Leite* was CEO at Unibuss, a bus transportation organization owned by the city of Oslo. When Unibuss was to buy new buses for their transportation system in the city, they had several potential vendors. One vendor – the German MAN corporation – suggested to procurement executives at Unibuss that they specify buses with a length of exactly 18 meters and 75 centimeters. In the procurement papers, buses of this length were specified. The only manufacturer of buses this size was MAN. So MAN got the contract, at the same time bribing a total of nine Unibuss executives.

After some time, a number of large-scale corruption scandals surfaced in Germany. One of them involved Siemens, another one was at MAN. By accident or luck, a Unibuss employee read a newspaper in Germany while on vacation. When returning home, he told a member of the board at Unibuss.

Former CEO Helge Leite was sentenced to 3.5 years in prison for receiving a bribe. Eight more executives were sentenced to prison. In terms of convenience theory, we find evidence of all three dimensions:

1. *Motive in the economic dimension: Greed for extending personal property and home.* Leite was managing quite a large organization, but his salary as a public employee was relatively modest. He wanted more money to rebuild his house.
2. *Opportunity in the organizational dimension: Offer of bribe by vendor.* Wiersholm (2012: 21) write in their investigation report:

   > There has been a culture that bus vendors have paid for restaurant meals for Unibuss employees. The dinners have been connected to, for instance, Christmas festivities.
   >
   > Employees of Unibuss have been travelling with people who work on tenders and equipment specifications. There have been a number of factory visits and individual journeys of a seemingly private nature. The people have also enjoyed expensive socializing at sporting events. The relationships appear to be unfortunate.

   One of the sporting events that Leite attended, and which was paid for by a vendor, was the Rupholding biathlon.

3. *Deviance in the behavioral dimension: Everyone does it in the procurement business.* Some of the bribes occurred as maintenance services on Leite's private home paid for by Unibuss vendors. Leite argued that it is quite common and that it should be legal, not illegal.

Wiersholm (2012: 3) write in their report:

> The investigation has revealed that a limited group of people over several years, regularly and in different ways, have drained the company of funds. Two senior executives have utilized their positions for personal gain in connection with purchase of goods and services and the disposal of used buses. One senior employee has abused his position to obtain private benefits in that Unibuss paid for extensive work on his residence. In addition, the person involved in the resale of used buses of a special kind has likely harmed the company. The three senior executives have received regular assistance from one employee outside any management function. None of the persons are employed any longer at Unibuss.

Based on the investigations reports of fraud examiners, we were able to identify the extent to which convenience orientation played a role in white-collar crime. We found support for all three dimensions of convenience theory with all seven convicted offenders. Based on this exploratory research, it should be possible for future empirical research to conduct case studies of convicted white-collar criminals in terms of financial motive, organizational opportunity and willingness to adopt deviant behavior.

## SOS Racism sentence

This case description is not based on an internal investigation report but on media reports and a court document where several defendants were given prison sentences. Convenience theory suggests that white-collar crime can be a convenient action when there is a financial motive to handle threats or possibilities, an organizational opportunity to commit and conceal crime, and a willingness to adopt deviant behavior. White-collar crime always occurs in an organizational context, with illegal activities hidden behind legal business activities. In this section we study a case of behavior aimed at defrauding the government, looking at an NGO that misrepresented its membership and activities to commit subsidy fraud. We find support for convenience theory in all three dimensions of motive, organization and behavior.

Government subsidy is an attractive area for convenient financial crime in countries where the government is wealthy and plays a dominant role in society. Norway is such an example, with its large government sector and its distribution of substantial government funding to a wide range of recipient bodies. Norway is a trust-based society where trust can easily be abused by white-collar criminals without likelihood of detection (Benson and Gottschalk, 2015; Gottschalk and Smith, 2016).

The purpose of this section is to demonstrate convenience in government subsidy fraud by means of a case study. The case study is concerned with an idealistic voluntary organization in Norway called SOS Racism. SOS Racism is a non-government organization (NGO) that is non-profit and funded by donations as well as government subsidies. This research is important as trust-based systems may need to be supplemented by control mechanisms that increase both the objective and the subjective probability of detection. It is in the organizational dimension that subjective detection probability can make a contribution to reducing the frequency of white-collar crime (Gottschalk and Smith, 2016; Wilberg and Gottschalk, 2014).

Kjell Gunnar Larsen (born 1956) was the leader of SOS Racism. The police had to use locksmiths to enter the premises of the organization during a search. The former leader of SOS Racism, Bård Eskild Frantzen (born 1978), had the week before appeared in the daily Norwegian newspaper *Dagbladet*, talking about a number of instances of misconduct and allied incidents in the organization. Examples included forged evidence and shadow wages, emptied bank accounts, and a burnt accounting sheet.

SOS Racism was sentenced by the district court to pay more than NOK 10 million (US$1.2 million) to the National Council for Norway's Children and Youth Organizations ('Landsrådet for Norges Barne- og Ungdomsorganisasjoner'). The verdict stated that SOS Racism had provided incorrect membership numbers to donors, including the government (Flydal, 2011). The verdict was also critical of Larsen as the organization's most powerful individual (Flydal, 2011):

> In the court's assessment, questions must also be asked about the democratic structure of the organization SOS Racism. Evidence has shown that only a handful of people appear in all the central parts of the organization as well as in the regional teams. This is not unusual in non-governmental organizations, where enthusiasts put themselves forward year after year and participate in all kinds of roles in the organization. What is worrying about SOS Racism, however, is that the vast majority of people defined by the organization as members are in fact deprived of any opportunity to influence decisions in the organization.

In addition to being the general manager of SOS Racism, Larsen was also a board member of the communist group Serve the People ('Tjen Folket'). He was a powerful man.

It was *Dagbladet* journalist Flydal who detected and revealed how SOS Racism had reported false courses, participants and members. Previous members told *Dagbladet* that SOS Racism produced lists of study activities that never occurred and did not exist. The fake lists were presented to gain subsidies for which there was no basis.

SOS Racisme (French origin) is a movement of NGOs that describe themselves as anti-racist. Their stated goal is to fight racial discrimination. Often the plaintiff in discrimination trials, the organization also offers support to immigrants and racial minorities that are facing discrimination. It is also heavily involved in protesting and publicizing examples of discrimination in society and in the law. Its Norwegian branch, which claimed to be both the largest chapter of SOS Racism and the largest anti-racist organization in Europe, was controversial for its marked Stalinist stance and for defrauding the government, resulting in the organization's conviction for fraud and its bankruptcy, as well as criminal proceedings against its leaders. The court sentencing that followed the criminal proceedings against its leaders is the case in this section (Flydal, 2013a, 2013b; Hofoss, 2013; Hvistendahl et al., 2014; NTB, 2012a, 2012b; Sørhus and Wold, 2012).

In Haugaland (2016) district court, a total of eight defendants were sentenced to prison: Larsen, two years and six months; Thorbjørnsen, one year and six months; Ormåsen, six months; Stokke, six months; Fuglemsmo, six months; Skretteberg, six months; Hansen, four months; and Frantzen, three months.

Content analysis can be defined as any methodology or procedure that attempts to identify specific characteristics within texts in order to make valid inferences (Krippendorff, 1980; Patrucco et al., 2017). Content analysis assumes that language reflects people's cognitive processes and how they understand their surroundings. Therefore, content analysis makes it possible to determine how a judge understands a case through the statements he or she makes about a defendant in the sentence document, which in Norwegian district courts may range from a few pages to several hundred pages. Similarly, content analysis also makes it possible to determine how a journalist understands a story he or she tells about a suspect or defendant in the media (McClelland et al., 2010).

McClelland et al. (2010) used a quantitative approach based on frequency counts of keywords in their content analysis. This approach assumes that the frequent appearance of particular words is indicative of the importance or centrality of the underlying construct these words represent. A two-stage approach means that researchers first develop a dictionary of words that can be used and then search for those words manually or electronically.

Patrucco et al. (2017) applied a two-stage approach in their content analysis of publications on public procurement. In the first double extraction process, each article was examined by two researchers, working independently of each other. In the second phase, the two researchers worked together on a small number of articles in which there were significant differences in coding decisions or some element of uncertainty existed.

In our own research we had access to the court document as well as newspaper reports. The court document from a district court in Norway turned out to be the final verdict, since appeals were unsuccessful: neither the court of appeals nor the Supreme Court were willing to look at certain aspects of the Haugaland (2016) district court verdict. The document from Haugaland (2016) is 341 pages long and provides useful insights into motives, opportunities and behaviors that can be studied by means of convenience theory. In addition, media reports provide insight into important perspectives of the case.

## SOS Racism convenience

Subsidy fraud and grant fraud seem to be common in Norway. When the Catholic Church was caught with a long list of individuals who were not members of the church, they refused to pay back subsidies to the government. It has been argued that the Catholic Church sometimes decouples itself from aspects of normal moral as well as social obligations by implementing their own rules and regulations, even when the decoupling leads to violations of criminal law in countries where the church operates. For example, Tjørholm (2016), a professor of religion at a university in Norway, suggests that the Oslo Catholic diocese adopted reprehensible methods when the church registered members to gain more state subsidies. When the church's illegal registration of assumed catholics was disclosed, the chief financial officer in the church was charged for fraud by the police. Bishop Bernt Eidsvig avoided indictment because there was not sufficient evidence of involvement.

SOS Racism seemed similarly decoupled from society when it abused government trust to commit fraud by way of false courses and non-existing participants as well as membership lists with individuals who were never registered. We will now analyze the case of SOS Racism by means of convenience theory.

## Economic dimension: motive

This is a case of corporate crime rather than occupational crime. Corporate crime is committed to benefit the organization financially, while occupational crime is committed to benefit the individual financially. The motive for the eight offenders, in particular Larsen, was power and influence. Claiming that SOS Racism was the largest within the Racism family in Europe seemed important to him. Maslow suggested a pyramid of human needs that can be adapted to the case of white-collar criminals. It seems that Larsen wanted to gain power, status, acceptance and, potentially, admiration and fame and was prepared to use fraudulent means.

Larsen had been in powerful positions before. He was a trade union activist and a communist politician in the municipality. He was a member of the communist party for many years before he was excluded from the party. Larsen started his career as a blue-collar worker in an aluminum plant. It was by means of a coup that Larsen and some other communists took over key positions in SOS Racism in the early 1990s. He became chairman of the property development company Activist Property ('Aktivisteiendom'). Larsen was nicknamed 'Joe S' after Josef Stalin, the Soviet dictator (Flydal, 2010). He was seen as the personal owner and head of the communist party Serve the People (Sjølie, 2008).

Some of the financial gain from government fraud was needed to finance the communist organization Serve the People. Several key individuals at Serve the People were employed by SOS Racism, receiving a salary but given no work assignments (Flydal, 2010). Thus, a secondary motive in the economic dimension for Larsen was being enabled to build a new communist party organization after being excluded from the Norwegian Workers' Communist Party.

According to the court document, Larsen was in charge of the money at SOS Racism (Haugaland, 2016: 49):

> Kjell Gunnar Larsen was elected main financial officer in SOS Racism in 1995 and had overall responsibility for finances in the organization until the bankruptcy of SOS Racism in May 2013. Kjell Gunnar Larsen handled the organization's accounts and approved invoices. As the main cashier, Larsen had responsibility for application processes in relation to various government support schemes. Kjell Gunnar Larsen had employer responsibility for employees in SOS Racism.

Several witnesses in court said that Larsen's "words were like a law" to them.

## *Organizational dimension: opportunity*

SOS Racism was organizing courses and seminars that were paid for by the government. Furthermore, the government subsidized the organization on the basis of the number of members. It was later found that some fictive course participants attended several courses at the same time in different locations. SOS Racism outsourced some of its courses to minority organizations that reported participant numbers greatly in excess of reality. A deal was made whereby SOS Racism got 25 percent of the surplus while the rest of the money was transferred to the minority organization. Larsen was in charge. He had a number of positions – including chief financial officer (CFO), head of the election committee, and member of the program committee and the national and employment boards – in addition to the position of secretary general.

## *Deviant behavior: willingness*

Larsen's employment of party leaders from Serve the People at SOS Racism can be understood in terms of neutralization theory (Sykes and Matza, 1957). He could justify crime by indicating a higher loyalty to the ideals of communism and the rule of the people. The offender appeals to higher loyalties. This technique is employed by those who feel they are in a dilemma that can only be resolved by violating a law or policy. In the context of an organization, an employee may appeal to organizational values or hierarchies. For example, an executive could argue that he or she has to violate a policy in order to get things done and achieve the strategic objectives of the enterprise.

Larsen might also have applied the neutralization technique of a dilemma where the benefits of the action outweigh the costs. The offender argues that a dilemma arose which prompted he or she making a reasonable tradeoff before committing the act. Tradeoff between many interests therefore resulted in the offense. Dilemma represents a state of mind where it is not obvious what is right and what is wrong to do. For example, the offense might be carried out to prevent a more serious offense.

We find evidence of convenience in all three dimensions of motive, opportunity and willingness. It is the organizational opportunity to commit and conceal crime that makes white-collar crime so different from other modes of financial crime. Haugaland (2016: 233) concluded about the main defendant Larsen:

> It is clear that Kjell Gunnar Larsen, by signing up as a teacher and participant at courses that he knew did not exist and confirming the attendance of persons who were not physically present, contributed to fraud. It is clear that Kjell Gunnar Larsen acted deliberately and that this was conscious behavior. Kjell Gunnar Larsen was the real head of the organization and was fully aware of the attendance sheets that were submitted and used as evidence that courses had been completed.

Larsen can be compared to a chief executive officer (CEO) in business and public organizations.

## CEOs in financial crime

There is probably no single position in the world that has met with a more systematic degree of naivety from its employers than that of the chief executive. Dating back to the views of Adam Smith, the motivation behind chief executive decision-making has been under continuous scrutiny and subjected to systematic influence. Adam Smith's point was that if indeed man is economically rational, any shopkeeper standing in for the true owner will be confronted with incentives to improve his own fortune rather than serving the interests of the owner. The shopkeeper's self-interested actions range from being softhearted towards employees and local environments to outright theft and embezzlement. With the advent of the joint stock company act of 1844, the shopkeeper's role changed into that of the chief executive (the CEO). Since a shareholding company with limited liability often has not one but several owners, the decision-making and disposition of the CEO is even less obvious to the individual owner. This viewpoint entered mainstream academia with the introduction of principal–agent theory and, since the 1990s, has evolved into a systematic instrument for assuring motives via the compensation systems of corporate governance (Eisenhardt, 1989; Treadway et al., 2009).

Khanna et al. (2015) found that the collective behavior of corporate leaders is often critical in corporate wrongdoing, and the CEO frequently plays a central role. They found that appointment-based CEO connectedness is positively related to the likelihood of corporate fraud and negatively related to the likelihood of detection if fraud takes place. Additionally, it decreases the expected costs of fraud by helping conceal fraudulent activity, making CEO dismissal less likely if fraud is discovered and lowering the coordination costs of carrying out illegal activity. Connections based on network ties through past employment, education or social organization memberships augment the connections that CEOs develop with top executives and directors through their appointment decisions.

It has been argued that goal-oriented management is a management approach that can inherently bring about more white-collar crime. Especially when goals are ambitious and the CEO is personally responsible for goal achievement and faces negative personal consequences of non-achievement, there might be a tendency for CEOs to use both legal and illegal means in the struggle to achieve goals. This is in line with the theory of profit-driven crime. In conformity with the managerial perspective in the business literature, which highlights the role of managers as agents for deciding enterprise strategies and operations as well as leading the activities required to implement corporate priorities, managers can develop and implement both legal and illegal strategies. Managers' perceptions and interpretations determine their commitment to certain goals over other goals (sub-goals).

Profit-driven crime by criminal business enterprises should be understood mainly in economic rather than sociological or criminological terms. In an attempt to formulate a general theory of profit-driven crime, Naylor (2003) proposed a typology that shifts the focus from actors to actions by distinguishing between market crime, predatory crime and commercial crime. The theory of profit-driven crime suggests that financial crime is opportunity driven, where executives and managers identify opportunities for illegal gain. This is in line with convenience theory in the organizational dimension. Opportunity is a flexible characteristic of financial crime and varies according to the type of criminal involved (Michel, 2008). An alternative to goal-oriented management is rule-based or value-based management (Jonnergård et al., 2010), where pressures to commit white-collar crime are less likely.

Cowen et al. (2016) suggest that employment contracts for CEOs should have a clause related to misconduct and crime:

> For example, a claw back could be triggered by a financial restatement that happens after an executive's dismissal or by new evidence that surfaces indicating he or she engaged in misconduct while serving as CEO. Claw backs can also force terminated executives to repay benefits if there is evidence their actions have violated restrictive covenants.

As suggested in agency theory, CEOs have a tendency to become opportunistic agents (Shen, 2003). Due to the charisma that is often a feature of CEOs in organizations, external stakeholders and board members lose control over CEO activities (Fanelli and Misangyi, 2006). For this reason, the employment contracts with a repayment option proposed by Cowen et al. (2016) might bring about a reduction in white-collar crime by CEOs.

Narcissistic organizational identification is one of several perspectives on CEO criminal behavior (Galvin et al., 2015: 163):

> It is not uncommon to learn of individuals in positions of power and responsibility, especially CEOs, who exploit and undermine their organizations for personal gain. A circumstance not well explained in the literature, however,

is that some of those individuals may highly identify with their organization, meaning that they see little difference between their identity and the organization's identity – between their interests and the organization's interest. This presents a paradox, because organizational identification typically is not noted for its adverse consequences on the organization.

Power is here emphasized by Galvin et al. (2015) as an explanation for criminal behavior. Similarly, Bendahan et al. (2015) found that power can cause CEO crime. If the CEO is in a position to make decisions that affect many employees or enjoys tremendous freedom and can make decisions on his or her own with significant consequences for others, then the temptation to abuse the power for personal or organizational gain is strong.

An example of CEO criminal behavior is involvement in transnational corporate bribery (Lord, 2016). CEOs sometimes find themselves in situations where they need to establish subsidiaries, get licenses or close deals in corrupt countries.

A distinction can be made between mundane offenders and serious predators among criminal CEOs. Mundane offenders commit mainly minor offenses of ambiguous criminality – that is to say, the criminal status of the act is contested (e.g. occasional use of bribes) or the act is petty and widespread among ordinary people. Unlike serious predators, mundane offenders are sensitive to moral considerations and are not unabashedly devoted to a criminal lifestyle. Most of the time it is important to them to be normal law-abiding executives who have some stake in social conformity. Their offenses tend to be committed intermittently and in situations that lack clear moral markers of their wrongfulness (Ceccato and Benson, 2016).

# 7
# MISCONDUCT INVESTIGATIONS IN SCANDINAVIA

While all the suspects in chapter 6 received prison sentences, none of the suspects in this chapter were prosecuted or convicted.

Fraud examiners are hired to conduct internal investigations in both private and public organizations. Prompted by suspicions of misconduct or crime, investigators from law firms and accounting firms enter client organizations to reconstruct past events. They interview people, search emails and other digitally stored information, and study documents and other sources. Examiners try to find out what happened, how it happened, why it happened, and who did what to make it happen or not happen (Brooks and Button, 2011; Button et al., 2007a, 2007b; Button and Gee, 2013; Gill and Hart, 1997; Gottschalk, 2015, 2016a, b, c, d; Lewis et al., 2014; Machen and Richards, 2004; Schneider, 2006; Wells, 2003, 2007; Williams, 2005, 2014).

## DNB bank in the Panama Papers

This case study is concerned with the corporate response when external accusations of misconduct and crime occur. The Norwegian DNB bank case in the Panama Papers scandal is an interesting example of corporate response. Based on convenience theory and agency theory, the response can be characterized by initial reluctance, then biased internal investigation, then promise of transparency, and finally complete silence. A key element in this response is the hiring of fraud examiners from a law firm that is the regular external legal service provider to the bank, even though an objective and independent investigation was supposed to be implemented.

DNB is a private bank in Norway, the DNB standing for Den Norske Bank (The Norwegian Bank). DNB was suspected of financial crime following the leakage of the Panama Papers. The suspicion was related to wealthy bank customers who wanted to hide their money in countries where there is no transparency. There were concerns of tax evasion, money laundering, fraud, bankruptcy crime, other kinds of financial crime and evading international sanctions.

The Panama Papers are 11.5 million leaked documents that detail financial and attorney–client information for more than 214,000 offshore entities. The documents that belonged to the Panamanian law firm and corporate service provider Mossack Fonseca were leaked in 2015 by an anonymous source.

This study looks at DNB executives' knowledge of and involvement in wealth management as well as the fraud examiners' private internal investigation at DNB. Critical issues in private internal investigations are discussed (Brooks and Button, 2011), the theory of convenience is applied to bank misconduct (Gottschalk, 2017) and principal–agent theory is used to study relationships at several levels (Bosse and Phillips, 2016) – that is, between the Norwegian ministry and the bank's board, between the board and corporate management, between management and subsidiary management, and between the bank and its clients.

This research is important because it shows how the media spotlight and international attention can force suspected entities to react to allegations of financial crime by white-collar offenders (Supernor, 2017). The case study illustrates how a stakeholder such as a major shareholder can put pressure on a suspected bank to reconstruct past events to a greater extent than it would otherwise have agreed to. The case study also questions the objectivity and independence of fraud examiners who are the legal bank advisors in normal times.

The leaked documents contain personal financial information about wealthy individuals and public officials. While offshore business entities in the Seychelles and other places are not necessarily illegal in home jurisdictions such as Norway, the United Kingdom and the United States, newspaper reports that studied the Panama Papers found that the Mossack Fonseca shell corporations were used for illegal purposes.

Andersen et al. (2017) argue that banks help rich people to hide their wealth. They suggest that banks take no responsibility for wealthy people's motives and behaviors such as tax evasion and money laundering. They find that political elites abuse public office for embezzlement and hide the money in tax havens. In countries with underdeveloped democratic governance, political elites can gain substantial rents by white-collar crime. The magnitude in poor countries is assumed to be substantial.

The newspaper *Aftenposten* was the Norwegian partner in the media consortium handling the Panama Papers. Aftenposten could reveal that DNB helped Norwegians and others to establish mailbox companies in tax havens. Norwegian newspaper reporters studied the Panama Papers and found a number of Norwegians on the Mossack Fonseca list. Their money had been hidden in the Seychelles by means of transactions through DNB private banking in Luxembourg. The bank service was labeled wealth management, and secrecy was a top priority. After the leakage, the Norwegian internal revenue service was interested in income and tax statements from Norwegians who had been serviced by DNB Luxembourg.

Also after the leakage, the Norwegian government as a major shareholder of DNB wanted to know if the bank had violated any Norwegian laws with their wealth management services. In April 2016, the chairperson at the bank sent a short report to the minister claiming that the bank had done nothing wrong. The minister was not happy with the statement and listed a number of questions to which she wanted clear answers.

## *Internal investigation*

The board at DNB then hired attorneys at local Norwegian law firm Hjort to conduct an internal investigation of the bank. Although the law firm was the permanent legal service provider for the bank, a role typically supportive of their client, the chairperson at DNB argued that Hjort would be objective and independent in the role of fraud examiners.

Law firm Hjort was commissioned to review DNB management's knowledge of tax havens. The assignment came from the board of DNB after Hjort had contributed to a report in April 2016 – a report that did not at all satisfy the largest owner, the government, represented by the Minister of Trade and Industry. The law firm received the assignment in April 2016, and the review was headed by the managing partner at Hjort. The investigation report was promised one month later, in May 2016, but it was not ready until September 2016, and it was only 18 pages.

In addition, the chairperson wrote a cover letter to the minister, in which compliance with the bank group's ethical guidelines was highlighted. Ethical guidelines are voluntary commitments that govern the behavior of a company and its employees towards external stakeholders beyond what is regulated elsewhere (Eriksen, 2016).

The suspicion of financial crime at DNB attracted considerable media attention in 2016. In addition to all the media coverage, a variety of letters and reports were made available to the public:

1. DNB's first report to the Ministry of Trade and Industry dated April 11, 2016 (Tanum, 2016a).
2. Questions from the Ministry to DNB dated April 12, 2016 (Wikborg and Stensland, 2016).
3. Report from law firm Hjort to DNB dated September 11, 2016 (Hjort, 2016).
4. DNB's cover letter to the Ministry dated September 16, 2016 (Tanum, 2016b).
5. Minister's reports to the Control and Constitution Committee dated September 30, 2016 (Mæland, 2016a) and November 4 (Mæland, 2016b).

The report of investigation by Hjort (2016: 2) starts by confirming that "a number of banks, including DNB Luxembourg S.A., had made it possible for customers to establish companies in so-called tax havens". Hjort was commissioned by DNB to "investigate how this service offer was established and practiced, what information about the service offer has been exchanged between employees and trust persons at DNB, and how that information has been handled by those who have received it". The mandate for the examination "stipulated that the investigation should include employees and trusted persons from: the board of directors of DNB Luxembourg, responsible business areas in DNB bank, the compliance function, the group audit, the control committee, the group management, and the boards of DNB".

Based on the examination, Hjort was asked to assess whether violation of guidelines applicable to bank business had occurred. Hjort's mandate did not include a review and examination of the individual companies that DNB Luxembourg had arranged to be established or the bank's dialogue with its individual clients. Furthermore, the examination did not include efforts to reveal how individual customers reported wealth and income to relevant tax authorities.

## *Investigation process*

The investigation team from Hjort consisted only of lawyers. Four lawyers worked on the case. While legal knowledge was certainly relevant to the investigation, it was surprising that other kinds of knowledge – from organizational behavior, management studies, sociology and psychology, as well as accounting and auditing – were absent. Given the legal background of the four examiners, they focused on formal documents rather than informal sources in their investigation. They studied all the DNB board minutes between 2004 and 2015. They studied all the reports from executive meetings over the same period. "Beyond this, the administration at DNB has sent documents that Hjort has requested or that the administration itself has considered relevant to Hjort's assignment" (Hjort, 2016: 2). "In addition to the documents that have been sent from DNB, Hjort has undertaken searches in electronically stored documents in DNB's Norwegian databases, both shared areas as well as personal email boxes".

It is interesting to reflect on the competence of investigators and the chosen sources of information in the investigation, given the mandate to examine information flows about tax haven services. Investigators looked into formal documents, such as minutes from meetings, to find traces of information flows. However, based on management studies, it is unlikely that bank services that may not stand the light of day are discussed and described in formal documents. Executives tend to discuss such matters outside meetings, during travel and in restaurants and other informal places.

Email searches may be more relevant, as executives and others tend to have a sender perspective when communicating, therefore not reflecting much about what the receiver may do with the electronic information. However, an email search is dependent on an intelligent search engine as well as expert selection of search words – synonyms as well as sentences – to be successful.

Hjort (2016: 3) also interviewed a number of people:

> As part of the inquiry, Hjort has also conducted talks with more than 30 people who in various ways were attached to the case complex. This applies to current and former employees and trust persons in the DNB group both in Norway and Luxembourg. All persons that Hjort has wanted to conduct conversations with, have met for conversations. In connection with the conversations, DNB has exempted the persons concerned from their duty of confidentiality vis-á-vis Hjort.

Violations of laws, regulations and guidelines were not the only criteria applied in the investigation. Examiners also emphasized the risk of loss of reputation. Hjort (2016: 10) seemed to think that misconduct is not really bad so long as it causes no damage to DNB's reputation: "As a general requirement, employees and trust persons shall refrain from conduct that may adversely affect the group's reputation".

## *Investigation result*

Law firm Hjort (2016: 8) introduces their conclusion with the following statement:

> In assessing whether a violation of rules and regulations applicable to DNB at the relevant times in connection with the relevant service offer, we have assumed that the general risk associated with banking activities in Luxembourg, with the rules of secrecy and discretion, was accepted within the group. Where risk assessments are relevant, therefore, it will primarily be a question of assessing the increased risk that the relevant service offer might have caused.

This statement seems to externalize potential blame for bank misconduct, which is in line with the blame game hypothesis (Gottschalk, 2016b). Examiners' attributions often suggest that the cause of an event is not within the control of the examined, thereby removing blame and responsibility (Lee and Robinson, 2000). As suggested by Sonnier et al. (2015: 10), "a negative effective reaction can influence the assessment of causation by reducing the evidential standards required to attribute blame".

Hjort (2016: 9) continues their externalization of blame by arguing that potential law violations must be attributed to bank customers and not the bank:

> Regarding external laws and regulations, DNB Luxembourg is governed by Luxembourg legislation, including anti-money laundering and terrorist financing. The inquiry we have conducted does not provide grounds for believing that the risk of breach of such rules increased as a result of the relevant service offer. We refer in this connection among others to the fact that shares in the Seychelles company, according to our information, were

registered to the customer's account in the bank, and that all transactions, according to our information, were made through the personal account of the customer.

As mentioned above, one of the criteria applied by examiners was potential damage to DNB's reputation (Hjort, 2016: 13):

> As we consider it, it should be assumed in this situation that the current service offer as such would harm the group's reputation. This was irrespective of whether the customers followed the call to report income and assets properly and regardless of which procedures DNB Luxembourg followed before accepting a new corporate structure as a customer (...)
>
> When the situation in 2008 was such that the service offer could potentially harm DNB's reputation and management at DNB Luxembourg was doubtful if it was something to be continued, it is in our view difficult to reconcile the practice with guidelines and thus understand why the service offer was nevertheless continued.

The final issue in the report of investigation is concerned with the question: should the misconduct at the subsidiary in Luxembourg have been noticed by the CEO and the board at DNB in Norway? Hjort (2016: 17) answers no to this question for the following reason:

> As stated above, and based on the inquiry we have conducted, we cannot find evidence of information flow about the relevant service offer at any time to the CEO, executive meetings or board members until the case emerged in the media in 2016.

Again from a blame game point of view, it is interesting that examiners use formal documents such as minutes from meetings to determine whether or not someone at the top of the bank in Norway had knowledge of harmful practice in tax havens by the subsidiary in Luxembourg.

Furthermore, it is interesting to note that the service offer in Luxembourg was immediately terminated when the Panama Papers were published in Norwegian newspapers. DNB board and management did not wait for the Hjort (2016) report to stop the practice that harmed the bank's reputation and potentially represented misconduct and crime.

We now turn to convenience analysis in the DNB case. Convenience theory suggests that misconduct and crime can be a convenient alternative when making business decisions (Gottschalk, 2017). Rather than avoiding gray zones in business practice, wealth management seems so attractive to banks that they are willing to accept the risks involved. Access to resources such as private examiners from law firm Hjort enabled bank management to control what information was available to the inquiry and the perspectives applied in the investigation based on the mandate.

When private investigators conclude that no violations of Norwegian law have occurred, then Norwegian law enforcement agencies have a tendency to look the other way. For example, when Hjort's (2016) conclusions were published, the Norwegian National Authority for Investigation and Prosecution of Economic and Environmental Crime (Økokrim) decided not to open a police investigation case.

The Økokrim decision is interesting, especially in the light of crime detected at a competing Swedish bank. Nordea is a bank in Sweden that also appeared in the Panama Papers. An investigation concluded that Nordea in Luxembourg had backdated documents for their wealth management customers. Backdating is illegal in both Sweden and Norway (Gottschalk, 2016a).

In line with the theory of convenience, it may be said that it is convenient for banks such as DNB to reveal misconduct but not crime. By hiring their own law firm to conduct an internal investigation, the bank board can assume that examiners will avoid evidence of crime and that the Norwegian police will not pursue the case. Furthermore, Pontell et al. (2014) point out that some people are too powerful to blame.

It seems that internal investigators failed in their crime signal detection in this case.

## *Principal–agent analysis*

In principal–agent analysis, agency theory suggests that problems in terms of conflicting preferences, knowledge asymmetry and different attitudes towards risks are three fundamental problems in a principal–agent relationship. In private internal investigations, the client is the principal and the fraud examiner the agent. Agency theory is based on the assumption of narrow self-interest of both agent and principal (Bosse and Phillips, 2016).

Both principal and agent may behave opportunistically. Agents such as fraud examiners are believed to be rational actors who are interested in maximizing their individual utility, even at the expense of the principal. Since DNB is an important client for law firm Hjort, and the tax haven investigation was just a minor assignment, the law firm may have simply planned to produce an investigation report that satisfied the client and met expectations.

Agents are believed to be opportunistic, and a key goal of an investigation mandate is for the principal to manage opportunism through two major mechanisms: financial incentive and examination mandate (Dawson et al., 2016).

As mentioned in the introduction, principal–agent theory can also be applied to relationships at several levels in the DNB case, as well as how these levels are treated by Hjort in their investigation report (2016). First, there is the relationship between the Norwegian Ministry of Trade and Industry and the board of directors at DNB. The board felt pressure from the ministry to initiate the investigation (Mæland, 2016a). The ministry even influenced the mandate for the investigation (Mæland, 2016b). Already in April 2016 there was no room for opportunism in the form of closing the case since the media were filled with Panama Papers stories. The only available opportunism was hiring the bank's permanent legal advisors at Hjort to conduct the investigation.

Next, there is the relationship between the bank's board and its management. While bank executives have their primary position in the bank, the position of board members is secondary. Preferences, knowledge and risk attitude are agency problems that can easily occur in situations of crisis management. However, in the DNB case there is no evidence of significant divergence between board and management.

Then there is the relationship between DNB headquarters in Norway and the DNB subsidiary in Luxembourg. Although not evident in the report, it seems that headquarters were happy when the subsidiary made money, and they were not particularly interested in knowing how that money was made. Norwegians on the board of DNB Luxembourg were mainly interested in setting ambitious financial targets and checking that targets were reached. They were not really interested in how it was done.

Finally, there is the relationship between the bank and its clients. At the time of writing, the internal revenue service in Norway is looking into bank account statements of Norwegians at DNB Luxembourg, and some bank clients would like to present a case that blames the bank. They argue that they asked the bank to place their money appropriately and did not know that the bank set up potentially illegal structures for them.

In conclusion, the Norwegian DNB bank case in the Panama Papers scandal is an interesting example of corporate response to accusations of misconduct and financial crime – interesting also because the Swedish bank Nordea made a similar response. The response can be characterized by initial reluctance, then biased internal investigation, then promise of transparency and, finally, complete silence. The retired group auditor was blamed, while no top executives in post were blamed. Although we need to be careful in generalizing from a case study, it seems from previous research that private internal investigations by fraud examiners have a tendency to concentrate on clarifying critical post circumstances while avoiding white-collar crime suspicions against the top executives who hired them.

Future research may build on critical issues in private internal investigations, the theory of convenience in white-collar misconduct and crime, as well as principal–agent theory for relations between client and examiner and between different managerial levels to try to find an integrated explanation of corporate response to external accusations of misconduct and crime.

## Police Immigration Unit

The business of fraud examiners in private internal investigations is important to many auditing firms and law firms. They are hired by public and private organizations when there are suspicions of misconduct and financial crime. Suspicions are sometimes disclosed by whistleblowers who attempt to reveal what they perceive as illegal, immoral or illegitimate practices. This study presents a case from the Norwegian police in which whistleblowers expressed concerns about overtime, use of private cars and the procurement of equipment for personal use. The main whistleblower was also the ombudsman in the organization, where he repeated his accusations and allegations so frequently that he ended up being the main subject in the private internal investigation.

Whistleblowers attempt to disclose information about what they perceive as illegal, immoral or illegitimate practices (Atwater, 2006; Bjørkelo et al., 2011; Vadera et al., 2009; Vadera and Aguilera, 2015). Private internal investigators are hired to reconstruct the past after suspicions of misconduct, often reported by whistleblowers (Brooks and Button, 2011; Green and Podgor, 2014; Miller, 2010). Whistleblowers are supposed to be treated as information sources by internal investigators, and they are supposed to be protected against reprisals and revenge. Investigators should never play the blame game (Gottschalk, 2016a, b, c, d).

However, the practice is sometimes very different. As illustrated in this case study, private internal investigators turned against the whistleblower. The case study is from the Norwegian police, which has been hit by several whistleblowing scandals. Because of all the scandals, the major union for police officers in Norway advised its members not to "blow the whistle" any more (Andersen, 2016).

This case study is important because the involvement of fraud examiners in private internal investigations is growing without the activity being subject to any regulation in most jurisdictions (Button and Gee, 2013; Schneider, 2006). We analyze the case by means of the blame game hypothesis (Gottschalk, 2016a, b, c, d).

Whistleblowers are an important source of information for many fraud investigators. In the following we discuss both the characteristics of whistleblowers and their trustworthiness as information sources in a situation where identified persons are to be considered innocent until proven guilty (Bjørkelo et al., 2011). Since persons are neither prosecuted nor convicted, and since persons may indeed be innocent, the quality of information from the whistleblower is problematic. Rather than representing a case where the whistleblower was in the end shown to be right, this case study presents a situation where the whistleblower might have been wrong.

Suspicions of misconduct and crime in organizations often arise when whistleblowers disclose information about potential wrongdoing (Atwater, 2006). Since misconduct and white-collar crime is difficult to detect and prosecute, whistleblowers represent important information sources (Vadera et al., 2009). Whistleblowers may be able to provide forensic evidence in addition to witness statements (Vadera and Aguilera, 2015).

However, there are problems associated with whistleblowers as information sources in fraud investigations. The trustworthiness of both source (the whistleblower) and information (the facts) has to be evaluated carefully by investigators before they are included as relevant pieces in an investigative puzzle.

## Whistleblowing

The focus on organizational members who speak out about perceived wrongdoing has increased in recent years. Whistleblowing has gained recognition as an organizational social control instrument because it can end wrongdoing and bring offenders to justice (Bjørkelo et al., 2011).

Whistleblowing is a distinct form of active reaction consisting of four elements (Johnson, 2005): the person acting is a member or former member of the organization where he or she has observed something, his or her information is about nontrivial misconduct in that organization, he or she intends to disclose and expose the wrongdoing in an acceptable manner, and he or she acts in a way that makes the information available to someone who can do something about the situation.

Vadera et al. (2009) define whistleblowing similarly as the disclosure by a former or current organizational member of unethical, immoral, illegitimate, or illegal practice to a person in the organization that may be able to effect action to investigate and stop the practice.

Atwater (2006) applies a similar definition by defining whistleblowing as an act by which an individual reports observed deviant behavior within the organization to a person in position of authority who can rectify the situation.

Bjørkelo et al. (2011: 208) summarize the variety of definitions by arguing that the most widely applied definition in research is "the disclosure by organizational members (former or current) of illegal, immoral or illegitimate practices under the control of their employers, to persons or organizations that may be able to effect action".

Like any other term, the concept of whistleblowing can be defined narrowly or widely. If the concept is defined narrowly, then it is not considered whistleblowing if the individual is a victim of the misconduct reported.

In their research on whistleblowers and whistleblowing, Vadera et al. (2009) identified a number of characteristics. Whistleblowers are motivated by concern for others, they are high performers, they feel secure in their job positions, they are committed to their jobs, they are satisfied with their jobs, and they work in high-performing environments. Whistleblowers are emotionally angry at observed misconduct. Whistleblowing occurs more frequently when observers of wrongdoing hold professional positions, when they have positive reactions to their work, and when they recently were recognized for good performance. Whistleblowing is related to situational factors such as the seriousness of the offense and supportiveness of the organizational climate for whistleblowing.

Whistleblowers that do not have enough proof of perceived misconduct and crime are reluctant to report. Whistleblowers are also reluctant to report when there is no legal or management protection from negative consequences of blowing the whistle (Zipparo, 1999); for fear of retaliation.

Before concerns are expressed, employees can be encouraged by the development of a sense of moral identity and moral agency, by creating a tough anti-retaliation policy that permits disciplining or dismissing employees who retaliate against whistleblowers, and by disseminating such a policy through the intranet, in orientation materials and elsewhere. After concerns are expressed, employees can be encouraged to focus on the wrongdoing alleged in the complaint and not on the complainant, to investigate reports fully and fairly, and to take swift action when the complainant is well founded.

In a study of corruption in public procurement in the European Union, Wensink and Vet (2013) found that approximately 40 percent of fraudulent activities are detected by a whistleblower alert. They recommend furthering investment in well-functioning systems for whistleblowers, including proper protection. Legislation on whistleblowing as well as protection of whistleblowers represent areas that are not yet well developed.

Some observers are reluctant to blow the whistle because of loyalty to the organization. They believe that it is not a sign of loyalty to report on a colleague, and that reporting can hurt the reputation of the organization. The consider whistleblowing an act of betrayal of the organization, the employer, and colleagues. This phenomenon is called the loyalty paradox (Fehr et al., 2015).

## *National Police Immigration Unit*

Now we turn to the case. The National Police Immigration Unit in Norway is responsible for registering asylum seekers who come to Norway. The police have to establish their identity, forcibly return people without lawful residence and run the police immigration detention center.

In the fall of 2015, a record number of refugees reached Norwegian borders both in the south and from the Russian side. Norwegian police had the task of checking the identities of all the people who crossed the border. When people arrive in Norway, they must report to passport control or the nearest police authority to identify themselves and provide such information as is necessary to determine whether their entry into the country would be legal. If someone arrives in Norway from a country that participates in the Schengen police collaboration scheme, they are not subject to entry control. Every country that is part of the Schengen region undertakes control on its external frontiers on behalf of the whole Schengen territory. However, in the fall of 2015, parts of the Schengen system broke down, with national borders even temporarily introduced between Schengen nations.

In 2017, the police immigration unit had to downsize. Up to 80 employees were expected to leave the unit. Downsizing was a consequence of the fact that the flow of asylum seekers had almost stopped. Following the large increase in asylum seekers to Norway in 2015, the unit was boosting its budgets both towards the end of 2015 and in 2016, which led to a significant increase in staffing. Despite fewer asylum seekers from the middle of 2016, the police unit had the same number of deportations in 2017. The target for 2017 was 9,000 deportations (Wijnen, 2017).

The National Police Immigration Unit was in a state of emergency when the flow of asylum seekers entering Norway in late 2015 and early 2016 suddenly increased. It was during this period that the suspected misconduct and potential crime took place. In times of chaos and poor controls, social disorganization may occur, giving individuals in the organization ample opportunities to benefit themselves. The convenience of deviant behavior for personal enrichment increases in organizational settings where normal controls and procedures do not function properly (Gottschalk, 2017).

## *Internal investigation*

Now we turn to the investigation. KPMG is a professional service firm and one of the big four auditors along with Deloitte, Ernst & Young and PricewaterhouseCoopers. Based in Amsterdam, the Netherlands, KPMG employs 189,000 people and has three lines of service: financial audit, tax and advisory. Risk consulting, including private internal investigations, is one of KPMG's many business areas.

On January 27, 2016, investigators from KPMG in Norway were hired by the management at the National Police Immigration Unit to conduct an inquiry. The fraud examiners were to provide an assessment of possible misconduct incidents by trusted executives in the unit. The possible incidents were mainly concerned with suspicions of white-collar crime. KPMG delivered their 74-page investigation report on September 29, 2016. After several rounds of requests, we were able to obtain the report for research purposes in February 2017, when the report was made publicly available.

The mandate for the KPMG (2016: 6) investigation was as follows:

> KPMG is to conduct an independent factual survey of allegedly criticized conduct. An assessment shall be made of whether there is a violation of the Working Environment Act's rules regarding the psychosocial milieu or other misconduct behavior. KPMG shall conduct an independent factual inquiry into the use of overtime. There are allegations of favorable assignment of overtime, inadequate management and control, and that employees have had unlawful/unreasonable work load due to excessive overtime. A systematic investigation into overtime use will be conducted for a larger number of employees. It is necessary to assess whether there is a breach of the regulations of working hours, i.e. the Working Environment Act and the working time provisions for the police and if someone has or may have achieved illegal/unfair financial benefits after assignment of tasks that lead to overtime. Examiners shall also assess whether the police immigration unit have applied appropriate control and use of overtime. KPMG is to evaluate whether complaints, expressed concerns and allegations of misconduct behavior are covered by the Working Environment Act and Whistleblowing Regulations, including the immigration unit's internal routines for whistleblowing and the unit's policies against bullying, harassment and unlawful conduct. The factual survey shall be conducted in accordance with the Norwegian Labor Inspection Authority's guidelines for factual investigations.

The ombudsman's repeated whistleblowing was concerned with incidents that happened while the National Police Immigration Unit was overloaded with asylum seekers. Extraordinary efforts were required to handle the extraordinary situation, but there was also ample opportunity for deviant behavior for personal enrichment and abuse of power and position.

In the period from August 2013 to April 2016, management at the police unit received a total of 15 notifications from whistleblowers. The warnings were related to claims about systematic abuse of the overtime system, deviant procurements and negative relationships causing harm to the psychosocial working milieu. In addition, claims were made about critical circumstances related to the use of private cars in the service, temporary employment and the performance of temporary staff. The internal ombudsman for employee safety submitted seven of the alerts. In addition, on behalf of employees, the ombudsman provided another seven notifications. These 14 notices targeted three executives in the police unit. In addition, one of the executives submitted a complaint about the ombudsman.

In December 2015, the ombudsman reported the same three executives to the special affairs unit for police affairs, which is the Norwegian Bureau for the Investigation of Police Affairs. The role of the bureau is to investigate cases where employees of the police or prosecuting authority are suspected of committing criminal offenses in the course of duty. The bureau abandoned the notification with the argument that there was no reason to investigate whether a criminal offense had occurred. The bureau decision was appealed by the ombudsman to the Attorney General, arguing that there was insufficient case processing in the bureau, and that a thorough investigation should be conducted.

In autumn 2015 and spring 2016, the ombudsman went to the media where he repeated his criticism of the three executives. The three executives have rejected the criticism of the ombudsman and have perceived his repeated whistleblowing and other actions as harassment.

KPMG (2016) carried out 26 interviews with 23 persons. Among the interviewees were seven whistleblowers who had expressed concerns. Investigators had several meetings with local police union leaders and executives at the immigration unit. Investigators examined documents and data in systems related to overtime compensation. Documents regarding procurements were also examined. Thus, investigators used both primary information and secondary information in their examinations. Primary information included interviews and visits of relevant scenes, while secondary information included law data, management documents, circulars, instructions, annual reports, data from the payroll system and other documents.

Investigators developed an overview of all concerns expressed over time. They found that the concerns were mainly directed against three leading employees, with accusations of systematic abuse of the overtime system, irregular procurements for personal use, one irregular hiring process, use of private cars for unit work and violations of the working climate.

Investigators found that a very large number of employees had been paid for hundreds of overtime hours in 2015. Some employees had almost doubled their regular salaries by overtime compensation.

Concerning irregular procurements, different kinds of tool had been purchased by the unit. Investigators were unable to establish whether the tools were used by the unit or privately by some of the leaders.

Concerning the irregular hiring process, concerns had been expressed that a personal friend rather than the most qualified person had been offered a key position in the unit. Investigators were unable to reconstruct events and were thus unable to conclude whether or not irregularities had occurred.

Concerning the use of private cars for work, concerns were expressed that private cars were used for the transportation of prisoners. Car owners were reimbursed by the unit at very high rate since prisoners were being transported. Those who had used their own cars argued that no police cars were available. Again, investigators were unable to reconstruct past events and were thus unable to conclude whether or not improper use of private cars for immigration unit work had occurred.

Concerning the working climate, investigators did not blame managers, but suggested instead that there were serious conflicts involving the ombudsman (KPMG, 2016: 42):

> Generally, the notifications and interviews show that characteristics are derogatory and negative without any specifications or evidence. The descriptions of leadership behavior appear to be somewhat vague. The leader has in turn rejected most allegations, but acknowledged that he had a demanding leadership style during the current period. The leader says that he has always had a positive attitude towards all employees and demonstrated that he has raised matters about wage increases for four of the five who were directly reporting to him in the period.

KPMG (2016) concluded that the allegations made against three executives were not justified in substance. The three executives had not violated the duty of loyalty to their employer. There was no factual evidence of abuse of the overtime system, deviant purchases, misleading employment or repeated use of private cars for service duty.

KPMG (2016: 2) draws the following conclusion in relation to the ombudsman and whistleblower:

> From September 2015 until summer 2016, the ombudsman's notices, reports and use of media to promote his own views indicate that the accusations against the three were repeated and that the accusations escalated severely. We have conducted two interviews with the ombudsman, who in June 2016 chose to withdraw his explanations. The ombudsman has thus not wanted to help investigate matters that he himself had reported.
> 
> The repeated allegations and patterns of action of the ombudsman can in our view be regarded as misconduct. In our view, a major part of the

ombudsman's conduct goes beyond the right to waive the requirement for proper warning procedures. As of September 2015, this involves serious integrity violations of police employees who are particularly dependent on trust.

The ombudsman was a whistleblower, and he also communicated messages from other employees. His concerns were the original input to the investigation. Nevertheless, the ombudsman became the main focus of the examination, with investigators criticizing his actions, as stated above and in the following quote from the report (KPMG, 2016: 44):

> Our inquiry shows that there has been a conflict relationship between the ombudsman on one side and Leader 1 and Leader 2 on the other. The ombudsman has explained that the two leaders were famous for excessive overtime before they joined the police immigration unit. Leader 1 has indicated that the problems started when the ombudsman applied for but was not appointed to the post of senior police officer in the spring of 2013. It was Leader 1 who made the decision. The ombudsman appealed the decision and claimed that it was an act of revenge against him as ombudsman. His appeal was not successful. Leader 2 has indicated that the problems started when he took charge of organizational changes at the reception desk in the winter of 2015. Leading employee 3 was temporarily added to the reception desk during this period for six months. The ombudsman submitted a separate notice about these changes. The ombudsman has rejected the claims from both leaders.

As described above, the private internal investigators from KPMG (2016) turned against the ombudsman as the main whistleblower at the National Police Immigration Unit in Norway in their conclusions. According to the mandate, investigators were to examine allegations by the whistleblowers. They concluded that all concerns were unfounded. According to the mandate, investigators were also to examine the way concerns had been expressed. They concluded that concerns had been expressed in a very harmful manner.

An issue for discussion here is the violation of whistleblower protection (Dugstad, 2017). In the United Kingdom, whistleblowers are protected by the Public Interest Disclosure Act. In the United States, protection varies depending on the issue of concern. In Norway, the Working Environment Act protects against reprisals. Instead of protecting the ombudsman as a whistleblower, the mandate from police management encouraged investigators to criticize the impact of the expressed concerns on the work climate at the police unit.

A number of aspects of the KPMG (2016) investigation deserve to be problematized:

- The investigation should be based on the concerns of whistleblowers and not on an implicit assumption that it is all about claim against claim and accusation against accusation.

- The ombudsman should never have been the subject of the investigation. In both the role of ombudsman and the role of whistleblower, he should be immune from such allegations from executives about whom he has already expressed concern.
- The chief of police in the immigration unit was never interviewed by investigators. It seems that she played a role in the background by defining the mandate and monitoring the examination process.
- The private investigators express a number of negative opinions about the ombudsman without any hard facts or real evidence.

The fact that police immigration management was able to move the focus away from notifications, concerns and whistleblowing and onto the whistleblowers by adding a second part to the mandate is thought provoking. Even more thought provoking is the loyalty of fraud examiners to this second part of the mandate. It must have been pretty obvious that the police immigration management wanted to divert attention away from their own potential mismanagement in a difficult situation and onto those who pointed out weaknesses, mistakes and misconduct. As pointed out by many researchers in the past (e.g. Brooks and Button, 2011; Gottschalk, 2016a, b, c, d; Schneider, 2006; Williams, 2005), the private investigation business is problematic as long as it is not regulated. Although the result of an examination in the form of an investigation report is no court ruling or legal decision, it nevertheless carries weight and does often have serious implications for the people involved (Gottschalk, 2016a, b, c, d).

## *Blame game*

The blame game hypothesis suggests that suspected individuals are not necessarily subjected to a fair investigation by private examiners and financial crime specialists. Research on organizational justice and social accounts focuses on how explanations of negative events are publicly communicated to others. Explanations affect outcomes such as trust in the organization, feelings of anger, dissatisfaction, frustration and stress. Suspects find it unfair, especially when suspicions develop into more-grounded or less-grounded accusations (Gottschalk, 2015, 2016b).

The term blame game is often used to describe a phenomenon that happens with groups of people when something goes wrong. Essentially, all members of the group attempt to pass the blame, absolving themselves of the responsibility of the issue. Lack of causal accounts increases disapproval ratings of the harm carried out by placing the blame for harmful acts on others. For example, by attributing corruption to an executive in the organization, terming him a rotten apple, the suspect will feel betrayed by other executives who, in his opinion, belong to the rotten apple basket (Gottschalk, 2015, 2016b).

External attributions place the cause of a negative event on external factors, absolving the account giver and the investigation client from personal responsibility. However, unstable attributions suggest that the cause of the negative event is unlikely to persist over time, which mitigates the severity of the predicament. Uncontrollable attributions suggest that the cause of the event is not within the control of the attributor, further removing any blame or responsibility for the unjust act from the account giver (Lee and Robinson, 2000).

The reasons for private internal investigations include lack of facts and lack of accountability. Nobody will blame themselves for a negative event. The account giver, the private investigator, absolves others from blame and responsibility for the negative event. Even in cases of self-blame, investigations are required to ensure that the self-blame is justified. Self-blame is attributing a negative event to one's own behavior or disposition (Lee and Robinson, 2000).

Some are too powerful to blame (Pontell et al., 2014). Status-related factors such as influential positions, upper-class family ties and community roles often preclude perceptions of blameworthiness (Slyke and Bales, 2012).

From a principal–agent perspective, attributions for negative events may deflect blame away from the real perpetrators. Investigators are motivated to assume power and project control over causal relationships. This motivation to appear in control might lead the account giver to use internal and controllable attributions in their accounts by deflecting blame. Blaming others when a negative event has occurred is simply attractive.

When the blame game hypothesis is applied to the current case of the National Police Immigration Unit in Norway, we find many elements from the theory present. For example, by attributing management failures and organizational misbehavior to repeated concerns expressed by the ombudsman as a whistleblower, executives in the unit successfully engaged KPMG (2016) in removing attention away from themselves.

In conclusion, the police case serves to raise awareness of problematic fraud examiners regarding their potential lack of professionalism, integrity and objectivity in private internal investigations. At the same time, fraud examiners face dilemmas that police investigators can avoid. For example, there is a client with certain expectations that need to be met in order to get the final product accepted and paid for.

The treatment of whistleblowers is a particularly problematic issue in this case. A whistleblower is supposed to be protected against revenge and reprisals. However, as illustrated by the case, problematic behavior by the whistleblower – for example, repeating accusations and allegations – can cause investigative attention to move away from concerns and onto the whistleblower.

It seems that internal investigators avoided crime signal detection in this case.

## Dale Property Development

The case of Dale Property Development serves as an empirical demonstration of the theory of convenience. The purpose is to demonstrate convenience in all three dimensions of convenience theory: financial motive, organizational opportunity and personal willingness. Deviant economic behavior in an organizational context can be explained by convenience theory. At the core of convenience theory we find organizational opportunity, where offenders have the resources for misconduct and also ample opportunities to hide misconduct so that it is only detected by accident. Agency theory suggests that agent and principal may be dissimilar in three respects. First, they may have different preferences and even conflicting values. Next, there is an asymmetry in available knowledge about the organization and its business, where the agent knows much more than the principal. Finally, differences in attitude towards risk may exist, where they have different risk aversion and risk willingness. Because of such differences, the CEO may demonstrate opportunistic behavior by making decisions that benefit himself or herself as the principal at the expense of the board. In the Dale case, it seems that all three agency problems arose.

Financial crime by elite members in an organizational context is at the core of convenience theory. Convenience is a relative concept concerned with efficiency in time and effort as well as a reduction of problems and pain that are compared to actual or potential costs. Convenience is concerned with the relative attractiveness and accessibility of economic behavior (Berry et al., 2002; Collier and Kimes, 2013; Farquhar and Rowley, 2009; Higgins, 1997; Mai and Olsen, 2016; Sari et al., 2017; Sundström and Radon, 2015).

At Dale outside the city of Stavanger in Norway, Rogaland County politicians wanted to create an especially attractive residential area. Millions of dollars were poured in, but no shovel was ever put in the ground. Investigative journalists from a Norwegian newspaper found out and revealed how it all went wrong. The newspaper discovered how the money was spent, and journalists questioned the board's responsibility. NOK 254 million ($30 million) was spent on the project, of which NOK 88 million came from Rogaland County (Risa et al., 2017a).

The newspaper revealed the scandal in January 2017; the control and quality committee in Rogaland County made a decision in April to conduct an internal inquiry, and the police began their investigation the following month (Risa et al., 2017b). The control and quality committee in Rogaland County subsequently decided to suspend its inquiry until the police had secured their evidence in the corruption case. Only a large number of architectural drawings in three dimensions remained from the dream that so many shared. All the money was gone (Aas et al., 2017b).

In this section, deviant economic behavior in an organizational context is explained by convenience theory. The case of Dale Property Development illustrates white-collar misconduct in the form of abuse of public funds. However, at the time of writing, crime signal detection has not occurred.

Numerous restaurant visits and trips abroad provided experiences that the participants enjoyed. In the years from 2011 to 2014, Dale Property Development paid for 180 bar and restaurant visits. In total, the food and beverage bill amounted to NOK 416,414 of taxpayers' money. NOK 132,061 went on champagne, wine, drinks and beer (Risa et al., 2017a).

The chief executive officer (CEO) of Dale Property Development participated in 27 of the 34 trips abroad (Risa et al., 2017a). Architects received millions of Norwegian kroner without any assignment bid, and an advertising agency and a communications advisor received work assignments that far exceeded the value limit for tender competition in public procurement (Aas et al., 2017a).

A Dale employee claimed travel expenses of over 400,000 Norwegian kroner. Her work place and position were moved from Dale outside the city of Stavanger to Brussels in Belgium when her husband got a job there. When she was home in Stavanger, she stayed at the Radisson Blu Royal hotel. During 2013 and 2014, hotel expenses alone amounted to NOK 170,000 (Risa et al., 2017b).

The police started investigating possible corruption after representatives from seven small business enterprises appeared anonymously in the newspaper with information that they were offered lucrative work at Dale if they lowered the price for construction work at the CEO's private residence (Aas et al., 2017b). The police stepped up their investigation after interviewing several construction executives who talked about work in the CEO's private property (Risa, 2017).

A consulting firm invoiced for more than NOK 10 million, the largest project in the history of the firm. And then everything just ended up in a drawer. Consultants just produced a number of plans and then billed Dale Property Development, while nobody followed up.

## *Organizational opportunity*

Rogaland County had no control over its own property company, which was organized as a limited company with the county as sole shareholder. The board at Dale Property Development was politically appointed, with representatives from the political parties in the county. The seats on the board were distributed between the political parties as part of an election settlement, when various committee positions were also distributed.

The board exercised no real control in the company. Board members were pleased to know that the administration's total spending remained within budget and were reassured by the auditor who approved all accounts. The board relied on and trusted management and audit because they did not have the competence or experience to take a more critical line. Board members did not ask any questions that might have been unpleasant or challenging. The board checked that company spending did not exceed company budget, but no concerns were raised regarding whether spending was relevant or in the company's interest.

"We have received budgets and accounts on the board table; this has never been a problem. The budgets have been held all the way," said the former chairperson of the board (Johnsen, 2017a). The chairperson also confirmed that she had never questioned a single travel bill or any other expense sheet from the CEO, but approved those that had been submitted. Thus, both wine and champagne was able to flow freely without anyone reacting.

That assignments demanding an open competitive bid were put out to tender was simply "taken for granted in a publicly owned company" (Johnsen 2017a), and the practice was therefore never overseen by the board. The board did not consider it to be their responsibility to ensure that the administration followed current procurement legislation in the public domain in Norway, which requires that contracts worth more than 500,000 Norwegian kroner should always be based on a form of public tender.

The CEO presented a fairy-tale castle in a fantasy world to the board, which it did not understand. The deputy chairperson on the board told the newspaper that he saw the CEO as simply having no contact with reality and that he had lost confidence in the CEO. But the deputy chairperson never did anything to express his distrust of the CEO at the meetings of the board. "When I questioned what management did, then I got the feeling that I was lacking competence" (Risa et al., 2017a: 15).

The county councilor in Rogaland had no real control opportunity as Dale Property Development was an independent legal entity where they lacked any sort of role. There was no requirement that the chairperson of the board should certify or approve the CEO's travel bills and other expenses. She often did it reluctantly, nevertheless. "There was nothing in the governance structure or power of authority that required any controls, there was procurement without limitations. We had an oral understanding" (Risa et al., 2017a: 18). "I have never seen any reason to question the business," said Dale's chairperson for 15 years (Risa et al., 2017a: 21).

"Yet once again it has been demonstrated that boards of directors exclusively recruited from political parties to govern public projects do not exercise adequate oversight. The competence is simply not there" (Skjæveland, 2017: 21).

Rogaland public audit conducted a management audit and company control of Dale Property Development in 2015, but revealed no misconduct, fraud or financial crime (Rogaland Revisjon, 2015).

When asked why so much money was spent, the CEO neutralized potential guilt by claiming that he did not "know there was any regulatory framework for this" for Dale Property Development:

> We never received any feedback or signals that our business practice was beyond the acceptable, neither specifically nor in general. ... On several occasions, the chairperson, or representatives from the county, also attended these events with their spouses. In other words, I had no reason to think that Dale's practice differs from the practice of the county council.
> 
> *(Risa et al., 2017a: 18)*

The chairperson always signed off the CEO's travel bills and other expense sheets when they were presented, and he interpreted this as indicating that everything was in order. By approving and signing all his bills, she took on – in his mind – responsibility for all the expenses that arose from his activities.

"In international projects (...) there will always be a lot of travel, where cultural and knowledge development in Europe is an essential part of the purpose" (Risa et al., 2017a: 18). The CEO also believes that part of the purpose of the study tours conducted has been to "provide valuable information and experience" (Risa et al., 2017a: 18). That architects were awarded contracts without a bid was because it is "more expensive with a bid" (Aas et al., 2017a: 10).

The newspaper revealed in May 2017 that the CEO was previously reported to the police by his former employer, Kristiansand Municipality, after it was discovered that he had double-billed hours so that he was paid an unwarranted extra 40,000 kroner. In response to this charge, the CEO wrote an email to the newspaper saying that the duplication of billable hours was caused by the heavy workload he experienced in 2007 and 2009. The case was closed by the police in 2009 because of lack of evidence.

For many years (1997–2009), the Dale company dealt exclusively with fairly ordinary property management and rental of properties that until the late 1990s were used as a psychiatric hospital. The properties were later used mainly as housing for refugees and asylum seekers under the auspices of a business organization specialized in refugee reception areas, camps and integration. Thus, the county's wholly owned property development company was for a number of years profitable from rental income.

It was the initiation of an EU project in 2009 that changed the direction of the company. Although Norway is not a member of the European Union, it participates in many EU activities through the European Free Trade Association.

The EU project was something new for Dale Property Development. Its main focus was to deliver innovative, sustainable and solid demonstration projects in line with its name: CONCERTO – communities towards optimal thermal and electrical efficiency of buildings and districts. Fourteen partners from four countries represented a consortium of scientific knowledge, building expertise, solar power specialists, architects, building associations, public authorities, service providers and municipality representatives. The project took off in December 2009 and was initially set for three demonstration venues. Dale in Norway was chosen to run a project at its old hospital property.

In the EU project, retrofitting old buildings and constructing new buildings needed to occur by using front-running technology for the various parts. Two of the three demonstration projects – in Hungary and Spain respectively – succeeded. The third demonstration project, Dale in Norway, lost all the money.

On the EU website, www.pimes.eu, downloaded July 10, 2017, all three projects are listed. The Dale project is marked "project terminated". It says, "Situated at the end of the beautiful Gandsfjord, Dale area will be developed as a modern residential area over the coming years," followed by "Dale project was stopped by Rogaland County Council in June 2014. The property is undergoing preparation for new ownership or sales".

The organizational opportunity to conduct and conceal misconduct and abuse of funds is at the core of convenience theory. In the Dale case, control was supposed to be exercised by the board. However, research shows that control initiatives by some board members can frequently be ignored by other board members. CEOs have a tendency to become opportunistic agents (Shen, 2003). Often because of a CEO's charismatic leadership style, board members lose control over CEO activities (Fanelli and Misangyi, 2006). The CEO at Dale had a reputation for dreams and visions that people shared because of his charisma.

The CEO is supposed to be controlled by the board, but the board only meets once in a while to be updated by the CEO on matters and issues of the CEO's choice. In the theoretical perspective of principal and agent, the CEO is the agent in a relationship with the board as the principal. Hambrick et al. (2015) found that boards often fail in their monitoring responsibilities. One of the reasons is that many board members lack some of the following attributes: independence, expertise in the domain, bandwidth and motivation. In the Dale case, board members seem to have considered board meetings as an arena for political rivalry between left and right. To be capable of dispassionate monitoring, a board member must be independent and objective about the organization's executives and their policies. Being an effective monitor requires expertise – that is, in-depth knowledge and understanding of the domain being monitored.

The fourth attribute by Hambrick et al. (2015) is motivation, here defined as eagerness to exert oneself on behalf of Rogaland County. It requires a board member to ask for additional information, which requires more time and effort and might raise eyebrows. To voice a substantive concern, an act that fellow board members might see as non-collegial, time consuming and even provocative, is no easy task. The CEO may perceive it as criticism (Tingstad, 2016: 28):

> The real challenge lies in each board member's courage and willingness to challenge management, ask tough questions and take intractable positions on the board. Such courage could of course mean that you end up in a minority position, but also that you are frowned on by the board and among executives, are perceived as problematic, and eventually disappear from the board.

## Nordea Bank in the Panama Papers

Although fraud examiners and other investigators have been in business for many years, there are fundamental limits to their work. Organizations that may be subject to some form of fraud or other white-collar crime call in investigators to examine any concerns they may have and to produce a report on whether there is evidence to substantiate such concerns.

They are hired to reconstruct the past and find reasons why negative events occurred. Client organizations have the resources to involve fraud examiners. However, the blame game, lack of integrity and objectivity, and other issues can call into question the value of investigation reports.

This section presents the case of the Scandinavian bank Nordea, in which Nordea executives were suspected of involvement in tax evasion, money laundering and other forms of financial crime in tax havens as a result of information leaked in the Panama Papers.

When suspicion of misconduct and white-collar crime occurs in a business enterprise, there is a tendency to hire fraud examiners from a law firm or an accounting firm to conduct an internal inquiry. The purpose of a private investigation is similar to that of a police investigation in that it is about reconstructing the past (Osterburg and Ward, 2014). Past events and their sequence are to be reconstructed as objectively and completely as possible. Investigators should avoid bias and abstain from sympathy and antipathy. An investigation should be independent and apply information sources and knowledge categories that are relevant to the case. Investigators may assess past events, but they should not pass judgment on individuals.

There are many problematic issues related to private investigations (Brooks and Button, 2011; Button et al., 2007a, 2007b; Williams, 2005, 2014). First, a client pays for the work and asks investigators to do what the client has defined in the mandate. Second, the inquiry is limited in scope since the client is only willing to spend a limited amount of money on the task. Third, private investigations are characterized by secrecy so that neither the police nor the public gain knowledge of procedures and results. Finally, the client sometimes has a desired outcome from the investigation that may influence the work of fraud examiners.

Other limits are concerned with the role of fraud examiners that sometimes extends beyond inquiry into prosecution and sentencing. For example, some private investigators conclude in their reports that there is misconduct, but no crime, thereby "acquitting" their client who is paying for the investigation. While this may be a desirable result for the client, it is an unacceptable outcome for the criminal justice system in democratic societies. Private fraud investigators are not to suggest private settlements when penal laws are violated as this would represent a privatization of law enforcement (Schneider, 2006).

In this section we study the case of a private internal inquiry at Nordea. Media coverage of the so-called Panama Papers in April 2016 portrayed Nordea International Private Banking in Luxembourg as a provider of tax haven structures for its clients. As a response to what was reported in the media, Nordea issued a statement that the bank strongly denounces tax evasion, that other than in exceptional cases Nordea does not assist in setting up offshore companies, and that Nordea does not accept clients that are non-transparent towards relevant tax authorities. As a further response to the revelations in the Panama Papers, Nordea initiated an internal inquiry of adherence to relevant laws and regulations as well as policies and instructions in connection with offshore structures (Mannheimer Swartling, 2016; Nordea, 2016).

## *Nordea Bank*

The Scandinavian bank Nordea is headquartered in Stockholm, Sweden and has a presence in 19 countries around the world, running full service branches, subsidiaries and representative offices. Nordea international private banking has its headquarters in Luxembourg and branches in Switzerland and Singapore. Nordea is the largest bank in Scandinavia. Despite warnings from the Swedish Financial Supervisory Authority, Nordea has been active in offshore structures in tax havens, as leaked by the Panama Papers. The Nordea section in Luxembourg has in the years 2004–2014 set up nearly 400 offshore companies in Panama, the British Virgin Islands and the Seychelles for its customers. The Swedish authority has pointed out serious deficiencies in how Nordea monitors money laundering as well as tax evasion. In 2015, Nordea had to pay the maximum fine of over five million euro in Sweden.

The Panama Papers are 11.5 million leaked documents that detail financial and attorney–client information for more than two hundred thousand offshore entities. The leaked documents were created by Panamanian law firm and corporate service provider Mossack Fonseca. The leaked documents illustrate how wealthy individuals and public officials are able to keep personal financial information private. While offshore business entities are often not illegal, media reporters found that some of the shell corporations were used for illegal purposes, including fraud, tax evasion and money laundering. "John Doe", the whistleblower who leaked the documents to German newspaper *Süddeutsche Zeitung*, remains anonymous.

In 2012, Nordea asked Mossack Fonseca to change documents retrospectively and change dates on signed documents. The chief executive officer at Nordea Luxembourg at that time was from Denmark, while a bank executive from Norway was chairman of the board. The Swedish minister of finance characterized the conduct of Nordea as a crime and totally unacceptable. Politicians in Norway condemned the Norwegian executive's support of secrecy for wealthy bank clients and suggested that she should resign from another chair position in Norway (Ekeberg, 2016e).

## *Internal investigations*

Two parallel investigations were initiated at Nordea in April 2016. Both investigation reports are publicly available. One investigation was internally conducted by the bank's group compliance and group operational risk functions. The other was conducted by law firm Mannheimer Swartling. They both produced investigation reports, of 12 pages and 20 pages respectively. Both reports describe misconduct, but not crime. Both reports suggest that the misconduct has stopped.

Where crime signal detection occurred in the form of illegal backdating of documents, the internal Nordea (2016: 11) report concluded as follows:

> The investigation has found deficiencies in the procedures regarding renewal of Powers of Attorney (POA). In at least seven cases investigation has shown that backdated documents have been requested or provided

during the last six years, which is illegal when it aims at altering the truth. The previous backdating of a POA took place in 2012, and the backdating of a proxy took place in 2014. However, to be convicted of the criminal offence of forgery or use of forgery, certain conditions need to be met cumulatively. These conditions do not all seem to be met for the cases at hand. At least one of the conditions seems not to be met, which is the clear benefit or illicit advantage of the employee asking for backdating, the bank or another third party or causing prejudice or potential prejudice to a third party. However, the procedures are in violation of the Nordea Code of Conduct.

Internal investigators from the group compliance and group operational risk functions also drew a conclusion of misconduct rather than crime. Similarly, Mannheimer Swartling (2016: 6) pointed out that neither lack of tax evasion control nor money laundering is considered a crime in Luxembourg:

> There are several laws and regulations in place in Luxembourg in relation to the fight against money laundering and terrorist financing. Luxembourg has transposed the relevant EU directives on anti-money laundering (AML) to date. It may be noted that Nordea has the same duties on AML and know-your-customers controls regardless of whether the client uses an offshore structure or not. It may also be noted that, also for the time being, Luxembourg banks do not have any legal obligation to make sure that their clients are tax compliant. The fourth EU directive on AML has not yet been transposed into Luxembourg law and tax evasion is therefore not yet treated as predicate money laundering crime under Luxembourg law. There are also bank secrecy rules in place that prevent banks from reporting on tax evasion to the public prosecutor or their holding company. Tax information sharing is only allowed for in certain limited circumstances and exclusively to the Luxembourg tax authorities or to the prosecutor, as part of investigation conducted by such authority.

The internal inquiry at Nordea (2016) only studied documents, while the investigation by law firm Mannheimer Swartling (2016) also interviewed key personnel. They interviewed wealth partners in Luxembourg, current and former board members at Nordea, and management and employees at Nordea.

Mannheimer Swartling (2016: 4) used interviews to confirm information from other sources:

> Unless otherwise expressly stated, a mention in this report to that we have been "informed" of a certain circumstance or that a fact has been "confirmed" or "explained" or the like is a reference to information provided to us during these interviews. The information in the documents together with the information received during said interviews is referred to as the material. The review is based solely on our understanding of the material.

With regard to misconduct, Mannheimer Swartling (2016: 18) concluded as follows:

> While operations associated with offshore structures as such are not illegal in Luxembourg, such structures could be used by clients as instruments for money laundering or tax evasion. In view of this, as well as the result of the investigation, it is therefore a fair conclusion that both the Nordea board and executive management should have identified a need for a particular risk awareness related to the operations associated with offshore structures, and that such risk awareness should have been incorporated in risk assessment processes and the risk appetite framework. If this had been the case, it would have facilitated for the risk and capital and/or the compliance functions to integrate related risks into their respective risk assessment and control processes, and internal audit would possibly have performed audits with this in focus.

Nordea (2016) suggested that the next step following the completion of the internal investigation relating to private banking should be the development of advice on how to mitigate the deficiencies.

## *Evaluation of investigation*

This discussion section is structured as follows. The convenience perspective is discussed first, followed by the resource-based perspective. The blame game hypothesis is discussed next, and finally other limits to private internal investigations.

In the convenience perspective, helping bank customers to set up offshore companies for the purpose of wealth secrecy is not a crime. Wealthy customers are important in private banking, and Nordea competes with other banks globally to attract such clients. Nordea and other banks may suggest to their clients that they avoid tax evasion by being open with their own national authorities about their money placements. Nordea and other banks may also suggest to their clients that they avoid money laundering by avoiding sums that may stem from criminal activities such as corruption, embezzlement, fraud and the drug trade, as well as pointing out that money should not be transferred from tax havens for the purpose of terrorist financing.

Nordea may find it convenient to manage the wealth of important clients without really knowing where the money is coming from or where it is going. Clients may commit financial crime, but bank executives do not really know about it (Ekeberg, 2016b, 2016c, 2016d).

In the resource-based perspective, bank executives have access to financial crime specialists who can investigate when they are accused of white-collar crime. For bank executives, the leakage of the Panama Papers was extremely unfortunate. It became public knowledge that banks such as Nordea helped set up secret offshore structures. Politicians and the media criticized Nordea for unethical business practices. To respond to the criticism and avoid police investigation, Nordea initiated two internal investigations by Nordea (2016) and Mannheimer Swartling (2016). Nordea had access to resources by hiring examiners and by defining the mandates for both investigations.

The blame game hypothesis suggests that the client can indicate where investigators should place the blame for misconduct such as offshore structures and for potential contributions to financial crime such as money laundering and tax evasion. The blame game hypothesis implies that suspected individuals are not necessarily subjected to a fair investigation by private examiners and financial crime specialists (Gottschalk, 2016c).

Lee and Robinson (2000) found that almost nobody will blame themselves for a negative event. Self-blame is attributing negative events to own deviant behavior. Self-blame is very rare. When self-blame occurs, investigators have to ensure that self-blame is justified by being sceptical of potential motives for self-blame. Investigators have to establish the facts and identify accountability. Investigators have to augment knowledge, resolve doubt, ask more questions, test alternative hypothesis, and keep an open mind as long as possible before a conclusion is drawn.

Sonnier et al. (2015) conceptualize blame in terms of personal control. The assessment of an actor's control over a harmful event is influenced by the desire to blame someone whose behavior, reputation or social category has aroused negative reactions. Blaming implies forming affective reactions to aspects of negative events and to the people involved. Private investigators judge how much control the actor exerted by analyzing the structural linkages of volition, causation and foresight while also spontaneously, relatively and unconsciously forming affective reactions. The central question in assessing control and blame attribution is whether the actor desired, caused or foresaw the harmful outcome. Attribution is affected by the investigator's view of what other actors would do in the same situation. When investigators feel that the actor should have foreseen or anticipated the negative consequences of their acts, they are more likely to lay the blame on the actor. The need to lay blame arises out of the need to feel that similar occurrences can be avoided in the future.

Nordea (2016: 12) blamed local employees at Nordea Luxembourg for offshore arrangements: "The communication has mainly been handled by a limited number of employees in wealth planning and client relationship units".

Mannheimer Swartling (2016) blamed local employees at Nordea Luxembourg for illegal backdating of documents. The firm blamed the local board headed by a Norwegian bank executive for not having implemented a code of conduct.

The chief executive officer at Nordea is not blamed in the reports. That comes as no surprise, since he initiated both investigations. Similarly, Valukas (2014) never blamed CEO Mary Barra for the ignition switch failure cover-up at General Motors, maybe because she initiated the investigation.

A number of other potential limits to the investigations are relevant. First, independence. The internal Nordea (2016) report was produced by people whose promotion was dependent on chief executives in the bank, which indicates a lack of independence. Next, integrity. Nordea (2016) investigators have avoided being criticized by Group Compliance and Group Operational Risk, normally responsible for preventing misconduct and crime, which indicates lack of integrity – as well as lack of objectivity, since biases should not affect understanding and assessment. Finally, there is the attempted privatization of court work by Mannheimer Swartling (2016), who concluded that Nordea would not be convicted of forgery.

This section has looked at private inquiries in the corporate sector using the case study of Nordea. It has produced some interesting insights into how the private sector approaches such cases, which is rare in the broader literature. The case indicates that there are a number of limits to private internal investigation of white-collar crime suspicions. While an investigation should reconstruct past events by finding out what happened, how it happened, when it happened and why it happened, reports of investigations have a tendency to suffer from:

1. *Mandate bias*. The mandate for the investigation points in a certain direction and excludes other directions for scrutiny.
2. *Report bias*. The investigation report has selected a partial perspective and does not present a complete picture of the matter under investigation.
3. *Lack of contradiction*. The investigators do not give suspects and witnesses an opportunity to contradict statements in the report. For example, the board chairperson from Norway at Nordea Luxembourg disagrees with the criticism, but there is no evidence of contradiction in the reports.
4. *Privatization of law enforcement*. Investigators try to acquit suspected executives for illegal backdating of documents.
5. *Blame game*. The investigation conclusion blames others than those paying for the investigation.
6. *Roles*. Investigators take on the roles of police, prosecution and judge.
7. *Lack of independence*. Internal compliance officers are not independent of their superiors.
8. *Lack of integrity*. Internal compliance officers might blame themselves for not preventing negative events.

Given such fundamental limits to private investigations, it is important that decision-making is also based on other sources when it comes to conclusions about past negative events. Alternatively, fraud examiners should learn how to avoid these problems so that investigation reports can play a more trustworthy role in the future.

## Regional public management

Here we look at an investigation conducted in Denmark in 2015. There was suspicion of fraud by a leading politician. The law firm Kromann & Reumert was asked to reconstruct events related to changes found in invoices from external suppliers. There was suspicion that invoice text did not represent the real services provided.

The fraud investigation case started when a journalist started to ask questions in a media inquiry on September 24, 2015, in the region of Southern Denmark. The journalist claimed to be in possession of documents that showed that in February 2013 the region had asked an external supplier to change and anonymize the text in an invoice. In a follow-up to the media inquiry on October 1, regional council chairperson Stephanie Lose requested that an external investigation into the matter be initiated. She asked regional director Jane Kraglund, as senior manager of administration, to implement an examination of the case, including whether or not there were grounds for believing that there might be other similar cases (Trenskow and Mosbek, 2015).

The Southern Denmark case received considerable public attention in Denmark in the autumn of 2015. Regional governor Carl Holst was suspected of abusing his position, both for writing political speeches at the expense of the regional administration and for hiring a political advisor paid by the region. The political advisor was hired not to assist him in the region but rather to help him develop a political career nationally. When Holst resigned as regional governor, it was to take up the position of defense minister in the Danish government. However, soon after he had to resign as defense minister due to the emerging scandal related to his former position as regional governor. The scandal centered on the suspicion that Carl Holst, in his period as regional governor, had abused regional funds for private, including party political, purposes. Among other things, during his election campaign he had used a regional employee and paid another employee to be his personal advisor in his parliament ('Folketinget') election campaign. Later on, the regional supervisory authority issued a public criticism of Holst for misuse of regional funds. Holst resigned as minister of defense in the autumn of 2015 and was granted leave from the Danish parliament in the spring of 2016.

## *Description of the case*

Until spring 2012, the preparation of public speeches for the regional governor Carl Holst was handled internally in the region by several employees. When some of these speechwriters resigned from their positions, the region lacked resources in terms of speech writing. New employees were hired, but the regional administration had a problem meeting the standards that Holst requested for his public speeches. After a while, Holst decided to hire an external speechwriter.

In the following period the external speechwriter prepared a number of public presentations for the regional governor to use at different events. When the talks were received, the drafts were reviewed and completed by administrative staff from the region. Internal reviewers started to question the relevance of the speeches for the region. Skepticism grew following an internal memorandum in August 2010, which stated that there should be a clear distinction between party politics and tasks for the region, especially in relation to speech writing. The administration was therefore aware that there was a limit to the kinds of public talk that could be prepared at the region's expense. However, notice was seldom given when the limit had been exceeded. Regardless of such discussions and warnings, all speeches for governor Carl Holst were paid for by the region.

On December 20, 2012, the external supplier of speeches sent an invoice regarding four drafts to the regional governor. The invoice had the heading, "Invoice for preparation of talks and articles for Carl Holst". The expense items for the four speeches were described as follows: "Compilation of written remarks for the Circle 19/11", "Speech at the debate in the Boarder Association at Mors 23/11", "Speech at New Year's 4/1" and "Lecture on Grundtvig in Munkebjerg Church 10/1".

After the invoice arrived at the regional administration, internal discussions became more heated. As a result of these discussions, an email was sent on February 19, 2013 to the external supplier of speeches, asking for a change of text on the invoice. The likely reason for this email being sent almost two months later is the workload in the regional administration. The speechwriter was asked to anonymize the heading by changing it to: "Invoice concerning preparation of drafts". The four expense items were rephrased as: "Comment on November 19, 2012", "Preparation November 23, 2012", "Preparation January 4, 2013", and "Preparation January 10, 2013". The speechwriter added two more items to the invoice: "Preparation January 20, 2013" and "Preparation February 3, 2013". The speech on February 3 was for a debate in the Liberal Educational Association. This was a speech that Holst had personally ordered after the administration pointed out to him that the first speech did not refer to regional interests and thus could not be paid for by the region (Trenskow and Mosbek, 2015).

## *Information retrieval*

The investigation report from law firm Kromann & Reumert was prepared by Trenskow and Mosbek (2015). The report is compressed into 27 pages. In addition, the regional council had a meeting on November 23, and a report from the meeting was published on the website www.regionsyddanmark.dk. The minutes of the meeting reflect the regional council's decision to tighten guidelines (Region Syddanmark, 2015a). A third source of information about the case is the actual mandate for the investigation – called 'kommissorium' – concerned with change and anonymization of the invoice. The mandate is dated October 22, 2015, and the mandate states that the examination should include (Region Syddanmark, 2015b):

1. Statement of the case process, including background and motives.
2. Assessment of the case process, including the extent to which rules of professional administration have been complied with and whether there has been an infringement of other rules.
3. If the investigation detects that there is reason to believe that there are similar cases, these cases are also requested to be examined.
4. Any potential recommendations that the examination may lead to support.
5. If any other circumstances are encountered during the investigation that appear surprising and require special attention, they must be included as well.

A fourth source of information is a letter from the lawyers Nemeth and Azzouzi (2015) at the law firm Nemeth & Sigetty. The letter is dated November 19 and is

18 pages. The letter is a defense statement on behalf of former regional governor Carl Holst in connection with the investigation.

A fifth source of information is media coverage of the Holst case. Examples are Laursen (2015), who writes that Holst's lawyers demand an inquiry into the leakage from the case, and Møller (2016), who writes that the investigation report cost taxpayers 1.3 million kroner (about US$140,000).

A sixth source of information are the emails that Holst's lawyers attached to their response to the investigators. One example is Holst's message to the investigators where he asks them to explain statements in their preliminary report that he cannot understand. Another example is a message from examiner Mosbek to defense lawyer Nemeth in which Mosbek rejects the request for more time to comment on the draft report. A third example is a message from examiner Mosbek to defense lawyer Nemeth in which Mosbek apologizes for the leakage of the preliminary report. Mosbek writes that leakage is unacceptable and subject to criticism and that "the media coverage based on the leakage has put your client in an unfair situation".

All these sources of information can be used to arrive at an assessment of the investigation work and to pass a judgment on the investigation report by Trenskow and Mosbek (2015).

## *Investigation process*

The regional administration provided all the relevant written material. There were also meetings with persons whom investigators thought were relevant to the examination. The investigators from Kromann & Reumert prepared a short summary of each conversation, which the individual had an opportunity to acquaint themselves with. Trenskow and Mosbek (2015) interviewed both current and former employees. These interviews were conducted according to special guidelines designed to ensure they were a reassuring process for those involved.

The region wished that there should be complete anonymity for people interviewed. Therefore, the investigation report is anonymized in relation to both who the examiners talked to and who said what. For the same reason, the report's reproduction of the case process and the examiners' recommendations were kept at a general level.

The internal investigators were aware that in the state administration and at the prosecutor's office there were simultaneously public investigations of a number of concrete issues in relation to former regional governor Carl Holst in connection with his election campaign. In agreement with the authorities, the internal investigators' examination did not include such circumstances, and therefore these issues were not addressed in the conducted interviews.

When internal investigators had surveyed a number of concrete issues, which raised questions about the region's coverage of irrelevant costs, Holst was contacted. Investigators gave Holst the opportunity to get acquainted with and comment on the information and preliminary assessments. A preliminary report was prepared for Holst on November 5 and he was given a deadline of November 9. Investigators intended to send their report to the regional executive committee on November 11. Holst asked in a phone call on November 5 that his remarks be taken directly into the report. The investigators agreed to this, but brought the deadline forward to November 8.

Later the same day the investigators were contacted by Holst's lawyer, who told them that he was abroad and could assist Holst when he returned to Denmark on November 9. The investigators concluded that it was not possible to receive Holst's response and finalize the draft report before the meeting of the executive committee on November 11. Therefore, the examiners prepared a preliminary report on November 9 for use at the business meeting on November 11. The investigators received the consultation response from Holst's lawyer on November 19.

The preliminary report of November 9 was leaked to the press. The person or persons who gave the draft report to the media violated their obligation of secrecy and put Holst in a difficult position, as confirmed by the investigators.

In the final report by Trenskow and Mosbek (2015), investigators incorporated Holst's comments where the investigators considered them relevant. The report was prepared for political consideration at the regional council meeting on November 23 (Region Syddanmark, 2015a).

## *The suspect's defense*

In their defense of suspect Carl Holst, attorneys Nemeth and Azzouzi (2015) wrote an 18-page report. The attorneys claimed that the investigators have "conducted inquiries and concentrated on Carl Holst's role without Carl Holst ever being contacted". Through the attorneys' letter, Carl Holst rejected that he had anything to do with text changes on the invoice. Holst strongly denied that he had in any way contributed to the invoice changes. He had neither initiated the modification of the invoice nor known that it was modified.

The attorneys critized several biased statements in the investigation report. One example was where the report argues that there was a poor working environment in the regional office, characterized by fear, while the annual work environment surveys painted a completely different picture. Investigators claim in their report that those who worked closely with the regional governor Carl Holst were particularly exposed to this, but the claim could not be documented. Since interviews were anonymized in the report, no one can say who put investigators onto such lines of reasoning.

It was news to Carl Holst that the leadership and management structure should have been unclear. It was also news to him that a dispute between board members could have been the reason for the change of the invoice. Holst did not know of any unfortunate work environment, or that his employees had been afraid to challenge or oppose him. It may seem strange that people in the regional administration were afraid of challenging Holst, since the investigation report says that the same people strongly criticized Holst for his speech at the Liberal Education Association.

Defense attorneys Nemeth and Azzouzi (2015) criticized investigating attorneys Trenskow and Mosbek (2015) for failure to reconstruct events and the sequence of events. For investigators to remain objective and secure integrity, signal detection is of utmost importance. The defense attorneys also criticized the investigating attorneys for poor legal work. For example, investigators did not base their review on the managing authority that is actually assigned to a regional governor.

The defense attorneys argued that it was quite natural for Holst to give lectures and speeches in different contexts and arenas. In his capacity as regional governor he was invited to speak at a number of events and about a variety of societal issues. It was a natural part of his job to attend events that focused on public education and colleges and, in that context, Grundtvig, a Danish philosopher.

Holst thus claimed – contrary to his critics who spoke to the investigators – that he attended all events in his capacity as regional governor. As a regional governor, Holst was a politician, and it was therefore meaningless of investigators to criticize him for acting as a politician when he spoke at public appearances. Holst's lawyers therefore concluded that the assistance the administration gave to Holst for his participation at various events complied with the regulations. For example, it did not seem contrary to the regulations that the administration should prepare a political speech for the regional governor on a subject that lies within the region's area of responsibility. A line may be crossed if the administration is asked to formulate party politics, but Holst claimed that he never took such an initiative. He claimed that all his talks had obvious relevance to regional policy.

The investigators accused Holst of having illegitimately charged the region for language courses. As regional governor for Southern Denmark he had a large number of representative tasks in relation to other countries for which it was necessary for him to master English at a high level. It is stated in the regional act that the regional council is to cooperate with authorities in other nations.

The examiners in their report of investigation also criticized Holst for attending an INSEAD course, "High Performance Leadership", in France. Holst's lawyers point out that, first of all, the details were wrong, as Holst attended an IMD course in Switzerland. Second, the lawyers pointed out that the cost of the course was not as high as the investigators were claiming.

The investigators further criticized Holst for engaging in a consultancy business. This involved providing organizational advice and assistance in connection with the appointment of board members and other senior executives in the region's management.

The investigators also criticized Holst for subscribing to a number of newspapers at the expense of the region. However, the newspapers were not delivered to Holst, but to the secretariat, and were used by the entire secretariat.

## *Investigation evaluation*

The investigation report by Trenskow and Mosbek (2015) illustrates the main challenges related to private internal investigation for the client, involved persons and, not least, the many different stakeholders, including the media and the public in general. When the investigation, under the auspices of a reputable Danish law firm, began in November 2015, Carl Holst was the Danish defense minister. The contracting authority was the Southern Denmark region ('Region Syd-Danmark'), which in light of massive press coverage, among other things, asked the law firm to assess whether the administration in the region had asked a supplier to change the text in an invoice so that the items of expenditure were more anonymous, and if there were reasons to believe that there were other similar cases, and whether there were other conditions that seemed surprising, etc.

The completed internal investigation immediately reveals themes that illustrate some of the issues associated with investigations, such as uncertain legal status of the suspect, insufficient account of the suspect's version, and leakage of the review report before the suspect had the opportunity to comment on and possibly refute some of the accusations. The report uses, and attaches considerable importance to, anonymous sources, which reduces the suspect's potential defense opportunities. Misconduct signals should be reported by evidence, not by accusations from anonymous sources (Kristensen, 2016).

The investigation had a very broad mandate ('kommissorium'). For example, investigators were asked to examine "other circumstances that appear surprising". One might argue that the investigation would therefore only cover what the region was interested in, which could threaten justice for the suspect. Such bias might also distort the opinions of involved persons, public opinion and opinions expressed in potential future court proceedings (Kristensen, 2016).

The broad mandate is not necessarily matched by access to information and the short-term perspective of the investigation. In terms of crime signal detection, the mandate may cause random detection and random lack of detection, since "other circumstances" may emerge at any point depending on what investigators stumble upon.

The investigation by Trenskow and Mosbek (2015) seems far from thorough, dealing as it does with only a few aspects, more or less randomly selected. Among signals not detected by the investigators is the private alarm in Carl Holst's residence allegedly paid for by the region.

The justice situation for others involved in the investigation is also unclear. Although interviews were anonymous, it might be possible, through archival insight requests by lawyers and the media, to identify interviewees. What significance would the potential exposure of anonymous information sources have had for the confidentiality relationship between interviewers and interviewees?

The region ended up reporting Holst to the police, although in fact, Holst had already been reported to the police by several local citizens. Moreover, a police investigation is not dependent on external reports. It is assumed that the police also monitor newspapers and other media and react appropriately where there is suspicion of white-collar crime.

In an evaluation we have to ask: what benefits does such an investigation provide? Is it only a performance for the gallery, designed to reassure the public that the region is at least doing something in response to possible negative events?

Investigators were asked in the mandate to explain the process that took place when invoice text was changed. They were asked to examine the background and find the motive. But the investigators were not able to do this. According to Kristensen (2016), they failed. Instead, investigators in their report focused on a number of subjective and biased assessments for why the invoice was changed, including the allegation of a working environment characterized by fear of Holst as regional governor.

Defense attorneys Nemeth and Azzouzi (2015: 6) seem to be right in stating that the investigation violated Danish law association guidelines: "It must be assumed that the guidelines have been overridden in various ways. Carl Holst had no access to contradiction, and he had no legal support from the region". Nemeth and Azzouzi (2015: 17) formulated their criticism of Trenskow and Mosbek's report as follows:

- The report has been prepared without those responsible for the report having conducted sufficient investigations of the factual or legal basis.
- The conclusions drawn by the inquiry are random, undeveloped and tendentious in nature.
- The investigation has been conducted without observing the legal guarantees that should be granted to anyone subject to an investigation.
- The investigation has been conducted in violation of the guidelines for legal investigations.
- The investigation has been conducted in a manner that must be characterized as a serious breach of correct law practice.
- The study is based on anonymous explanations from interviewees, which neither Carl Holst nor ourselves have been made aware of.
- The investigation has been completed without either Carl Holst or ourselves having had access to all relevant documents.
- The documentary material presented is completely inadequate, it does not give a true picture and is only presented to draw attention to some apparently significant expenses, which further inquiry – an inquiry by Kromann Reumert that they did not undertake – would show do not concern Carl Holst.
- The preparation of the so-called interim report of November 9, 2015 should have awaited Carl Holst's comments.
- There was not the least basis for handing the interim report to members of the Regional Council (members of the Executive Committee) before the report was final.
- Anyone familiar with the regional policy system had to be aware that the report would be immediately leaked, which made it profoundly risky to hand over such an incomplete report.
- The followed approach shows that it is a political attack on Carl Holst and an attempt at character assassination.
- The produced report can be characterized as extremely poor craftsmanship, both as regards the processing of the facts and in terms of law.

Many of these points are purely subjective entries by Holst's attorneys. While Trenskow and Mosbek (2015) are supposed to be objective, accountable and trustworthy and demonstrate integrity in their reconstruction of past events, Nemeth and Azzouzi (2015) are allowed to be subjective in their defense of their client. However, some of the points are highly relevant as evaluation criteria. For example, that Holst did not have reasonable time to contradict allegations is justified criticism. That a preliminary report was so widely circulated is also a justified point of criticism. That many conclusions seem to have such a weak and biased basis is clearly another valid criticism.

At the beginning of the investigation, investigator Nemeth advised the suspected Holst not to hire an attorney. This was a bad advice, and we can only speculate about the motive, given that investigators ended up accusing Holst of white-collar crime (Kristensen, 2016).

## *Investigation consequences*

Carl Holst was born in 1970. He is a Danish politician and a member of parliament ('Folketinget') for the liberal party ('Venstre'). He felt pressured to leave his ministerial post and take a leave of absence from Folketinget as a result of several issues, including the investigation by Trenskow and Mosbek (2015). Other matters included the disclosure that he might have received a double salary for a period of time. Holst resigned after 93 days as defense minister (NTB, 2015b):

> Denmark's defense minister Carl Holst resigns, three months after joining Lars Løkke Rasmussen's government. There has been a storm around Holst since he became the defense minister. He has, among other things, been criticized for insane statements about Denmark's participation in the Iraq war and poor handling of the conflict with the Danish military's combat plane mechanics. It probably peaked when Danish media recently revealed that Holst in his former position as regional governor in Southern Denmark had used a communications officer in the region as his personal assistant in the election campaign earlier this year. Holst has rejected this, but this week it came out that the assistant had sent hundreds of emails about the election campaign.
>
> "I have today informed the prime minister that I resign as minister of defense and minister of Nordic cooperation," Holst said in a press release, giving as his reason the "shadows" from his past in the Southern Denmark region.

The Southern Denmark authority decided to report the former regional governor to the police, and the state government subsequently concluded that something illegal had taken place. In February 2016, a local chairman stood down in protest when it became known that Carl Holst would run for a new seat in Folketinget (Ritzau, 2016).

In March 2017, the attorney general in Denmark concluded that there was no basis for criminal proceedings against the former regional governor (Holler, 2017):

> The Attorney General has today decided not to raise a criminal case for job abuse and misconduct against the former regional governor of Southern Denmark, Carl Holst (V). This is confirmed by state prosecutor Jens Røn from the Attorney General. The prosecutor has investigated whether Christian Ingemann performed campaign work for Carl Holst during the parliamentary elections of 2015. Ingemann was employed as a communications officer for the region, not to spend his time assisting with a campaign for a parliamentary candidate. According to state prosecutor Jens Røn, the investigation has shown that people employed in the region have carried out campaign work for Carl Holst.
>
> But there is no basis for criminal proceedings against the former regional governor, he said. The prosecutor is of the opinion that it will not be possible to prove in a criminal case that these tasks have been carried out at the expense of the communication officer's duties as an employee of the Southern Denmark region.
>
> Jens Røn explains:
>
> "This is because, among other things, the communications officer has had considerable freedom to organize his working hours. It also applies to what times of the day he chose to carry out his work for the region," says state prosecutor Jens Røn. The prosecutor states that today's decision is based on 18 months of investigation. Among other things, interrogations of 31 persons have been conducted and a comprehensive review of the case documents has been made. This includes 8,200 emails.

People in the region were not happy with this decision. In August 2017, the regional administration initiated another internal investigation into Holst's spending of public money. At the same time, Holst was not happy with the decision of the police not to press charges against those who leaked the draft report to the media (Suurballe, 2017).

## Tipping point decision-making

Tipping points in decision-making by police detectives have been subject to empirical study. This section explores tipping points in decision-making by fraud examiners in private internal investigations. Fraud examiners are hired to conduct internal investigations when there is suspicion of white-collar crime in public and private organizations. Fraud examiners make decisions regarding investigative approaches and information relevance. Investigative approaches include interviews, document reviews, digital searches and tips receipts. Information relevance is concerned with information quality and well as source reliance.

Content analysis of investigation reports indicate that both secondary and primary sources lead to identification of suspects.

The main purpose of a fraud examination is to establish if, how, where, when, why and by whom financial crime was committed. Examiners need to discover, collect, check and consider pieces of information from various sources to construct a coherent account of past events (Gottschalk, 2016a, b, c, d). Examples of investigations in the United States include Enron investigated by Powers et al. (2002), General Motors investigated by Valukas (2014), Lehman Brothers investigated by Valukas (2010), Peregrine investigated by Berkeley (2013), Walters investigated by WilmerHale and PwC (2008), Wildenthal investigated by Breen and Guberman (2012), and WorldCom investigated by Wilmer and PwC (2003).

Mistakes in examiners' decision-making may be the most common type of error in criminal investigations. Fahsing (2016) suggests that problems typically arise when examiners prematurely shift from evidence-based investigation to suspect-driven case building, without considering competing explanations or collecting all the available evidence. Just as in the police force (Dean et al., 2008), there is a need for highly specialized expert detectives to make relevant and optimal decisions during a private internal investigation.

There is a need for more research on what makes a good fraud examiner. This section makes a contribution. There is also a need to translate research findings into sound investigative practice and acknowledge detective expertise (Fahsing and Ask, 2016).

Based on a sample of 60 investigation reports in Norway, this section presents empirical results regarding decision-making by fraud examiners. This section addresses the following research question: *How do fraud examiners make decisions in white-collar crime investigations?* We focus on tipping points in decision-making – that is, decisions that can change examiners' mindset to point out a suspect or suspects (Fahsing and Ask, 2013). We search for triggers that caused narrowing shifts in mindsets of fraud examiners. Triggers are conceptualized as pieces of information that change the state of knowledge and cause a mindset to point out a suspect or suspects. While Fahsing and Ask (2013, 2016) applied tipping points to police investigations, this research applies tipping points to private investigations by fraud examiners. This research is important, as inherent biases can be present in criminal detectives' judgments and decision-making.

Fraud examiners make decisions about investigative strategies as well as information that has been collected. Fahsing (2016: 10) suggests that a common denominator can be noted in different accounts of criminal investigative failures whereby investigators strive to confirm their initial hypothesis while seemingly ignoring or downplaying conflicting information: "Accordingly, a number of studies from different traditions have identified decision-making abilities as the core in making an effective detective".

Decision-making is a cognitive process resulting in the selection of a belief or a course of action from among several alternative possibilities. The course of action chosen represents an alternative that seems superior to other alternatives in terms of its advantages compared to its disadvantages.

Convenience theory suggests that people tend to choose alternatives that represent savings in time and effort, as well as avoidance of pain and experience of satisfaction (Gottschalk, 2017). Just as white-collar criminals may find convenient ways for their offenses, internal investigators may find convenient ways in their examination efforts. Fraud examiners have to make decisions regarding the allocation of people and man-hours (Brooks and Button, 2011).

Fahsing and Ask (2013) asked investigators to identify decisional tipping points – that is, decisions that could change detectives' mindset from suspect identification to suspect verification, together with situational and individual factors relating to these decisions. In a content analysis, two types of decision were identified as typical and potentially critical tipping points: (1) decision to point out a suspect, and (2) decisions concerning main strategies and lines of inquiry in the case.

Investigative psychology is primarily directed towards detectives' cognitive tasks such as the processing of information, the identification of different investigative scenarios, and decisions on the best investigative strategies or lines of inquiry (Fahsing and Ask, 2016). The decision to point out a suspect may come to nothing as a result of the blame game. The blame game hypothesis suggests that suspected individuals do not necessarily become subject to a fair investigation by private examiners and financial crime specialists. Research on organizational justice and social accounts focuses on how explanations of negative events are publicly communicated to others. Explanations affect outcomes such as trust in the organization, feelings of anger, dissatisfaction, frustration and stress. Suspects find it unfair, especially when suspicions develop into more-grounded or less-grounded accusations (Gottschalk, 2015).

External attributions place the cause of a negative event on external factors, absolving the account giver and investigation client from personal responsibility. The account giver who places the blame on someone is not necessarily capable of defining a cause-and-effect relationship. Therefore, the claimed causality will not always persist over time. The cause of an event is not within the control of the attributor. However, uncertain and attributions can remove potential blame from the account giver (Lee and Robinson, 2000).

Fraud examiners' decision-making environment is often far from ideal. There are budget constraints imposed by the client, there are agreed time constraints, there are access problems regarding certain information sources, such as personal emails, and there are missing documents. Fraud examiners can be exposed to pressures internally in the client organization, internally in their own auditing or law firm, and externally from the media. In such a problematic decision-making environment, fraud examiners may often rely on their own intuitions, field experience and rules of thumb.

The theory of tipping points, which has its roots in epidemiology, is based on the insight that once beliefs and energies are engaged in a specific direction, conversion to and trust in an idea will gather speed like an epidemic, bringing about fundamental change in an inquiry very quickly (Kim and Mauborgne, 2003). The theory suggests that such a movement – pointing at a potential suspect, for example – can be "unleashed" by an examiner who arrives at a conclusion by making a decision about causality. An investigative tipping point puts a detective in a goal-directed mindset focused on verifying the guilt of a suspect (Fahsing and Ask, 2013, 2016).

Content analysis can be defined as any methodology or procedure that works to identify specific characteristics within texts attempting to make valid inferences (Krippendorff, 1980; Patrucco et al., 2017). Content analysis assumes that language reflects both how people understand their surroundings and their cognitive processes. Therefore, content analysis makes it possible to determine how a white-collar offender perceives their personal experiences as an inmate (McClelland et al., 2010).

Investigation reports by fraud examiners are the subject of content analysis in an archival study. Unfortunately, reports are difficult to find and obtain. As explained by Gottschalk and Tcherni-Buzzeo (2017), there are a number of reasons why client organizations keep reports secret and do not disclose them to the public or police. First, there is a group of reasons concerned with business and enterprise management and maintaining control over the situation, where the company would like to avoid any interference with its business:

1. *Reputation*. If it becomes known that the police are investigating the case, it could lead to negative publicity and financial loss.
2. *Exclusion*. As long as the company is under investigation by the police, contracts may be put on hold in both the public and private sectors.
3. *Effort*. Crime is not reported because it takes too much time and effort. The police will ask for all kinds of documentation and access to computers.

Next there is a group of reasons concerned with the consequences of law enforcement:

4. *Law enforcement penalty*. Reaction against the company may be a reason for not going to the police.
5. *Protection from law enforcement*. Shielding both individuals and the organization from police investigation is another reason for not disclosing evidence of white-collar crime to the police.
6. *Bargaining with law enforcement*. Plea bargaining is available to varying degrees in different countries.

Third, there is a group of reasons concerned with lack of trust in the police:

7. *Police passivity*. Police often demonstrate passivity when approached about possible offenses.
8. *Police competence*. Investigating white-collar crime suspicions requires highly specialized expertise, which is often not available in the police at the time a potential financial crime is reported.
9. *Police capacity*. There is an inability of the state unilaterally to cope with the rising tide of economic crime due to limited resources.
10. *Police failure*. Just as a private investigation can fail to establish facts, so police investigations can fail to find the truth about a negative incident.

Finally, there is a reason for non-reporting that is concerned with the judgment of whether the situation actually constitutes a crime:

11. *Grey area.* What happened is considered insignificant.

Despite these challenges, we were able to identify and retrieve a total of 60 investigation reports in Norway. Detection occurred when there was media coverage of cases and when people in the business and public sectors knew we were looking for reports. We spent almost three years searching until we had an acceptable sample. Unfortunately, we have no way of telling whether these reports are in any way representative of the vast number of reports actually produced. Therefore, because these reports were the only ones available to us, the sample has to be labeled a convenience sample. All 60 reports are listed in chapter 6.

## *Research findings*

We are looking for tipping points for suspects described in investigation reports. We have to exclude reports where no suspect(s) were identified. All reports listed in chapter 6 are summarized in Table 7.1 in terms of tipping point findings.

More than half of the investigations had no tipping point. One reason for this is that some investigations concluded that no misconduct or crime had occurred. Another reason is that some investigations were mainly focused on preventative routines rather than investigative findings. A third reason is that some investigators failed to get to the bottom of the case.

Among the tipping point cases, Table 7.1 shows that it was the discovery of documentary and other secondary source content that led to the identification of suspects. In a few tipping point cases, primary sources such as witness statements led to the identification of suspects.

Fraud examiners in private internal investigations perform an integrated set of purposeful work activities. Work and work settings can be defined based on variations in knowledge that underlies work practices. Work practice means the way in which work gets done and the knowledge how to do it. Practices are the actions engaged in by individuals to accomplish the ongoing work of an investigation. The focus should be less on detectives as knowledge workers and more on detective activity and practice, meaning the type of work and the desired performance outcome (McIver et al., 2013).

Detectives apply tacit knowledge where the extent of inseparability from action can be found in the unobservable sequences, routines, capabilities and systems for doing work (Fahsing and Ask, 2016). Knowledge is embedded in work and co-dependent on unidentified aspects of the local investigative context (McIver et al., 2013).

Fraud examiners in global auditing firms and local law firms can participate in communities-of-practice concerned with knowledge in private internal investigations. Such communities view learning as situated in the context of the activity or

**TABLE 7.1** Tipping points when suspects are identified

| # | Case | Tipping point(s) | Suspect(s) |
|---|---|---|---|
| 1 | Adecco | Overtime sheet for employees | Local managers at nursing home |
| 2 | Ahus | No tipping point | - |
| 3 | Andebu | No tipping point | - |
| 4 | Betanien | Bank statements | CEO in foundation |
| 5 | Briskeby | No tipping point | - |
| 6 | Demokrat | Bank statements | Party leader |
| 7 | DNB | No tipping point | - |
| 8 | Drammen | Witness evidence | Manager in municipality |
| 9 | Eckbo | No tipping point | - |
| 10 | Fadderbarna | No tipping point | - |
| 11 | Forsvaret | Fake invoices | Colonel in the army |
| 12 | Forsvaret | Lack of approval | Colonel in the army |
| 13 | Forsvarsdep | Violation of routines | Colonel in the army |
| 14 | Furuheim | Illegal transactions | Board members |
| 15 | Gassnova | No tipping point | - |
| 16 | Grimstad | No tipping point | - |
| 17 | Hadeland | Personal transactions | CFO in company |
| 18 | Hadeland | Personal transactions | CFO in company |
| 19 | Halden | No tipping point | - |
| 20 | Halden | No tipping point | - |
| 21 | Hordaland | Whistleblowing | Chief of Police |
| 22 | Kraft | Witness statements | CEO |
| 23 | Kragerø | Minutes of meetings | CEO |
| 24 | Kvam | No tipping point | - |
| 25 | Leksvik | No tipping point | - |
| 26 | Lindeberg | Violation of regulations | Councilman |
| 27 | Lunde | Fraudulent transactions | CEO |
| 28 | Moskva | Lack of contracts | Headmaster |
| 29 | NAV | No tipping point | - |
| 30 | Nordea | No tipping point | - |
| 31 | Norges | No tipping point | - |
| 32 | Norsk | Private property | CEO |
| 33 | Næringsdep | No tipping point | - |
| 34 | Omsorg | Construction cost sheet | CEO |
| 35 | Omsorg | No tipping point | - |
| 36 | Oslo | Lack of contracts | Chief of Sanitation |
| 37 | Oslo | No tipping point | - |
| 38 | Politi | Overtime accusations | Safety representative |
| 39 | Rana | No tipping point | - |
| 40 | Region | Private expenses paid | County mayor |
| 41 | Romerike | Embezzlement documents | CEO |
| 42 | Samferdsel | Corruption documents | Department manager |
| 43 | Sandefjord | No tipping point | - |
| 44 | Skjervøy | Mismanagement of public funds | Former mayor |

| # | Case | Tipping point(s) | Suspect(s) |
|---|---|---|---|
| 45 | Stange | Transaction of shares | Board members |
| 46 | Stavanger | No tipping point | - |
| 47 | Sykehus | No tipping point | - |
| 48 | Telenor | Whistleblowing | Two senior executives |
| 49 | Tomter | No tipping point | - |
| 50 | Troms | No tipping point | - |
| 51 | Undervis | Fake invoices | Property manager |
| 52 | Undervis | Fake invoices | Project manager |
| 53 | Unibuss | Whistleblowing | CEO |
| 54 | Utenriksdep | Embassy expenses | Local manager |
| 55 | Utenriksdep | Grant funding | CEO |
| 56 | Utenriksdep | Lack of approval | CEO |
| 57 | Utlending | No tipping point | - |
| 58 | Verdibanken | No tipping point | - |
| 59 | Video | No tipping point | |
| 60 | World | Illegal game | CEO |

practice and emphasize the importance of understanding how easy or difficult it is to learn to do a particular kind of investigative work. The learnability of a practice consists of the type and amount of effort, study and accumulated comprehension needed to perform certain kinds of work (McIver et al., 2013).

Knowledge is a key ingredient in decision-making (Earl, 2001). Traditionally, a distinction has been made between two different knowledge management strategies: personalization and codification (Imran et al., 2017). Decision-making relies heavily on personalized knowledge. Information is the raw material for knowledge. Information refers to facts and data that can be understood, stored and transferred. Know-how refers to skills and expertise that are action based (McIver et al., 2013).

Tacit knowledge is a form of knowing that is inseparable from action because it is constituted through doing. Tacit knowledge is the unspecifiable process of knowing-in-action that is difficult to teach and difficult to articulate (McIver et al., 2013). It is difficult to capture because it is hard to formalize and not easily visible. It is difficult to share with others because it is highly context dependent or firm specific.

In conclusion, tipping points are an interesting phenomenon in decision-making. Based on 60 reports of investigations, we explored the extent and content of tipping points. We found that both secondary material (such as documents) and primary material (such as witness statements and whistleblowing) can be tipping points leading to a suspect being identified, whereupon all efforts are focused on that suspect.

# 8
# CRIME INVESTIGATIONS IN THE UNITED STATES

Most reports from private internal investigations, both in Norway and the United States, are not available to the public because of secrecy. Reasons for this include business secrets and other confidential information, data protection of sensitive information about identified individuals, and general avoidance of public attention (Gottschalk and Tcherni-Buzzeo, 2017). However, we were able to identify and obtain a few U.S. reports.

## Enron Corporation

Enron was investigated by Powers et al. (2002). Enron was an American energy, commodities and services company based in Houston, Texas. The company employed 20,000 people in the areas of electricity, natural gas, communications, and pulp and paper. In the 1990s, the company ran into financial problems. Enron was in need of a rescue plan. One possibility was to sell off subsidiaries and close down unprofitable businesses. Another was to let a competing business enterprise take over Enron, restructure it and merge it with similar activities. A third possibility was to replace top management with a new skill team to change product lines, marketing strategy and organizational structure. A fourth was for the failing top management team to commit white-collar crime.

The top management team consisted of Kenneth Lay, Jeffrey Skilling and Andrew Fastow. They decided to implement alternative four, considering it to be the most convenient. By committing white-collar crime, they believed that they could rescue Enron. They thought the financial problems were temporary and would disappear after some years. They thought they might be able to correct their crime when profits flowed in again. They were convinced Enron would recover.

Alternatives one to three were less attractive. They had built an empire that was associated with success, status and influence. Ken Lay was a close friend of the

Bush family, including the president. Enron made large campaign contributions to Bush and headed several important committees in the Republican party. From their prestigious positions, it was unacceptable to Lay, Skilling and Fastow to hand over the business to others. It was unacceptable to reveal to the world that Enron was performing poorly.

White-collar crime was thus a convenient option. By presenting financial results that were far more favorable than indicated by the real situation, they were able to stay on top of an apparently successful, expanding and profitable business enterprise. It was the threat of collapse and bankruptcy that made white-collar crime a seemingly convenient way out of performance difficulties. If Enron had recovered, the white-collar crime would have been successful and probably nobody would have learned about the offense. It would have served to protect Enron's interests.

Some quotes from the internal investigation report by Powers et al. (2002) illustrate convenience in the economic dimension:

- "Enron used this strategy to avoid recognizing losses for a time" (page 14).
- "One perceived solution to this finance problem was to find outside investors willing to enter into arrangements that would enable Enron to retain those risks it believed it would manage effectively, and the related rewards" (page 36).
- "On June 18, 1999, Fastow discussed with Lay and Skilling a proposal to establish a partnership, subsequently named LJM Cayman. Fastow would serve as the general partner and would seek investments by outside vendors" (page 68).
- "Fastow and Glisan developed a plan to hedge the Rhythms investment by taking advantage of the value in the Enron shares covered by the forward contracts" (page 78).
- "In late 1999, at Skilling's urging, a group of Enron commercial and accounting professionals began to devise a mechanism that would allow Enron to hedge a portion of its merchant investment portfolio" (page 99).
- "It is particularly surprising that the accountants at Andersen, who should have brought a measure of objectivity and perspective to these transactions, did not do so" (page 132).
- "The Board of Directors was denied important information that might have led it to take action" (page 148).

Powers et al.'s (2002) investigation report reveals that it was not only a threat motive that made white-collar crime a convenient option. There was also an element of greed, especially as regards Fastow:

- Andrew S. Fastow, Executive Vice President and Chief Financial Officer of Enron, is the managing member of LJM1's general partner. The general partner of LJM1 is entitled to receive a percentage of the profits of LJM1 in excess of the general partner's proportion of the total capital contributed to LJM1, depending upon the performance of the investments made by LJM1" (page 184).

- "The failure to set forth Fastow's compensation from the LJM transactions and the process leading to that decision raise substantial issues" (page 187).

Unfortunately for Lay, Skilling and Fastow, their white-collar crime was not successful. It did not solve the problem. Enron went bankrupt and the executives went to prison.

While the economic convenience of white-collar crime in the Enron case is mainly characterized by need for success and fear of falling (Piquero, 2012), the organizational convenience is characterized by opportunities of advanced manipulation techniques that are available to top executives (Benson and Simpson, 2015). The behavioral convenience can be found in a corporate culture dominated by Lay, Skilling and Fastow focusing on goals that justify (illegal) means (Jonnergård et al., 2010) and neutralization of potential guilt feelings (Stadler and Benson, 2012).

## Philadelphia Police Department

The Pennsylvania Crime Commission published an investigation report on police corruption and the quality of law enforcement in Philadelphia. The report documents evidence of systematic patterns of corruption in Philadelphia among some police officers. The commission found that police corruption in Philadelphia was ongoing, widespread, systematic and occurring at all levels of the police department (Pennsylvania, 1974).

In an economic convenience perspective, it was convenient for police officers to receive improper cash payments by gamblers, racketeers, bar owners, prostitutes, illegal construction companies and others. Since salaries for police officers were not great and law enforcement actions against organized crime was a challenge, it was much more convenient to cooperate with criminals than arrest them. By cooperating with criminals, police officers made additional money that enabled a slightly better lifestyle for their families. By cooperating with criminals, police officers avoided threats and dangerous situations.

While it was convenient for police officers to receive bribes, criminals avoided the inconvenience of law enforcement by giving bribes to police officers (Pennsylvania, 1974: 170):

> If the police were to enforce strictly all the laws, ordinances, and regulations governing the activities of construction companies, it would cause much inconvenience for the companies involved. Because of pressures to get work finished, the companies are willing to pay the police and other public employees to avoid the situation.

Convenience among police officers took the form both of receiving bribes and of planting evidence to get the wrong person arrested to protect bribing criminals (Pennsylvania, 1974: 204): "My partner really wanted this guy busted so we went in to search, right. So my partner conveniently comes up with the pinch". Patrols by police officers among bribing criminals were scheduled conveniently for offenders (Pennsylvania, 1974: 220): "We would call them up or either stop by and see them and let them know that they would inform us which time was most convenient".

In addition to the convenience of receiving bribes and avoiding confrontations with serious criminals, there was also the convenience of playing along with colleagues in the police force. The occupational culture in the police was that police officers better not challenge the corruption culture. Interviewed police officers told investigators that fraudulent behavior was the rule rather than the exception (Pennsylvania, 1974: 228):

> The young officer begins to realize that one who does not participate in corrupt activities is ostracized. One officer in New York who did not participate in taking money described the system as follows:
> "To other police officers your participation (in taking money) was another strong link in a chain of fraternity and had no reflection whatsoever on your honesty. Conversely, your refusal meant certain ostracism and a cross-eyed look as someone not in full possession of all his mental faculties. It cannot be emphasized enough that taking money was such a tradition, such a habit, and was so common all around, that the police officers I talked with did not think of it with any more regard than the habit of smoking – you know it's bad for you and you shouldn't do it, but you do it anyway."
> In Philadelphia, police officers have similarly described the peer pressure with which they were confronted. A member of the Philadelphia police force testified before the Commission that after he noticed vice activity at certain locations within his sector, he talked to an older officer who said, "Don't worry about it, kid; I'll be taking care of it. Or you walk a beat."

Convenience theory is concerned with white-collar crime. It might be argued that corruption among police officers is not a typical case of white-collar crime. However, there was a system of weekly payments based on rank in the police department: policemen received $5, sergeants received $10, and captains and special vice investigators received $15. The payments were usually made between the hours of 8 a.m. and 4 p.m. Criminals made regular payments of a sizable sum to a large number of person in exchange for protection against gambling raids and other law enforcement activities.

Towards the end of their internal investigation report, the Pennsylvania (1974) crime commission summarized their corruption investigation experience. They argued that a corruption investigation of a police department is one of the most difficult tasks that an investigatory agency can undertake. When another law enforcement unit is the target of the investigation, there are additional problems for the investigators. Police are very protective of each other, and law enforcement units are exceedingly reluctant to investigate other law enforcement units.

## Chief Technology Office

The Acar fraud involved a series of loosely related fraudulent schemes over the course of a three-and-a-half-year span from September 2005 to March 2009. While none of these schemes were particularly complex according to fraud examiners Sidley (2010), they all escaped detection and would likely have remained undiscovered but for the cooperation of an informant. Over time, these schemes grew more brazen, reflecting Acar's growing confidence that there were no mechanisms in place to detect their fraud. The initial plan was a basic corruption scheme with kickbacks from Sushil Bansal. Bansal's company, AITC, had been awarded a contract to provide temporary contractors in the security division. Bansal had tendered a number of candidates, but Acar and his co-workers had rejected them as unqualified.

After these failed attempts to place AITC contractors, Farrukh Awan, a contractor who had been offered a full-time position at the Office of the Chief Technology Officer (OCTO), approached Acar and proposed the following: Acar would independently locate qualified candidates for the security division positions and allow Bansal to hire those individuals as AITC employees. Bansal would then offer the contractors to OCTO, and Acar would approve them. In exchange, Acar and Awan would each receive a kickback from Bansal for part of the value of each contract. Acar explained to Sidley (2010) that, from his perspective, the arrangement provided him with a bonus payment for hiring individuals he would have hired anyway, with the additional benefit of allowing him to do his job at OCTO more effectively by retaining more competent contractors.

Therefore, in the behavioral dimension of convenience theory, Acar argued that his corruption scheme did no damage and had no victim. In the organizational dimension of convenience theory, Acar had the opportunity to involve himself in the kickback scheme because his position at OCTO enabled him to hire people.

Over time, Awan's role was phased out, but Bansal and Acar continued the arrangement on their own. The next scheme they developed was a "ghost employee" fraud. Under this scheme, AITC either submitted false timesheets to Acar that inflated the contractor's actual hours or submitted timesheets for fictional AITC contractors. In some circumstances, Acar would identify contracts in the security division awarded to AITC in which work was completed, but the contract remained open. Acar would approve timesheets submitted by Bansal on those contracts. In exchange for the approvals of ghost-employee timesheets, Bansal would kickback a share of the billings attributable to the ghost employees.

The final form of fraud engineered by Acar and Bansal involved the purchase of software licenses. OCTO approved Acar's request for the purchase of 2,000 software licenses, and the contract was awarded to AITC. However, AITC delivered only 500 of the 2,000 licenses OCTO purchased. Acar certified that OCTO received the complete order, and the district paid AITC for the entire contracted amount (Sidley, 2010).

In order to impede detection of these acts, Acar engaged in several other improper practices. For example, while working as a district employee and awarding government contracts, Acar had an undisclosed interest in Circle Networks, a company that contracted with the district and was allegedly used to launder illegal kickback payments from Bansal to Acar. Acar's ownership interest in Circle Networks represented a conflict of interest for a district employee, yet the district never detected it. Similarly, Bansal created shell companies nominally controlled by other individuals in order to create an appearance of competitive bidding on contracts that Acar would award to AITC. Finally, Acar used the access he had to electronic data in the security division to monitor emails to and from the OCTO leadership to determine whether his activities were in any danger of being discovered by the Office of the Inspector General during its audits (Sidley, 2010).

Yusuf Acar was in charge of hiring consultants to the security division. He was also in charge of buying software licences. In addition, he was able to monitor emails by others. Acar had thus ample organizational opportunities to commit white-collar crime in convenient ways.

As of March 15, OCTO had 231 full-time employees and employed 267 contractors, most of whom were full-time. OCTO had a longstanding contractor culture, with contractors drawing a salary from a third-party vendor that contracted with the district government. Numerous, simultaneous, one-time modernization projects were managed by contractors.

Some quotes from the internal investigation report by Sidley (2010) illustrate convenience in the organizational dimension:

- "Acar told us that the genesis of the first kickback was a 2005 contract for forensics engineers in the security division. Acar was going to supervise these engineers, and he was among the OCTO employees with input on the hiring decisions" (page 22).
- "Acar would manipulate the requirements listed in the procurement requests to direct hiring decisions towards Bansal's candidates" (page 23).
- "Acar and Bansal concocted a plan whereby bills for individuals who had finished their work at OCTO without exhausting all the allotted hours in the purchase order would continue to be issued for the remaining time in the contract by using fraudulent timesheets" (page 24).
- "This overbilling scheme evolved into a plan in which Acar and Bansal would bill the remaining time in the name of individuals who had never even worked at OCTO" (page 24).
- "Acar and Bansal also collaborated to get the agency to overpay for software purchased by the security division" (page 25).
- "In 2009, Acar began monitoring incoming District emails to OCTO employees to detect any communications from the Office of the Inspector General" (page 26).

- "OCTO's internal controls failed to detect or prevent Acar's various fraudulent activities" (page 27).
- "Many OCTO employees attribute Acar's prolonged success to what they describe as the isolation of the Security Division. Because the Security Division has access to all District email and telecommunication messages, OCTO treated the Division differently from its other programs" (page 30).
- "For several years before discovery of the fraud, Acar was a key decision maker in the hiring of contractors for the security division, which facilitated his kickback scheme. Moreover, on several occasions he served as acting program manager of the department, at which time he was able to make procurement decisions without any careful, third-party scrutiny. Further, as the acting leader of the group, Acar was able to expand the fraud by exercising substantial control over the division's annual budget request. The lack of external scrutiny prevented these decisions from receiving the sort of oversight that might have prevented the fraud" (page 31).

According to the investigation report by Sidley (2010), the internal controls at OCTO played no role in detecting Acar. Some OCTO employees claimed that reforms initiated by CTO Kundra adequately addressed the Acar fraud, and several expressed the belief that these changes actually led to the detection of the fraudulent schemes. The fraud examiners' review contradicts those assessments. Many of the fraudulent transactions took place during and after reforms, and Acar himself said to investigators that the reforms did not meaningfully impede his ability to conduct his criminal activities.

Sidley's (2010) investigation focused on identifying the organizational and institutional vulnerabilities both inside and outside of OCTO that allowed Acar's fraudulent activities to escape detection over a prolonged period of time. The identified vulnerabilities fall into two general categories. First, Acar exploited several OCTO-specific deficiencies. Second, at least two broader issues involving procurements throughout the district government allowed Acar and his co-conspirators to engage in these schemes. Although OCTO responded to several of these vulnerabilities after the Acar scandal became public, investigators argued that there were remaining institutional vulnerabilities to be addressed.

## Tax and Revenue Office

Harriette Walters worked in the tax and revenue office in Washington DC She embezzled substantial amounts of money for many years. The case of Harriette Walters is one of economic convenience in that it involved helping friends, family and herself financially. She let friends participate in her fraudulent schemes. For example, Walters relied on a long-time relationship with a local bank teller named Walter Jones. Walters also involved three family members in the scheme. All three – her brother, nephew and niece – used different companies that did not own property in the District of Columbia.

Some quotes from the internal investigation report by WilmerHale and PwC (2008) illustrate convenience in the economic dimension:

- "Jones deposited the fraudulent payments into accounts controlled by Walters, her family, or her friends" (page 40).
- "In early March 2007, Walters created an $85,000 credit on a property associated with Samuel Earl Pope, Walters' friend" (page 47).
- "Walters apparently provided cover stories to explain her generosity. According to one rumor, she was from a wealthy family and had inherited large sums of money. According to another rumor, she had a wealthy boyfriend or a second job and was good at 'budgeting' her money" (page 60).

Walters' motive was private spending money for herself, her friends and her family. Unfortunately, the investigation by WilmerHale and PwC (2008: 8) "did not attempt to trace the stolen money or to determine how the money was distributed or spent".

WilmerHale and PwC (2008: 2) describe Walters' scheme, which illustrates the organizational dimension of convenience theory for white-collar crime:

> Harriette Walters was a long-time employee and starting in 2001, a low-level manager in RPTA. As Walters explained to us, she first became involved in a fraudulent tax refund scheme in the mid-1980s when she learned from a co-worker how to process fake refunds, how to waive penalty and interest charges in exchange for gifts and cash, and how to cash refund checks that were returned to RPTA when the taxpayer recipient had died. According to Walters, she eventually concluded that her co-worker, whom she described as a substance abuser, was unreliable as a partner in these activities. Walters then embarked on her own embezzlement scheme in the late 1980s, which focused on the issuance of fraudulent real property tax refund checks. From the late 1980s through late 2007, Walters stole more than $48 million from the District, which, according to the *Washington Post*, is the largest known government-related embezzlement scandal in the District's history. Despite the long duration and scope of Walters' scheme, it was accomplished in a relatively simple and mundane fashion. Walters started small. Her first two fraudulent refunds in the late 1980s were for less than $5,000 each and were issued payable to a friend who agreed to participate in the scheme. Soon, however, Walters discovered she could issue significantly larger refunds without incurring any additional risk of detection. In the early 1990s, Walters began processing fraudulent refunds to her friends and to her friends' companies for more than $10,000 per transaction. By the late 1990s, Walters was issuing fraudulent refunds in excess of $100,000 each. After becoming a manager of her unit, she increased the amount of the fraudulent refunds further still. By 2004, she was processing fake refunds for $350,000 or more. During the course of her scheme, Walters processed two fraudulent refunds

in excess of $500,000 – one for $543,423.50 in July 1997 and another for $541,000.74 in May 2007. These fraudulent refund requests appeared on the surface to be legitimate. The requisite vouchers attached what seemed, at first glance, to be valid supporting documentation containing property descriptions and proof of tax payments. But the documentation often did not relate to the properties or property owners identified for the refund. Instead, the supporting materials were frequently copied from legitimate tax refunds for unrelated properties or were simply fabricated. Many of the refunds were issued directly to entities that did not own property in the district. The names of these entities were sometimes slight variations on legitimate businesses operating in the district. On at least one occasion, it appears that Walters simply strung together letters to create a nonsensical payee name. In still other instances, Walters processed fraudulent refunds in the names of legitimate property owners, but directed that payments be made "care of" companies that did not own or bear any relationship to the referenced property. Walters also processed refunds in care of, or to the attention of, prominent real estate attorneys. (We saw no indication whatsoever that these attorneys were involved in, or aware of, the scheme.) In all of these cases, Walters arranged for the refund checks to be delivered to her rather than mailed to the recipients. She then passed the checks to other participants in the scheme for deposit into bank accounts that they controlled, in later years with the help of a corrupt bank employee. To put the scale of Walters' scheme in perspective, the average value of legitimate real property tax refunds in the District from October 1998 through January 2008 was about $7,300. By contrast, the average fraudulent refund processed by Walters during that time frame was over $275,000. Between October 1998 and January 2008, 21% of real property tax refunds between $100,001 and $200,000 were fraudulent, 45% of real property tax refunds between $200,001 and $300,000 were fraudulent, and 68% of real property tax refunds between $300,001 and $400,000 were fraudulent. Most significantly, 81% of real property tax refunds between $400,001 and $500,000 were fraudulent. Between 2005 and 2007, Walters' fraudulent refunds accounted for nearly 35% of all real property tax refund dollars. Although some of Walters' subordinates helped prepare vouchers for the fraudulent refund requests and received gifts and/or substantial payments from her, we could not establish that any of them actually knew the refunds were in fact fraudulent. The subordinates we interviewed denied knowing about Walters' scheme, although one key witness who initially faced criminal charges that were later dropped refused through her attorney to talk to us. We also could not establish that more senior managers or other employees of the District were aware of Walters' scheme.

While the economic convenience for Walters was consumption, by having spending money far in excess of personal income for herself, friends and family, and the organizational convenience was tax returns and other special transactions she was able to manipulate, the behavioral dimension is difficult to understand from the investigation report by WilmerHale and PwC (2008). She pleaded guilty to federal charges related to theft of over $48 million of District of Columbia funds.

## WorldCom Corporation

Ebbers at WorldCom was investigated by Wilmer and PwC (2003). Ebbers directed significant energy at building and protecting his own personal financial empire, with little attention to the risks these distractions and financial obligations placed on the company that was making him one of most highly paid executives in the country. It was when his personal financial empire was under the greatest pressure – when he had the greatest need to keep WorldCom's stock price up in order to avoid margin calls that he could not meet – that the largest part of the fraud occurred. And it was shortly after he left that it was discovered and disclosed.

The fraudulent corporate culture began at the top. Ebbers created the pressure that led to the fraud. He demanded the results he had promised, and he appeared to scorn the procedures (and people) that should have been a check on misreporting. When efforts were made to establish a corporate code of conduct, Ebbers reportedly described it as a "colossal waste of time". He showed little respect for the role lawyers played in corporate governance matters within the company. While we have heard numerous accounts of Ebbers' demand for results – sometimes emotional, sometimes insulting, with express reference to the personal financial harm he faced if the stock price declined – we have heard none where he demanded or rewarded ethical business practices.

Ebbers was autocratic in his dealings with the board, and the board permitted it. With few exceptions, the members of the board were reluctant to challenge Ebbers even when they disagreed with him. Like most observers they were impressed by the company's growth and Ebbers' reputation, even if they were sometimes perplexed by his style. This was Ebbers' company. Several members of the board were experienced and knowledgeable, yet the board were deferential to Ebbers and passive in its oversight until April 2002.

An example of this was the board's failure to challenge Ebbers on the extent of his substantial outside business interests (and the consequent claim on his time and energies). Those interests included a Louisiana rice farm, a luxury yacht-building company, a lumber mill, a country club, a trucking company, a minor league hockey team, an operating marina and a building in downtown Chicago. Most properly run boards of directors would probably not permit a chief executive officer to pursue an array of interests such as these, certainly not without careful examination of the time and energy commitments they would require. Yet there seems to be no evidence of any such challenge.

Ebbers dominated the board meetings, which followed a consistent format. Each meeting opened with a prayer. A series of presentations – generally done fairly quickly – followed. Typically, the chairmen of the audit committee and the compensation and stock option committee, Max Bobbitt and Stiles Kellett, respectively, both reported to the board. Michael Salsbury, general counsel, reported on legal and regulatory issues.

The fragmentation of the legal department was Ebbers' choice. None of the company's senior lawyers was located in Jackson. He did not include the company's lawyers in his inner circle and appears to have dealt with them only when he felt it necessary. He let them know his displeasure with them personally when they gave advice – however justified – that he did not like. In sum, Ebbers created a culture in which the legal function was less influential and less welcome than in a healthy corporate environment.

WorldCom marketed itself as a high-growth company, and revenue growth was clearly a critical component of WorldCom's early success. In the 1990s, WorldCom was often cited as a top "growth stock". Analysts marveled at the company's ability to "outgrow an industry that was outgrowing the overall economy" (Wilmer and PwC, 2003: 137), and Ebbers repeatedly trumpeted the company's impressive record on revenue growth during his quarterly conference calls with analysts. As Ebbers stated in 1998, "[WorldCom's] industry leading and accelerating revenue growth, combined with a demonstrated track record of margin expansion, are cause for optimism as we continue our relentless pursuit of increasing shareholder value" (Wilmer and PwC, 2003: 137). This growth was critical to both WorldCom's stock market valuation and its ability to use its stock as currency for compensation and expansion.

Beginning in September 2000, the compensation committee extended to Ebbers a series of loans and guarantees which, by April 29, 2002, reached approximately $408 million (including interest). These loans and guarantees enabled Ebbers to avoid selling most of his WorldCom stock in order to meet the demands of banks from which he had borrowed substantial sums of money. The loans from WorldCom provided Ebbers with funds with which to conduct his personal business affairs at advantageous interest rates. In making these loans and guarantees, WorldCom assumed risks that no financial institution was willing to assume. The company did not have a perfected security interest in any collateral for the loans for most of the time period during which they were outstanding.

The price of WorldCom stock continued to decline during 2000, and Ebbers continued to face margin calls from his lenders. By September 6, 2000, the day of a scheduled meeting of the compensation committee, the stock price was down to $30.27 a share. Shortly before the meeting, Ebbers told Stiles Kellett, the committee's chairman, about the margin calls he was facing and they discussed the possibility that the company would give him a loan. There is conflicting evidence regarding who first suggested the loan. Kellett agreed to take the matter to the committee. At the meeting that followed, the committee directed the company to give Ebbers a $50 million loan and – as part of the retention bonus program then being applied to many WorldCom employees – pay him a $10 million bonus.

At some point, in-house counsel to the compensation committee discovered that Ebbers was withdrawing money from the direct loans for use in connection with his other companies' operating expenses. When confronted with this fact,

Ebbers justified the use of the money for these other businesses as necessary in order to avoid impairing the value of these assets. Instead of objecting and demanding that Ebbers use the loans only for their intended purpose, the committee accepted this rationale, concluding that it was in the company's interest that these assets remained unimpaired so that Ebbers could sell them, if necessary, and repay WorldCom.

After discovering Ebbers' other uses of the loan proceeds, the company characterized the purpose of the loans more neutrally in its filings with the SEC:

> We have been advised that Mr. Ebbers has used, or plans to use, the proceeds of the loans from WorldCom principally to repay certain indebtedness under loans secured by shares of our stock owned by him and that the proceeds of such secured loans were used for private business purposes.

In the economic dimension of convenience theory, Ebbers was a greedy person who enjoyed exposure of wealth and consumption. In the organizational dimension of convenience theory, Ebbers had control over board and management and could do what he liked. In the behavioral dimension of convenience theory, he felt entitled since he claimed to have created the corporate business success of WorldCom.

# 9
# MISCONDUCT INVESTIGATIONS IN THE UNITED STATES

While all suspects in the previous chapter were given prison sentences, none of the suspects in this chapter were even prosecuted.

## Lehman Brothers

In their classic article on the absence of prosecutions after the 2008 financial meltdown, Pontell et al. (2014: 1) suggested that some companies were too big to fail and too powerful to jail:

> These companies had balance sheets that were saturated with securities containing toxic subprime mortgages. They collapsed, were bought by competitors, or were bailed out by the federal government with huge infusions of taxpayer money. For most onlookers, including criminologists and the public in general, the corporate actions represented intricate and arcane business practices that were difficult to understand fully and to portray as sound bytes [sic] – and therefore tended to become trivialized in regard to their failure components.

One of the companies mentioned in their article is Lehman Brothers, which went bankrupt. A private internal report of 2,208 pages written by fraud examiner Valukas (2010: 16) concluded: "The business decisions that brought Lehman to its crisis of confidence may have been in error but were largely within the business judgment rule".

In this section we study the issue of too big to fail and too powerful to jail (Pontell et al., 2014) in the context of convenience theory (Gottschalk, 2017), based on the private internal investigation report of Lehman Brothers by Valukas (2010). Convenience theory was introduced to integrate a number of theoretical approaches to explaining and understanding white-collar misconduct, which was first defined by Sutherland (1939).

Pontell et al. (2014: 10) argue that the financial meltdown shows the need to unpack the concept of status when examining white-collar and corporate offenses:

> The high standing of those involved in the current scandal has acted as a significant shield to accusations of criminal wrongdoing in at least three ways. First, the legal resources that offenders can bring to bear on any case made against them are significant. This would give pause to any prosecutor, regardless of the evidence that exists. Second, their place in the organizations assures that the many below them will be held more directly responsible for the more readily detected offenses. The downward focus on white-collar and corporate crimes is partly a function of the visibility of the offense and the ease with which it can be officially pursued. Third, the political power of large financial institutions allow for effective lobbying that both distances them from the criminal law and prevents the government from restricting them from receiving taxpayer money when they get into trouble.

These status elements are at the core of convenience theory. The legal resources that offenders can bring to bear make it less likely that law enforcement will prosecute them. It is often in the organizational context that such resources are available to suspects, or suspects have already accumulated sufficient wealth to pay top attorneys. Convenience emerges here as reduced future costs of misconduct because of unlikely prosecution.

The second status element suggests that the elite can blame others below them in the organization. The blame game is all about attributing negative events to others (Lee and Robinson, 2000). One way of allocating the cause of a negative event to someone else is to hire a private investigator and define the investigation mandate accordingly (Gottschalk, 2016b). Convenience emerges here in the organizational context where a white-collar offender may exploit their elite position for downward focus on misconduct and crime.

The third status element is at not the individual but rather the organizational level. The political power of large financial institutions makes them and their executives untouchable. Knowing this, executives find it convenient to commit financial crime if considered necessary to avoid threats and pain or to gain desired benefits that seem otherwise unattainable.

In January 2008, Lehman Brothers Holding Inc. reported record revenues and Lehman stock traded at US$65 per share. Eight months later, in September 2008, Lehman sought protection in the largest bankruptcy proceeding ever filed. Bank executives must obviously have manipulated accounting and committed other kinds of white-collar misconduct. Why were they were never prosecuted? One answer might be in the conclusions to the Valukas (2010) investigation report of 2,208 pages.

Valukas (2010: 2) starts out immediately distributing responsibility and presenting excuses for the collapse:

> There are many reasons Lehman failed, and the responsibility is shared. Lehman was more the consequence than the cause of a deteriorating economic climate. Lehman's financial plight, and the consequences to Lehman's creditors and shareholders, was exacerbated by Lehman executives, whose conduct ranged from serious but non-culpable errors of business judgment to actionable balance sheet manipulation; by the investment bank business model, which rewarded excessive risk taking and leverage; and by Government agencies, who by their own admission might better have anticipated or mitigated the outcome.

The above quote is an interesting case of the blame game, with even the government of the United States receiving blame for the collapse of a private bank. Blaming the business model moves responsibility from individuals to a model for which nobody is apparently responsible (Valukas, 2010: 3): "Lehman's business model was not unique; all of the major investment banks that existed at the time followed some variation of a high-risk, high-leverage model that required the confidence of counterparties to sustain". Valukas (2010: 16) repeats several times that executives were not to blame for the collapse, though they perhaps were for the cover-up:

> The business decisions that brought Lehman to its crisis of confidence may have been in error but were largely within the business judgment rule. But the decision not to disclose the effects of those judgments does give rise to colorable claims against the senior officers who oversaw and certified misleading financial statements – Lehman's CEO Richard S. Fuld, Jr., and its CFOs Christopher O'Meara, Erin M. Callan and Ian T. Lowitt.

It is interesting to note that one of the named persons, CFO Erin M. Callan, later wrote a book about her experience. She presents the following description of rivalry among executives a few months before the bank collapse (Montella, 2016: 175):

> In any event, I don't remember doing anything when I came into my office other than sitting at my desk, sipping some coffee, and waiting for the meeting. As it got closer to 7:30 a.m. my fellow executive committee members began to file past my office toward the conference room. It was next to my office so they could not avoid me. But, trust me, no one looked at me. They couldn't make eye contact. You'd think I'd be the one who couldn't look up from my desk, but it was the other way around. I was "dead man walking". No one wanted to go near me. I didn't want to go in there, though, until I thought everyone was seated. There was absolutely no way I was going to sit in there and make small talk until Dick showed up. When it seemed everyone was likely there, I walked in and took my regular seat by

the window in the middle of the table. In the middle of the action, as I always thought. The perfect spot to be engaged and relevant, or that was the idea.

Dick came in and sat down next to me. He started talking right away, announcing that Joe Gregory and I were resigning from our respective roles. And the scene blurs, like the fade-out in a movie. I know I started to cry. I wasn't outright bawling, just quiet tears down my face. I really did not want to cry. So stereotypical. I never cried about anything. But that was when it hit me. I was no longer the chief financial officer at Lehman Brothers.

Returning to the report of investigation, Valukas (2010: 47) concludes that Lehman executives cannot be jailed:

> Delaware law, which governs a Delaware corporation such as Lehman, sets a high bar for establishing a breach of the fiduciary duty of care. Officers' and directors' business decisions are generally protected from personal liability by the business judgment rule, and even if the business judgment rule does not apply, there is no liability unless the officer or director was grossly negligent. "In the duty of care context gross negligence has been defined as 'reckless indifference to or a deliberate disregard of the whole body of stockholders or actions which are without the bounds of reason'".

The remains of Lehman were taken over by others, so the bank was too big to fail completely. Maybe executives were too powerful to jail. Their behavior can be explained by convenience theory. In the case of Lehman, convenience theory suggests that the desire for success, the organizational opportunity to fool the market and the deviant behavior justified by neutralization caused executives to manipulate and conceal facts.

In the economic dimension of convenience theory, where we find the motive for misconduct, Lehman executives continued their "pursuit of this aggressive growth strategy" (page 44). It was "based on two important calculations by Lehman's management" (page 44). One of the calculations was that "Lehman had the opportunity to pick up ground and improve its competitive position" (page 45).

In the organizational dimension of convenience theory, nobody can stop executives from misconduct (Valukas, 2010: 46):

> Lehman senior management disregarded its risk managers, its risk policies, and its risk limits. Press reports prior to Lehman's bankruptcy stated that in 2007 Lehman had removed Madelyn Antoncic, Lehman's Chief Risk Officer ("CRO"), and Michael Gelband, head of its Fixed Income Division ("FID"), because of their opposition to management's growing accumulation of risky and illiquid investments.

In the behavioral dimension of convenience theory, where we find willingness for deviant behavior, Valukas (2010: 52) suggests that executives at Lehman did not notice that they were on a slippery slope: "Lehman's senior managers were confident making business judgments based on their understanding of markets, and did not feel constrained by the quantitative metrics generated by Lehman's risk management".

Executives probably suffered from differential association, where learning occurs in association with those who find their behavior and thinking favorable and in isolation from those who find it unfavorable. Differential association is the process whereby one is exposed to normative definitions favorable or unfavorable to illegal or law-abiding behavior (Sutherland, 1949).

Pontell et al. (2014: 11) argue that the "reason for lack of prosecution of senior, high-level executives in the current scandal illustrate the dynamics of keeping white-collar crime a non-issue, trivializing it more generally, and focusing enforcement efforts downward to lesser offending". Empirical evidence of this claim can be found in another internal investigation by Valukas (2014), where many below top executives were blamed for the ignition switch failure at General Motors.

In this section, we add another reason for lack of prosecution of executives in the elite group. The reason is private internal investigations. Law enforcement agencies are often happy when an internal investigation is initiated because it means they can avoid spending police detective resources on the case. When an internal investigation concludes that there has been misconduct but no crime, public prosecutors tend to be happy because they do not have to spend resources on the case in court.

In our convenience perspective, misconduct and crime by executives and other white-collar offenders remains a convenient course in situations characterized by threats. Lehman executives found it convenient to certify misleading financial statements. They considered the alternative much worse.

This section has discussed a reason for the lack of prosecution of senior executives. Powerful executives avoided police investigation, public prosecution and potential jail sentences because they were subject to private internal investigations. As long as internal investigators conclude there was misconduct but no crime, public prosecutors may prefer to stay away from the case.

## University of Texas

The internal investigation of Kern Wildenthal by Breen and Guberman (2012) documents misconduct motivated by convenience. Wildenthal had successfully created a medical center (known as UTSW) at the University of Texas, and he felt entitled to benefit from the success in the behavioral dimension of convenience theory.

Dr. Wildenthal had a broad mandate to spend the UTSW funds for fundraising, advancement of reputation and recruiting, which meant he could largely use his own discretion regarding his travel and entertainment expenses. Wildenthal's spending was generally consistent with a well-considered and successful fundraising strategy, which focused on a small number of individuals with the financial capacity to make large donations. However, he exercised questionable judgment in mingling his business and personal travel and entertainment expenses.

Breen and Guberman (2012) argue that as a leader of and key official at a public institution, Wildenthal's conduct was subject to public scrutiny and inevitably viewed by others at UTSW as an example of how to act. Nevertheless, at times his spending tested the boundaries of permissible travel and entertainment expenses under the UT System and UTSW rules.

UT System and UTSW had adequate policies, procedures and internal controls in place that provided a mechanism for approval, documentation, reporting and auditing of Wildenthal's spending, but they were not enforced at UTSW. His spending was not always sufficiently documented to show the main business purpose and benefit to UTSW, and as a result, it was not subjected to meaningful review. The information in Wildenthal's travel and entertainment expense reports was frequently inadequate and sometimes did not even include his signed acknowledgment. Such expenses were routinely approved by UTSW's chief business officer without any inquiry. The practices at UTSW disregarded UT System policies in place because Wildenthal was never questioned about the adequacy of the listed business purpose for his travel or benefit to UTSW.

The investigation by Breen and Guberman (2012) revealed that personnel at UTSW depended too much on the audit process. Individuals responsible for approving presidential expenses admitted to relying on the audit process, rather than themselves asking about questionable expenses or inadequate business purposes for expenses.

Dr. Wildenthal's mingling of business and personal affairs meant that he frequently had to decide which expenses were for business and which were personal. He was a busy man, and it was not always clear what could count as a business expense and what was properly a personal expense. For example, he traveled to New Zealand for more than two weeks in January 2010. The business purpose for this trip, as listed on Dr. Wildenthal's travel voucher form, was to "Visit the Medical School at the University of Otago". On the face of it, this might qualify as a legitimate business purpose, but the primary purpose of the trip does not necessarily appear to have been business. More days on the trip were designated as vacation days rather than work days, and he traveled with his family throughout New Zealand. UTSW reimbursed him for US$7,646.60, the cost of his airfare and six nights at a hotel. While Dr. Wildenthal later made a donation to UTSW for this exact amount, the fact remains that perhaps he should never have submitted these travel expenses and perhaps UTSW should not have paid for them.

In another instance, he traveled to France and Spain with his wife in September 2005. As part of the business purpose for this trip, he explained that he toured the Barcelona Opera House to view its construction because UTSW was carrying out its own construction projects at the time. This is not necessarily a legitimate business purpose. He split his time on this trip almost equally between work days and vacation days. He was reimbursed by UTSW for both his and his wife's travel expenses. While he made a donation to UTSW for some of his and his wife's travel expenses, the fact remains that at least some of these expenses should perhaps never have been submitted to or paid for by UTSW.

Investigators Breen and Guberman (2012) interviewed Wildenthal. He articulated business purposes for his trips that were within his broad spending mandate. He described the purpose of some of his trips as "borderline" between business and personal. He explained that the opportunity to introduce donors to opera singers backstage or at dinners was invaluable because it was an experience that he could provide, but which could not be purchased.

From a theoretical perspective, neutralization techniques applied by Wildenthal seem to include a sense of entitlement and an absence of injury or victim (Sykes and Matza, 1957). At the same time, reduced or limited self-control seems to have been present when making business travel decisions (Gottfredson and Hirschi, 1990).

## General Motors

Anton R. Valukas investigated General Motors (GM) in 2014. He inquired into and submitted a report to the board of directors of General Motors Company regarding ignition switch recalls. His internal report details GM ignition cover-up (Valukas, 2014). According to Jones (2014), the internal report commissioned by General Motors into the recall of vehicles with a potentially lethal ignition defect presents a devastating picture of corporate indifference to public health and safety for financial gain.

Anton R. Valukas was the United States attorney for the Northern District of Illinois from 1985 to 1989. The most notable event of Valukas' four-year term was Operation Greylord, which was an investigation into judicial corruption in Cook County in Illinois that ultimately resulted in the indictment of 92 people, including 17 judges. Valukas returned to Chicago law firm Jenner & Block, where his practice focused on white-collar criminal defense. He became the chairman of Jenner & Block in 2007, in which capacity he gained notoriety in 2009, when he was appointed bankruptcy examiner in the bankruptcy of Lehman Brothers.

Jenner & Block is a U.S. law firm of approximately 450 attorneys with offices in Chicago, New York, Los Angeles, and Washington, DC. The firm works on litigation cases involving anti-trust and competition law, bankruptcy, copyright, intellectual property, media and first amendment, privacy and information governance, real estate and construction, and white-collar defense and investigations. The firm also does work in transactional areas such as corporate finance, employee benefits, mergers and acquisitions, real estate, and tax practices (www.jenner.com).

General Motors hired Valukas to help lead an internal probe of an ignition switch failure tied at that point to at least 13 deaths (by December 2014 this number had risen to 42 death claims). "He sounds like a good choice because he has prosecutorial experience and has done other outside controversial investigations," said Joan Claybrook, a former administrator of the National Highway Traffic Safety

Administration and long-time consumer advocate who has been critical of GM's response (Green and Plungis, 2014).

On February 7, 2014, General Motors recalled 800,000 of its small cars due to faulty ignition switches, which could shut off the engine during driving and thereby prevent the airbags from inflating. The fault had been known to GM for at least a decade prior to the recall being declared. The company was facing multiple lawsuits because they did not attempt to fix these faulty ignitions sooner.

Most private investigations by financial crime specialists start with the mandate. A mandate is an authorization to investigate a specific issue by reconstructing the past. This was also the case in the GM investigation. GM's CEO, Mary Barra, and its board directed the examiners to investigate the circumstances that led to the recall of the Cobalt and other cars due to the flawed ignition switch. Examiners were to investigate what happened, why it happened and what GM should do to ensure that it never happened again. Investigators were also asked to focus on the knowledge of specific senior executives, as well as GM's board (Valukas, 2014: 12).

## *Internal investigation*

Valukas and his team identified 300 document custodians for collection. Many of those custodians were identified early on in the investigative process, and additional custodians were added as new information and investigative leads were obtained. Multiple sources of custodial and non-custodial data were collected and reviewed, including: (1) forensically imaged hard drives, (2) server-based emails and electronic share drives, (3) legacy electronic data collections, (4) hard copy documents, and (5) database collections from various GM electronic databases, such as Global Document Management system and Problem Resolution and Tracking system. Search terms were designed to identify the most relevant subset of information (Valukas, 2014: 13).

Valukas and his team identified a number of people to be interviewed. Every request for an interview of a GM employee was granted. A number of former GM employees and third parties were also interviewed as part of the investigation. In all, over 230 witnesses were interviewed over a period of approximately 70 days. Because certain witnesses were interviewed more than once, the total number of interviews conducted was over 350. All interviews were conducted by at least two investigators (Valukas, 2014: 14).

Law firm Jenner & Block started its investigation of General Motor on March 10 and completed it on May 29, in less than two months, producing a report of 325 pages (Valukas, 2014). Valukas and his team were to determine how and why it took so long for GM to recall the Cobalt. The investigators were given free access to witnesses and documents and asked for an objective account.

Valukas' (2014) report documents that there were multiple, interrelated factors that led to GM's decade-long failure to recognize the safety defects in the Cobalt and initiate a recall. The lessons learned from these factors are summarized in terms of recommendations for the future, which at the same time indicate where it went wrong:

A. *Organizational structure* is the result of organizational choices related to job specialization, behavioral formalization, design of positions, unit grouping and unit size. Furthermore, organizational structure is concerned with the design of decision-making systems in terms of power to make decisions down the chain of authority. Formal power is transformed into informal power – for example, control over knowledge resources and information gathering and advice (Donk and Molloy, 2008).

The organizational structure at GM did not work. Responsibilities were not adequately and appropriately defined. Sufficient resources for executives to properly address safety and compliance issues were not ensured. Departments, divisions and groups did not have responsibilities spelt out concerning the identification, investigation or remediation of safety issues. They had no reporting line leading up to higher management. There was no coordination with legal staff. Several units had independent and parallel responsibilities for identifying and resolving a safety defect.

Safety executives did not have direct access to the CEO or the board in crisis situations. The responsibilities of safety executives were not appropriately defined. There was no clear owner when areas of overlap emerged.

B. *Organizational culture* is a set of shared norms, values and perceptions, which develop when the members of an organization interact with each other and the surroundings. It is holistic, historically determined, socially constructed and difficult to change (Hofstede et al., 1990). Organizational culture might determine how the organization thinks, feels and acts. It represents basic assumptions made up of beliefs, values, ethical and moral codes, and ideologies that have become so ingrained that they have dropped out of consciousness. These assumptions are unquestioned perceptions of truth, reality, ways of thinking, and feeling that develop through repeated success in solving problems over extended periods of time. Important basic assumptions are passed on to new members, often unconsciously. Organizational culture represents an imperfectly shared system of interrelated understandings shaped by its members' history and expectations. It defines the "should" and "oughts" of organizational life (Veiga et al., 2000).

No regular communication with employees about safety took place at GM. There was no awareness of safety issues. Employees were not encouraged to raise any concerns they had about safety or compliance. There was a culture of fear of retaliation when employees reported concerns regarding actual or potential safety-related defects or potential non-compliance with federal standards. There was no communication to suppliers about the importance of safety and GM's potential expectation that suppliers should promptly and accurately identify any potential safety issues. Suppliers were not encouraged to speak up for safety. Employees were reluctant to classify issues as safety issues or potential safety issues. Words and phrases about safety issues that might be deemed too sensitive or inflammatory were avoided. No communication to employees on safety policy issues came from the top of the organization. Employees were afraid of escalating unresolved safety issues because of possible consequences for themselves. Top management was absent in safety issues, making employees believe that they were irrelevant and not "smart" to pursue. In every corporate culture, the tone from the top signals what is important and what is not. Signals from the top at GM were not about safety issues. Personnel dealing with quality issues were not considered key people in the company. People who were tracking and reporting safety concerns were not popular in the organizational culture.

C. *Individual accountability* refers to situations in which someone is required or expected to justify actions or decisions. Accountability has been called the "mother of caution". Accountability means that mechanisms are in place to determine who might have taken responsible actions and who is responsible. Systems and institutions in which it is impossible to find out who took what action are inherently incapable of ethical analysis or ethical action. If top management refers to itself as a team, personal accountability might be diminished. Professionals such as safety experts should be held accountable to their own professional group. Accountability is the acknowledgment and assumption of responsibility for actions, products, decisions and policies, including the administration, governance and implementation within the scope of the role or employment position. Accountability encompasses the obligation to report, explain and be answerable for consequences (UNODC, 2006).

No employees or executives at GM felt responsible for raising safety issues, and no employees felt responsible for addressing safety issues once they were identified. Executives did not take steps to ensure that employees were aware of their safety-related responsibilities or that individuals are accountable for addressing the safety issues they have a responsibility for. Owners of safety and compliance issues could not be identified at GM. Therefore, accountability could not be addressed. Internal roles did not define the responsibilities and accountability of those involved in processes related to the evaluation and resolution of safety issues, including responsibilities around feeding items into the relevant work process. The roles of committees were not clarified. There was no person on each committee designated as a safety liaison, with responsibility for elevating safety issues. Appropriate identification, elevation and resolution of safety and compliance issues was not included as a factor in employee performance evaluations. Employees were not required to certify that they had reported any safety issues they were aware of or to identify, as part of that certification, any safety issues they were aware had not been resolved.

D. *Communications between and within groups* is the purposeful activity of exchanging information and meaning across space and time using various technical or natural means. Distinctions can be made between the communication of data, information, knowledge and wisdom. In business, the level of knowledge communication is the most important, where knowledge is defined as information combined with interpretation, reflection and context. Knowledge integration processes involve social interaction among individuals using internal communication channels for knowledge transfer and knowledge development to arrive at a common perspective for problem solving. Where organizational units hold specialized knowledge, inter-unit linkages are the primary means of transferring that knowledge. Such knowledge transfer permits knowledge reuse, and the recombination of existing knowledge is an important antecedent of uncertainty resolution in organizational service innovation (Mitchell, 2006).

Breakdowns in communication between and within groups were a critical part of the failures at GM described in the report by Valukas (2014). Inadequate communication was found at all levels and in all aspects of safety issues. Regular written and oral updates by legal staff for relevant engineering groups on alleged or potential defects were not provided. Coordination between groups was never formalized, and there was no coordination between different engineering teams with accountability for safety and compliance issues. There was no cross-functional committee to track and review potential safety issues and set action items. Due to this lack of coordination, there was only random communication of warranty claims and other safety issues. There was no assessment of the adequacy of mechanisms for ensuring coordination between groups handling different subsystems of the same vehicle regarding safety-related information and items that might affect safety performance. For example, nobody ensured that those working on the ignition switch understood how it interacted with airbag deployment.

E. *Communication with national regulator* is the purposeful activity of exchanging information and meaning externally with competent people having the power to enforce guidelines. It is argued that an effective communication effort in general on the part of a corporation can improve corporate social responsibility (Walker, 2010). An advantage of informing the regulator is that information is passed on and stored in a government agency that cannot be manipulated by the CEO or any other company representative (Williams, 2008).

GM did not consider the regulator as an ally in the effort to ensure that the company's vehicles were as safe as they could be. Interactions with the regulator were not consistent with that type of relationship. A consent order requires the company to have monthly and quarterly meetings with the regulator and be prepared to address various issues at those meetings. As part of this effort, GM did not ensure that both the quality and the frequency of communications were sufficient to keep the regulator fully informed of safety-related issues. There was no individual at GM responsible for this communication. Management at GM paid no attention to communication with the regulator. There was no timely notification to the regulator of safety-related defects. There was no evaluation of reporting requirements.

F. *Role of lawyers.* Lawyers are defined as knowledge workers who are competent in general legal principles and procedures and in the substantive and procedural aspects of the law. They are supposed to have the ability to analyze and provide solutions to legal problems. Lawyers are professionals who have gained knowledge through formal education (explicit) and learning on the job (implicit). A lawyer is a knowledge worker specializing in the development and application of legal knowledge to solve client problems. Lawyers represent their clients in legal matters by presenting evidence and legal arguments as well as providing counsel to clients concerning their legal rights and obligations.

The legal staff at GM did not play a critical or unique role in assisting with the identification, analysis and resolution of safety issues that had given rise to customer claims. There were no regular discussions between product litigation attorneys and practice area managers regarding whether trends could be observed or potential safety issues in lawsuits or not-in-suit matters were recognized. Nobody within the legal staff was designated to provide regular reports on safety-related issues identified in matters handled by legal staff. There were no regular meetings between safety groups and legal staff. The safety organization had no regular arena where they could present significant or unresolved safety issues to legal staff. Engineers responsible for different specialties such as power steering had no regular arena for discussing observed trends and potential safety issues in their specialty field. The claim administrator was not involved. When safety issues were identified, it was not ensured that the global process leader for litigation was informed. It was not ensured that at the onset of litigation the legal staff would generate a list of all recalls, product investigations and issues for the subject vehicle make and model. This information was thus not provided to outside counsel at the onset of litigation. Early technical assessments did not reflect considerations of whether there were relevant recalls, product investigations or issues in the process that could affect the integrity of the make and model involved. There was no process instituted to elevate unresolved technical issues expeditiously. Legal staff did not provide specific guidance concerning the types of issue that could become relevant in terms of safety problems and unresolved safety challenges. In-house counsel was not aware of the expectation that they should respond appropriately if they became aware of any threatened, ongoing or past violation of a federal, state or local law or regulation, a breach of fiduciary duty, or violation of GM policy, including the expectation that if they raised such an issue and believed it has not been addressed properly, they would bring the situation to the attention of their supervisors, and if they believed their supervisors had not addressed it appropriately, to higher levels if necessary. There was no guidance provided for product liability attorneys on how to recognize and communicate safety issues to ensure that they were properly addressed notwithstanding ongoing litigation or claims activity, while fulfilling their obligations to defend the company in litigation and appropriately protect attorney–client privilege.

Valukas (2014) argues in the report that lawyers need to be winning with integrity. Integrity is defined as the quality of being honest and morally upright. Integrity issues imply misconduct (UNODC, 2006). Integrity implies that lawyers will take appropriate actions when any observed violation of law or GM policy occurs.

G. *Interactions with suppliers* is the next topic on Valukas' (2014) list of recommendations. The company's interactions with suppliers did not reflect the significance that supplier quality control has for vehicle safety.

H. *Data, storage, retrieval and analysis* is the next topic, where Valukas (2014) concludes that several of the problems discussed in his report could have been avoided or resolved much more quickly if the individuals involved had timely searched for or received accurate and complete data that in many cases was already in GM's possession. Computer systems were not up to date, and search functions were too complicated.

I. *Engineering processes and databases* did not have adequate arrangements in place for transparency, tracking and elevation of issues. The process for determining the correct severity classification was inadequate, as was review by supervisory personnel of initial severity determinations.

J. *Product investigation process* was not standardized. Collected and reviewed information did not give rise to product investigations.

K. *Recall decision-making process* was not in place. Too many steps were required before a final decision regarding whether to conduct a recall could be made.

L. *Policies and training* were missing. Personnel were not aware of what policies were relevant to help govern their decisions, and they did not sufficiently understand existing policy. Many employees received little or no training on policy and substantive issues relevant to their roles.

M. *Compliance, auditing and oversight* were missing. Nobody was asked to document any improvements in safety.

N. *Recordkeeping* was not adequate, which reduced the ability of product investigators and others with safety responsibilities to review past engineering and investigative measures that could impact on current investigations.

Valukas (2014) argued that these were the most important issues that had to be addressed by GM. He recommended that GM implement relevant measures and use the self-examination prompted by the ignition switch failures to learn how to handle consumer safety issues better in the future.

Based on these findings, it might be expected that top management were the first to be blamed and dismissed. But Valukas (2014) protects them by stating that they did not know about the problem and that they had sent out messages. He argues that CEO Mary Barra, Executive VP Mark Reuss and General Counsel Michael Millikin supposedly did not learn about the ignition switch's safety issues and the lengthy delay in addressing them until after a recall was decided on January 31, 2014.

As part of their involvement as investigators (Valukas, 2014: 227): "we were asked to prioritize our review of the involvement, if any, of these three current senior leaders in the events that led to the belated Ignition Switch recall. We conducted a thorough investigation that included ...". But investigators concluded that senior executives were not to blame. Similarly, Valukas (2014: 232) did not blame the board: "The Board's oversight of vehicle safety had multiple facets; no single committee of the Board was responsible for all vehicle safety-related issues".

## *Investigation result*

This acquittal of GM top executives by Valukas (2014) is interesting from a blame game perspective. Sonnier et al. (2015) argue that blame can be attributed to individuals who have personal control. Actors should have foreseen the harmful outcome. Attribution of blame implies that top executives should have foreseen the consequences of negligence. Top executives are to blame if it can be assumed that other actors would have behaved differently in the same situation. Thoughts about what could have been done differently to avoid the harmful event should have affected the investigator's assessment of blame. The investigation could have focused on what top executives might have done differently if they had kept themselves informed and acted accordingly. In this scenario, top executives would have foreseen negative events and tried to prevent consequences several years earlier.

On April 14, 2014, GM announced that two of its executives – Selim Bingol, senior vice president for global communications and public policy, and Melissa Howevell, senior vice president for global human resources – were leaving the company. GM did not say whether Bingol and Howell had resigned or were fired. Jones (2014) writes that, "After receiving the report, GM fired 15 low- and middle-level managers from its engineering and legal staff and disciplined five others. It now considers the matter closed and plans no further action".

Jones (2014) is critical to the investigation and consequences of the investigation:

> While the Valukas report outlines what can be best described as corporate criminality, it attributes GM's refusal to issue a recall to "errors" or "failure to connect the dots". This is an obvious whitewash. In reality the lives of scores if not hundreds of mostly young people were sacrificed on the altar of corporate profits.
>
> This is not just the product of the willful actions of executives, though GM officials should be held to criminal account. It above all expresses the incompatibility of the capitalist mode of production based on production for private profit with basic social needs. Corporations driven by the demands of Wall Street for ever-higher returns on investment are bound to ignore safety for the sake of cutting costs.

In September 2014 it was reported that the number of people who had died in connection with GM's failed ignition switch and were eligible for compensation had risen to 19. For example, Megan Phillips, 17, was behind the wheel of a 2005 Chevy Cobalt when the ignition switch led the car to lose power steering, power braking and the airbag's ability to deploy. Her friend Amy Rademaker, was in the front seat and died one week before her sixteenth birthday.

In the fall of 2014, federal prosecutors started to investigate GM's legal department for possible criminal liability in the way it handled the company's deadly ignition switch problem. The lawyers came under federal criminal investigation by the FBI for allegedly concealing ignition switch evidence. U.S. officials investigating the matter were seeking to determine whether lawyers working for GM, both internally and externally, concealed knowledge and evidence of the ignition switch defects. The police investigation was triggered by the internal Valukas (2014) report. GM had by then fired 15 employees, including several in its legal department. However, the head of GM's legal department, Michael Millikin, a 37-year veteran at the company, "has kept his position within the company, a circumstance that has drawn harsh disapproval and outrage from critics" (Niland, 2014).

Will GM be held criminally liable? Will executives at GM be prosecuted? Jones (2014) makes this case to a question of politics:

> The production of safe and reliable automobiles requires a high degree of conscious planning and foresight, including rigorous testing and public feedback. This requires the public ownership of auto manufacturing and other mass production industries under the democratic control of the working class.

## Coatesville Area School District

Auditing firm BDO was hired to investigate the Coatesville Area School District (CASD) in Pennsylvania. Pratt at BDO (2014a) wrote the report. In addition, investigative reports about the school district were written by Haverstick et al. (2014) at law firm Conrad O'Brien as well as by the Chester Grand Jury (2014), who investigated possible criminal charges. Issues included fiscal mismanagement, lack of accountability, abuse of power and the misappropriation, including theft, of school district funds.

For the initial report by Haverstick et al. (2014), investigators interviewed 93 current and former employees of the Coatesville Area School District, and the report makes a point of specifying that all of their interviews were completely voluntary. Investigators also interviewed individual vendors and contractors of CASD whose work crossed paths with the investigation. The Haverstick et al. (2014) report states that there were a number of individuals they wished to speak but who refused the request; they were blocked from speaking with one individual by the board of school directors. Particularly interesting is that in the supplemental report by Haverstick et al. (2014), investigators stated that they felt that the individual they were blocked from interviewing was important enough that they were willing to conduct the interview without charging CASD for their time.

The forensic audit was performed by BDO at the request of law firm Conrad O'Brien (Haverstick et al., 2014). The BDO investigator spoke with a number of district employees and made use of the school district's financial statements and accounting records. BDO (2014a: 8) described the scope of the report for CASD as follows:

> The scope of our report is specifically limited to the application of forensic accounting procedures and an analysis of the issues identified by CASD and its outside legal counsel. The issues identified include certain transactions involving former Superintendent Richard Como and former Athletic Director James Donato, specifically related to CASD Athletic Department revenue, Athletic Department expenses, and other particular issues. These other issues analyzed during our engagement include overall budgeting and financial reporting, purchasing, budget transfers, transfers between funds, bank account reconciliations, financial controls over Student Activities' Funds and the sale of delinquent tax liens.

The individuals that the reports primarily focus on are Richard Como, the superintendent of CASD; James Donato, the athletic director for CASD; and James Ellison, CASD solicitor. Other individuals that played a significant role in the events that triggered the investigation and the findings of the investigation included Abdallah Hawa, CASD director of technology, and Teresa Powell, CASD director of middle school education. Members of the board of school directors and others also played important roles.

The misconduct was initially detected based on a cell phone. In late spring or early summer of 2013, Donato requested a new cell phone from Hawa, the district director of technology. Hawa obtained the new cell phone and transferred Donato's information to the new device. Donato's old phone was put into storage to be reissued to another employee. On August 15, 2013, Hawa pulled out the phone with the intention of wiping it so that it could be reissued and discovered "numerous racist, sexist and bigoted messages", "primarily between Mr. Donato and Mr. Como" (Haverstick et al., 2014). Given the individuals that were involved, Hawa chose to go to Powell, specifically because he felt that she was not beholden to Como.

The major issue in the reports by Haverstick et al. (2014) is the financial irregularities associated with both Donato and Como. Irregularities were found in sales of football game tickets, as admission revenues had dropped sharply. The estimated total discrepancy in admission revenues during Donato's tenure was US$60,000.

The major issue in the report by BDO (2014a) was unusual and improper expenses totaling almost US$20,000. Some of this money was claimed to have been paid for fundraisers, but there were no corresponding deposits of money raised.

In total, Haverstick et al. (2014) and BDO (2014a) discovered a discrepancy of US$80,000. Both Como and Donato resigned from their posts, but they faced no criminal charges.

While the investigators identified several rotten apples in the form of the former superintendent, Richard Como, and former athletic director, James Donato, they also identified the factors that allowed the rot to become as extensive as it did in the district, which was poor management by the board of school directors. As superintendent, Como centralized hiring to the extent that he had almost complete control, allowing him to hire individuals with connections to either himself or the board of school directors. This could happen regardless of their qualifications, usually without the input and at times over the objections of the faculty and staff that were the supervisors of those Como hired. Como was able to keep faculty and staff in fear for their jobs if they objected, in part because the board of school directors failed to provide adequate oversight.

## Motorola Sales

The division of enforcement at the United States Securities and Exchange Commission (SEC) conducted an investigation into whether Motorola, Inc. violated federal securities law when one of its senior officials selectively disclosed information about the company's quarterly sales and orders during private telephone calls with sell-side analysts in March 2001. During those calls, Motorola's director of investor relations told analysts that first quarter sales and orders were down by at least 25 percent. Previously, in a February 23, 2001, press release and a public conference call, Motorola had said only that sales and orders were experiencing "significant weakness", and that Motorola was likely to miss its earnings estimates (SEC, 2002).

SEC (2002) found that the conduct in question was inconsistent with the disclosure mandate, which generally prohibits issuers from communicating material, non-public information to securities professionals without simultaneous public disclosure of the same information. When an issuer endeavors to make public disclosure of material information but later learns that it did not, in fact, fully communicate the intended message, and determines that further disclosure is needed, the proper course of action is not to selectively disclose the corrected message in private communications with industry professionals, but rather to make additional public disclosure.

According to the enforcement manual at SEC (2013), an investigation is an inquiry into potential violations of the federal securities laws. The purpose is to protect investors and the markets by investigating potential violations of the laws and litigating the SEC's enforcement actions. Values integral to that mission include integrity, fairness, passion and teamwork.

The main suspect in the investigation was the director of investor relations. He is blamed in the report and presented as a rotten apple. Motorola as company seems to avoid the rotten barrel label in the report. Blaming the director of investor relations without even interviewing the person is a shortcoming of the investigation. The report suggests that the director misinformed the public, then cleared it up with analysts, but neglected to inform the public again with a public release. Such allegations should have prompted investigators to interview the director to get what might be the other side of the story.

## Save the Children

Padakhep Manabik Unnayan Kendra (PMUK) is a non-governmental organization in Bangladesh. PMUK received US$5.2 million from Save the Children for HIV/AIDS work among children in Bangladesh. An investigation by the Office of the Inspector General (2012) was a result of irregularities found in multiple audits performed by the principal recipient, Save the Children USA (SCUSA). The investigation confirmed that there were acts of misappropriation and a fraud scheme between 2004 and 2009 identified through the audits. The loss of grant funds disbursed to PMUK amounted to US$1,894,426.

PMUK engaged in a scheme to divert the grant funds disbursed to them as a sub-recipient under the HIV/AIDS program. They concealed the diversion through fabricated documents for submission to SCUSA, including "a set of manufactured books and records to justify withdrawals that never actually took place, and then withdrew funds separately" (Inspector General, 2012: 3):

> The fictitious books and records included: (i) fabricated and falsified bank statements; (ii) accounting journals maintained for recording the false program expenditures and activities in detail; (iii) falsified bids and invoices for purchases of services and goods by third party vendors that did not in fact occur; and (iv) copies of checks allegedly issued to vendors that were never actually issued or presented for payment.

The documents were all created to justify the expenditures for a legitimate program purpose, but it was a program that never materialized. PMUK withdrew funds and diverted them to unknown locations. While the diversion of the program funds was well concealed through false documentation that appeared at face value generally complete and mutually consistent, on closer examination, indicators of fraud were evident (Inspector General, 2012: 4):

> For example, typographical and arithmetic errors appeared on the forged bank statements provided by PMUK. In addition, vendors who allegedly provided goods and services under the program confirmed in several instances that the bids and invoices bearing their companies' names were not authentic, that the vendors never provided the services/goods, and that these entities never actually received the money.

The investigation unit of the Office of the Inspector General is responsible for conducting investigations of fraud, abuse, misappropriation, corruption and mismanagement that may occur when grants are given for various purposes. Investigations aim to uncover the specific nature and extent of fraud and abuse of funds, identify the staff or private entities implicated in the schemes, and determine the amount of funds misappropriated. The office is an administrative body with no law enforcement powers (Inspector General, 2012).

Although PMUK was not able to detail their proper use of funds, investigators could not find out where PMUK had placed the money. Investigators were unable to locate misappropriated sums. The fabricated and falsified bank statements were evidence of fraud, but investigators failed to reconstruct the past in terms of historical financial transactions.

It seems that investigators entered Bangladesh without adequately appreciating its culture, as illustrated by the way they requested access to documents at the NCC Bank. Their confrontational and accusatory approach intimidated local staff and scared them away. It is likely that PMUK and bank employees were caught off guard because the U.S. investigators were viewed as outsiders and local staff were not sure how to handle external critics.

Investigators requested access to bank statements on May 26, 2011, but did not receive them until June 19, 2011. For about three weeks, investigators were messed about and stalled. It is understandable that Bangladesh executives were hesitant about giving up documents to foreign investigators. They did not want to incriminate themselves before someone they did not know or were familiar with. The investigators should probably not have barged into the country of Bangladesh without a better understanding of its culture or how local staff might feel. They might have gained – and deserved – the trust of executives in Bangladesh more if they had involved them in the struggle to reconstruct past events.

## Peregrine Financial Group

The investigative team at Berkeley Research Group was tasked with conducting a review of the National Futures Association's audit regulatory framework after the failed audit of Peregrine Financial Group (Berkeley, 2013). It was not the team's mandate to determine how former Peregrine Financial Group CEO Russell Wasendorf conducted the fraud that caused the failure of Peregrine, and the team did not conduct an exhaustive analysis of how he perpetrated the fraud.

The investigation found that National Future Association (NFA) auditors conducted a total of 27 audits of Peregrine from 1995 to 2012. The investigation further found that these audits were, for the most part, routine audits designed to review Peregrine's operations and systems and not specifically directed at a particular tip or complaint alleging that Wasendorf was conducting a fraud. Investigators inquired whether there were any such complaints and found none. Investigators also found that Wasendorf was able to conceal the fraud meticulously by providing numerous convincingly forged documents to NFA auditors (Berkeley, 2013).

Investigators found that, overall, the NFA audits were conducted in a competent and proper fashion, with the auditors dutifully implementing the appropriate modules that were required in the annual audits. However, they found that certain areas, such as internal controls, Wasendorf's capital contributions and Peregrine's accounts were not examined closely in the audits (Berkeley, 2013).

## Sandstorm banking

Sandstorm refers to a bank investigation by PwC (1991). The Bank of England was the client for the investigation. The investigation report is concerned with irregularities and related matters which came to the investigators' attention during the course of their work. Investigators reviewed correspondence and other files, and conducted interviews with former management.

According to Block (2001), the Sandstorm case involved the financial crime activities of the Bank of Credit and Commerce International (BCCI). The bank was founded in 1972 by Agha Hasan Abedi, a Pakistani financier. The bank came under the scrutiny of numerous financial regulators and intelligence agencies in the 1980s due to concerns that it was poorly regulated. Subsequent investigations revealed that it was involved in massive money laundering.

The Sandstorm case was one of the money laundering cases involving the bank. Sandstorm was a code name for BCCI (Wikipedia, downloaded March 28, 2015):

> In March 1991, the Bank of England asked Price Waterhouse to carry out an inquiry. On 24 June 1991, using the code name "Sandstorm" for BCCI, Price Waterhouse submitted the Sandstorm report showing that BCCI had engaged in "widespread fraud and manipulation" that made it difficult, if not impossible, to reconstruct BCCI's financial history.
>
> The Sandstorm report, parts of which were leaked to *The Sunday Times*, included details of how the Abu Nidal terrorist group had manipulated details and through using fake identities had opened accounts at BCCI's Sloane Street branch, near Harrods in London. Britain's internal security service, MI5, had signed up two sources inside the branch to hand over copies of all documents relating to Abu Nidal's accounts. One source was the Syrian-born branch manager, Ghassan Qassem, the second a young British employee.
>
> The Abu Nidal link man for the BCCI accounts was a man based in Iraq named Samir Najmeddin or Najmedeen. Throughout the 80s, BCCI had set up millions of dollars in credit for Najmeddin, largely for arms deals with Iraq. Qassem later swore in an affidavit that Najmeddin was often accompanied by an American, whom Qassem subsequently identified as the financier Marc Rich. Rich was later indicted in the U.S. for tax evasion and racketeering in an apparently unrelated case and fled the country.
>
> Qassem also told reporters that he had once escorted Abu Nidal, who was allegedly using the name Shakir Farhan, around town to buy a tie, without realizing who he was. This revelation led in 1991 to one of the *London Evening Standard*'s best-known front-page headlines: "I took Abu Nidal shopping."

Investigators from PwC (1991) emphasized that much of the information in their report was based on records that had previously been concealed from them. The documents only came to light as a result of investigators' insistence on the files being sealed, such records having been in the personal possession of top executives at the bank.

According to the Bank of England, the PwC (1991) report was the basis for the closure of BCCI in July 1991. The report was prepared for the Bank of England, though it was never finalized (http://visar.csustan.edu/aaba/BCCISandstormRelease.html). Some 1.4 million depositors lost between them US$11 billion.

While Agha Hasan Abedi was the founder of the bank, Zafar Iqbal was the chief executive and also general manager of the treasury of Grand Cayman. Ziauddin Akbar was bank treasury official; Swaleh Naqvi was bank executive and deputy to bank founder Abedi. These are some of the names presented in the investigation report by PwC (1991).

PwC (1991) writes that Abedi had "a grandiose vision of the bank, and the global role it should play". His deputy Naqvi "manipulated transactions". When Akbar resigned, he left a record of his activities with Naqvi, who "brought under his own control the amounts which had been financed by unorthodox means". Naqvi had a number of core documents in his personal possession when PwC (1991) started its investigation. Investigators found evidence of CEO Iqbal's "approval of certain questionable transactions booked through the accounts of the crown prince of Abu Dhabi".

The PwC (1991) investigation focused on the illegal money transfers that caused the bank to collapse. Transfers occurred from a bank in India to various entities. The report dealt with the implications of those money transfers and looked into which bylaws were violated during the money transfers.

PwC (1991) was unable to find out where the stolen money went. The team assigned to the investigation gleaned circumstantial evidence that the involved brokers did not always trade with the treasury and may have been involved with the manipulation of profits. The investigation was aimed at reaffirming the illegal money transfers made by Bank of India to different entities due to which the bank faced heavy losses. A special duties department was found to be involved in the fabrication of offshore accounts.

# CONCLUSION

The Wolf of Wall Street was famous for fraud and corruption. Jordan Belfort's story of greed, power and excess is a tale that he documented in his book (that later became a movie). Among the many episodes in his book, Belfort (2008: 151) tells how he as an American used a UK family member to conduct money laundering in a Swiss bank:

> Plausible deniability was obviously an international obsession among white-collar criminals (…) "But to answer your question, I'm planning to use a family member with a different last name than mine. She's from my wife's side, and she's not even a U.S. citizen, she's British. I'm flying to London tomorrow morning, and I can have her back here the day after tomorrow – passport in hand – ready to open an account at your bank."
>
> Saurel nodded once and said, "I assume you trust this woman implicitly, because if you don't, we can provide you with people who will use their own passports. These people are entirely unsophisticated – mostly farmers and shepherds from the Isle of Man or other tax-free havens such as that – and they are one hundred percent trustworthy. Furthermore, they will not be allowed access to your account. But I'm sure that you have already taken this woman's trustworthiness into consideration. However, I would still suggest that you meet with a man named Randall Franks. He is a professional with matters such as these, especially in the creation of documents. He can create bills of sale, financial letters, purchase orders, brokerage confirmations, and almost anything else within reason. He is what we call a trustee. He will help you form bearer corporations, which will further insulate you from the prying eyes of your government and allow you to break up your ownership of public companies into smaller increments, to avoid filing any of the requisite forms for over five percent stock ownership. He would be

invaluable to a man like you – in all aspects of your business – both foreign and domestic."

The social and economic impact of Belfort's fraud and corruption was enormous for all direct and indirect victims. Yet Belfort is just one of many white-collar criminals who abuse their trusted positions to harm individuals, organizations and nations for personal and business benefits. As is evident from his book, Belfort (2008) knew what he was doing, and he found it convenient. It was convenient to run his business illegally the way he did to enjoy power and wealth. The theory of convenience has emerged as an integrated explanation of white-collar crime. For members of the elite in trusted positions, financial crime is often a convenient solution to problems and a convenient path to explore and exploit possibilities. Convenience oriented people choose alternative actions that represent savings in time and effort, and avoidance of stress and pain. In a professional setting, white-collar offenders are able to commit crime as well as conceal crime among seemingly legitimate activities.

Belfort's (2008) book stands out as an exception among autobiographies by convicted white-collar offenders. Normally, suspected and convicted offenders tend to apply neutralization techniques when describing their activities. Neutralization techniques include denial of injury, denial of responsibility, loyalty to higher authority, and legal mistake.

Fraud is deliberate deception to secure unfair or unlawful gain. Fraud is an intentional perversion of truth for the purpose of inducing another in reliance upon it to part with some valuable thing belonging to him or to surrender a legal right. Fraud is a misrepresentation of facts with the purpose of causing someone else to do something financially that the person otherwise would not have done. Fraud is a criminal deception intended to result in illegal financial gain. Fraud is intended to deceive others, typically by unjustifiably claiming or being credited with characteristics, accomplishments or qualities. Fraud is an intentional misrepresentation or concealment of an important fact upon which the victim is meant to rely, and in fact does rely, to the harm of the victim. Fraud is an intentional deception of a victim by false representation or pretense with the intent of persuading the victim to part with something of value and with the victim parting with the valuables in reliance on the representation or pretense and with the perpetrator intending to keep the valuables from the victim. Fraud is often the crime of getting money by deceiving people. Fraud is deliberate actions taken by management at any level to deceive, swindle, or cheat investors, other key stakeholders, banks or others.

Fraud is an act or course of deception, an intentional concealment, omission, or perversion of truth, to (1) gain unlawful or unfair advantage, (2) induce another to part with some valuable item or surrender a legal right, or (3) inflict injury in some manner. Fraud is the crime of gaining money or financial benefits by a trick or by lying. Fraud is an intentionally deceptive action designed to provide the perpetrator with an unlawful gain. Fraud is a knowing misrepresentation of the truth or concealment of a material fact to induce another to act to his or her detriment. Fraud is an intentional act within the course of one's professional activity that is illegal.

A fraudulent practice is any act or omission, including a misrepresentation, that knowingly or recklessly misleads, or attempts to mislead, a party to obtain a financial or other valuable benefit or to avoid an obligation. Fraud consists of deceitful practice or willful device, resorted to with the intent to deprive another of his or her right, or in some manner to cause harm.

As documented in this book, signal detection theory may shed some light into why some private and public actors discover and disclose more fraud than others. There are a number of determinants of fraud signal detection. The detection of a stimulus depends on both the intensity of the stimulus and the physical and psychological state of the individual. A detector's ability or likelihood to detect some stimulus is affected by the intensity of the stimulus (e.g. how loud a whistleblowing is), the competence and experience of the potential detector and the potential detector's physical and psychological state (e.g. how alert the person is). Detecting persons may have varying abilities to discern between information-bearing recognition (called pattern) and random patterns that distract from information (called noise).

In the case of Jordan Belfort, the signal was certainly intense, but at the same time surrounded by noise. The Federal Bureau of Investigation (FBI) had high signal alertness, but probably limited pattern recognition. In the end, the Wolf of Wall Street was prosecuted and sent to prison. Afterwards he wrote his book that was later turned into a celebrated motion picture.

# BIBLIOGRAPHY

Aas, P., Risa, E. and Heimsvik, O. (2017a). Reagerer etter Dale-avsløringer (Reaction after Dale disclosure), *Stavanger Aftenblad*, January 30, pages 10–12.

Aas, P., Risa, E. and Heimsvik, O. (2017b). Dale-saken: Politiet starter etterforsking (The Dale case: The police start investigation), *Stavanger Aftenblad*, May 16.

ACFE (2008). *2008 Report to the Nation: On Occupational Fraud & Abuse*, Association of Certified Fraud Examiners, Austin, TX.

ACFE (2014). *Report to the Nations on Occupational Fraud and Abuse, 2014 Global Fraud Study*, Association of Certified Fraud Examiners, Austin, TX.

ACFE (2016). *CFE Code of Professional Standard*, Association of Certified Fraud Examiners, www.acfe.com/standards/.

Adler, P.S. and Kwon, S.W. (2002). Social capital: Prospects for a new concept, *Academy of Management Review*, 27 (1), 17–40.

Agnew, R. (2005). *Pressured into Crime: An Overview of General Strain Theory*, Oxford, UK: Oxford University Press.

Agnew, R. (2014). Social concern and crime: Moving beyond the assumption of simple self-interest, *Criminology*, 52 (1), 1–32.

Aguilera, R.V. and Vadera, A.K. (2008). The dark side of authority: Antecedents, mechanisms, and outcomes of organizational corruption, *Journal of Business Ethics*, 77, 431–449.

Ahrne, G. and Brunsson, N. (2011). Organization outside organizations: The significance of partial organization, *Organization*, 18 (1), 83–104.

Albrecht, C.C., Albrecht, W.S. and Dunn, J.G. (2001). Can auditors detect fraud: A review of the research evidence, *Journal of Forensic Accounting*, 2 (1), 1–12.

Anders, S.B. (2006). Website of the month: Association of Certified Fraud Examiners, *The CPA Journal*, 76 (8), 71.

Andersen, J.J., Johannesen, N., Larseen, D.D. and Paltseva, E. (2017). Petro rents, political institutions, and hidden wealth: Evidence from offshore bank accounts, *Journal of the European Economic Association*, forthcoming.

Andersen, Ø. (2016). Fraråder fortsatt politifolk å varsle (Still advises police officers not to whistleblow), *Dagbladet*, November 20.

# Bibliography 203

Arjoon, S. (2008). Slippery when wet: The real risk in business, *Journal of Markets & Morality*, 11 (1), 77–91.

Arnulf, J.K. and Gottschalk, P. (2013). Heroic leaders as white-collar criminals: An empirical study, *Journal of Investigative Psychology and Offender Profiling*, 10, 96–113.

Ashforth, B.E., Gioia, D.A., Robinson, S.L. and Trevino, L.K. (2008). Re-reviewing organizational corruption, *Academy of Management Review*, 33 (3), 670–684.

Ashkanasy, N.M. (2016). Why we need theory in the organization sciences, *Journal of Organizational Behavior*, 37 (8), 1126–1131.

Ashkanasy, N.M., Humphrey, R.H. and Huy, Q.N. (2017). Integrating emotions and affect in theories of management, *Academy of Management Review*, 42 (2), 175–189.

Atwater, K. (2006). Whistleblowers enforce procurement ethics, *American City & County*, October 23, http://americancityandcounty.com/mag/whistleblowers-enforce-procurement-ethics.

Baird, J.E. and Zelin, R.C. (2009). An examination of the impact of obedience pressure on perceptions of fraudulent acts and the likelihood of committing occupational fraud, *Journal of Forensic Studies in Accounting and Business*, Winter, 1–14.

Barney, J.B. (2001). Resource-based theories of competitive advantage: A ten-year retrospective on the resource-based view, *Journal of Management*, 27, 643–650.

BDO (2014a). *Report of Investigation of the Coatesville Area School District*, July 17.

BDO (2014b). *Gransking av Stiftelsen Betanien Bergen (Examination of the Foundation Betanien Bergen) – Anonymisert og revidert sammendrag (Anonymised and revised summary)*, BDO, Oslo, Norway.

Beasley, M.S. (2003). SAS No. 99: A new look at auditor detection of fraud, *Journal of Forensic Accounting*, 4, 1–20.

Belfort, J. (2008). *The Wolf of Wall Street*, Bantam Books, NY: New York.

Bendahan, S., Zehnder, C., Pralong, F.P. and Antonakis, J. (2015). Leader corruption depends on power and testosterone, *The Leadership Quarterly*, 26, 101–122.

Bendiktsson, M.O. (2010). The deviant organization and the bad apple CEO: Ideology and accountability in media coverage of corporate scandals, *Social Forces*, 88 (5), 2189–2216.

Benson, M.L. and Gottschalk, P. (2015). Public service motivation theory: differences between white collar criminals in the public and private sectors, *Journal of International Doctoral Research*, 4 (1), 56–68.

Benson, M.L. and Simpson, S.S. (2015). *Understanding White-Collar Crime*, Abingdon, UK: Taylor & Francis.

Berglihn, H. and Fosse, S.S. (2013). Meldte seg selv (Reported himself), *Dagens Næringsliv*, July 9, pages 8–9.

Berkeley (2013). *Report of investigation: Analysis of the National Futures Association's audits of Peregrine Financial Group Inc.*, Berkeley Research Group, January 29, www.nfa.futures.org/news/BRG/report_of_investigation.pdf, 160 pages.

Berry, L.L., Seiders, K. and Grewal, D. (2002). Understanding service convenience, *Journal of Marketing*, 66, 1–17.

Bjørkelo, B. and Matthiesen, S.B. (2011). Preventing and dealing with retaliation against whistleblowers, in Lewis, D. and Vandekerckhove, W. (editors), *Whistleblowing and Democratic Values*, London: International Whistleblowing Research Network.

Bjørkelo, B., Einarsen, S., Nielsen, M.B. and Matthiesen, S.B. (2011). Silence is golden? Characteristics and experiences of self-reported whistleblowers, *European Journal of Work and Organizational Psychology*, 20 (2), 206–238.

Bjørndal, B. and Kleppe, M.K. (2013). Mulig jeg har vært dumsnill (I may have been dumb nice), *Dagens Næringsliv*, October 21, www.dn.no/nyheter/politikkSamfunn/2013/10/21/-mulig-jeg-har-vaert-dumsnill.

Blickle, G., Schlegel, A., Fassbender, P. and Klein, U. (2006). Some personality correlates of business white-collar crime, *Applied Psychology: An International Review*, 55 (2), 220–233.

Blickle, G. and Schütte, N. (2017). Trait psychopathy, task performance, and counterproductive work behavior directed toward the organization, *Personality and Individual Differences*, 109, 225–231.

Block, A.A. (2001). *The Organized Criminal Activities of the Bank of Credit and Commerce International: Essays and Documentation*, Dondrecht, The Netherlands: Kluwer Academic Publishers.

Bogen, T. (2008). *Hvor var du, historien om mitt liv (Where were you, the story of my life)*, Oslo: Schibsted Publishing.

Bond, G.D. (2008). Deception detection expertise, *Law and Human Behavior*, 32, 339–351.

Bookman, Z. (2008). Convergences and omissions in reporting corporate and white collar crime, *DePaul Business & Commercial Law Journal*, 6, 347–392.

Bosse, D.A. and Phillips, R.A. (2016). Agency theory and bounded self-interest, *Academy of Management Review*, 41 (2), 276–297.

Bradshaw, E.A. (2015). "Obviously, we're all oil industry": The criminogenic structure of the offshore oil industry, *Theoretical Criminology*, 19 (3), 376–395.

Breen, K.M. and Guberman, P.A. (2012). *Special investigative report regarding allegations of impropriety by Dr. C. Kern Wildenthal relating to travel and entertainment expenses paid for by University of Texas Southwestern Medical Center*, Paul Hastings LLP, University of Texas, www.lrl.state.tx.us/scanned/archive/2012/18224.pdf, 365 pages (main report 46 pages).

Brightman, H.J. (2009). *Today's White-Collar Crime. Legal, Investigative, and Theoretical Perspectives*, Routledge, Taylor & Francis Group, NY: New York.

Brodahl, N. (2016). Korrupsjon i store virksomheter: Hvilke forutsetninger har en revisor i Skatteetaten til å avdekke korrupsjon? (Corruption in larger enterprises: What prerequisites does an auditor have in the tax authority to detect corruption?), term paper, BI Norwegian Business School, Oslo.

Brody, R.G. and Perri, F.S. (2016). Fraud detection suicide: The dark side of white-collar crime, *Journal of Financial Crime*, 23 (4), 786–797.

Brooks, G. and Button, M. (2011). The police and fraud investigation and the case for a nationalized solution in the United Kingdom, *The Police Journal*, 84, 305–319.

Buanes, F. and Valland, G. (2015). Førte timer for dag som ikke fantes (Registered hours for the day that did not exist), *Bergens Tidende*, February 4.

Bucy, P.H., Formby, E.P., Raspanti, M.S. and Rooney, K.E. (2008). Why do they do it?: The motives, mores, and character of white collar criminals, *St. John's Law Review*, 82, 401–571.

Button, M. and Gee, J. (2013). *Countering Fraud for Competitive Advantage: The Professional Approach to Reducing the Last Great Hidden Cost*, Chichester, UK: Wiley & Sons.

Button, M., Frimpong, K., Smith, G. and Johnston, L. (2007a). Professionalizing counter fraud specialists in the UK: Assessing progress and recommendations for reform, *Crime Prevention and Community Safety*, 9, 92–101.

Button, M., Johnston, L., Frimpong, K. and Smith, G. (2007b). New directions in policing fraud: The emergence of the counter fraud specialists in the United Kingdom, *International Journal of the Sociology of Law*, 35, 192–208.

Campbell, F. (1997) Journalistic construction of news: Information gathering, *New Library World*, 98 (2), 60–64.

Carson, D. (2013). Investigations: What could, and should, be taught? *The Police Journal*, 86 (3), 249–275.

Ceccato, V. and Benson, M.L. (2016). Tax evasion in Sweden 2002–2013: Interpreting changes in the rot/rut deduction system and predicting future trends, *Crime, Law and Social Change*, 66, 217–232.

CFCS (2013). *CFCS Certification Examination Study Manual*, 4th edition, Certified Financial Crime Specialist, Association of Certified Financial Crime Specialists, Miami, FL.

CFCS (2014). *CFCS Certification Examination Study Manual*, 4th edition, Certified Financial Crime Specialist, Association of Certified Financial Crime Specialists, Rivergate Plaza, Miami, FL.

Chang, J.J., Lu, H.C. and Chen, M. (2005). Organized crime or individual crime? Endogeneous size of a criminal organization and the optimal law enforcement, *Economic Inquiry*, 43 (3), 661–675.

Chattopadhyay, P., Glick, W.H. and Huber, G.P. (2001). Organizational actions in response to threats and opportunities, *Academy of Management Journal*, 44 (5), 937–955.

Chester Grand Jury (2014). *Chester County 18th Investigating Grand Jury's report re: Coatesville Area School District*, Court of Common Pleas of Chester County, http://casd.schoolwires.net/cms/lib8/PA01916452/Centricity/Domain/513/Grand%20Jury%20Report%20CASD.pdf, 114 pages.

Chokshi, N. (2017). Norway is no. 1 in happiness: The U.S., sadly, is no. 14, *New York Times*, March 20.

Chrisman, J.J., Chua, J.H., Kellermanns, F.W. and Chang, E.P.C. (2007). Are family managers agents or stewards? An exploratory study in privately held family firms, *Journal of Business Research*, 60 (10), 1030–1038.

Coburn, N.F. (2006). Corporate investigations, *Journal of Financial Crime*, 13 (3), 348–368.

Cohen, L.E. and Felson, M. (1979). Social change and crime rate trends: A routine activity approach, *American Sociological Review*, 44, 588–608.

Collier, J.E. and Kimes, S.E. (2013). Only if it is convenient: Understanding how convenience influences self-service technology evaluation, *The Scholarly Commons*, Cornell University School of Hotel Administration, http://scholarship.sha.cornell.edu/articles/826.

Comey, J.B. (2009). Go directly to prison: White-collar sentencing after the Sarbanes-Oxley act, *Harvard Law Review*, 122, 1728–1749.

Cowen, A.P., King, A.W. and Marcel, J.J. (2016). CEO severance agreements: A theoretical examination and research agenda, *Academy of Management Review*, 41 (1), 151–169.

Craig, J.M. (2017). The effects of social concern on white-collar offending, *Deviant Behavior*, 38 (7), 837–854.

Craig, J.M. and Piquero, N.L. (2017). The effects of low self-control and desire-for-control on white-collar offending: A replication, *Deviant Behavior*, 37 (11), 1308–1324.

Dahle, D.Y. (2011). Christer Tromsdal var politiagent (Christer Tromsdal was police agent), *Aftenposten*, October 19, www.aftenposten.no/nyheter/iriks/Christer-Tromsdal-var-politiagent-6369334.html.

Dawson, G.S., Denford, J.S., Williams, C.K., Preston, D. and Desouza, K.C. (2016). An examination of effective IT governance in the public sector using the legal view of agency theory, *Journal of Management Information Systems*, 33 (4), 1180–1208.

Dearden, T.E. (2016). Trust: The unwritten cost of white-collar crime, *Journal of Financial Crime*, 23 (1), 87–101.

Dearden, T.E. (2017). An assessment of adults' views on white-collar crime, *Journal of Financial Crime*, 24 (2), 309–321.

Dean, G., Fahsing, I.A., Gottschalk, P. and Solli-Sæther, H. (2008). Investigative thinking and creativity: An empirical study of police detectives in Norway, *International Journal of Innovation and Learning*, 5 (2), 170–185.

Dhami, M.K. (2007). White-collar prisoners' perceptions of audience reaction, *Deviant Behavior*, 28, 57–77.
Dion, M. (2008). Ethical leadership and crime prevention in the organizational setting, *Journal of Financial Crime*, 15 (3), 308–319.
Dion, M. (2009). Corporate crime and the dysfunction of value networks, *Journal of Financial Crime*, 16 (4), 436–445.
Distriktsrevisjonen (2007). *Rapport versjon II etter granskingsoppdrag fra styrene i Nedre Romerike Vannverk AS (NRV) og AS Sentralrenseanlegget RA-2 (RA-2) (Report on water supply unit)*, Nedre Romerike Distriktsrevisjon, Lillestrøm, May 30.
Dollar, D., Fisman, R. and Gatti, R. (2001). Are women really the "fairer" sex? Corruption and women in government, *Journal of Economic Behavior & Organization*, 46 (4), 423–429.
Donk, D.P. van and Molloy, E. (2008). From organizing as projects, to projects as organizations, *International Journal of Project Management*, 26, 129–137.
Dowler, K. and Sparks, R. (2008). Victimization, contact with the police, and neighborhood conditions: Reconsidering African American and Hispanic attitudes toward the police, *Police Practice and Research: An International Journal*, 9 (5), 395–415.
Drage, K. and Olstad, T. (2008). Ekstern revisor og økonomisk kriminalitet: En analyse av revisors ansvar og brukernes forventninger (External auditor and financial crime: An analysis of auditor responsibility and user expectations), BI Norwegian School of Management, Oslo.
Drammen tingrett (2014). 14-035842MED-DRAM, *Drammen tingrett* (Drammen District Court), October 24.
Dugstad, L. (2017). Lydig politi gjør varsling vanskelig (Obedient police officers make whistleblowing difficult), *Dagens Næringsliv*, January 20, www.dn.no.
Dupont, B. (2014). Private security regimes: Conceptualizing the forces that shape the private delivery of security, *Theoretical Criminology*, 18 (3), 263–281.
Durkheim, Émile. 1952. *Suicide: A study in sociology*, London: Routledge & Kegan Paul.
Earl, M. (2001). Knowledge management strategies: Toward a taxonomy, *Journal of Management Information Systems*, 18 (1), 215–233.
Eberly, M.B., Holley, E.C., Johnson, M.D. and Mitchell, T.R. (2011). Beyond internal and external: A dyadic theory of relational attributions, *Academy of Management Review*, 36 (4), 731–753.
Eddleston, K.A. and Kidwell, R.E. (2012). Parent-child relationships: Planting the seeds of deviant behavior in the family firm, *Entrepreneurship: Theory & Practice*, 36 (2), 369–386.
Edelbacher, M., Dobovsek, B. and Kratcoski, P.C. (2016). The relationship of the informal economy to corruption, fraud, and organized crime, in Edelbacher, M., Kratcoski, P.C. and Dobovsek, B. (editors), *Corruption, Fraud, Organized Crime, and the Shadow Economy*, Boca Raton, FL: CRC Press.
Eisenhardt, K.M. (1985). Control: organizational and economic approaches, *Management Science*, 31 (2), 134–149.
Eisenhardt, K.M. (1989). Building theories from case study research, *Academy of Management Review*, 14, 532–550.
Ekeberg, E. (2016a). Kritisk til granskinger (Critical to investigations), *Klassekampen*, May 27.
Ekeberg, E. (2016b). Visste om lyssky kontoer (Knew about shady accounts), *Klassekampen*, Friday, July 22, pages 4–5.
Ekeberg, E. 2016c). Nordea fant lovbrudd (Nordea found law violations), *Klassekampen*, Tuesday, July 26, pages 12–13.
Ekeberg, E. (2016d). Tar paradisene i forsvar (Tax havens in defense), *Klassekampen*, Wednesday, July 27, pages 10–11.

Ekeberg, E. (2016e). Skuffet over Telenor-toppen (Disappointed in Telenor heads), *Klassekampen*, July 28, pages 6–7.

Elnan, T.S. (2016). Kriminelle er ofte mer innovative enn folk flest (Criminals are often more innovative than other people), *Aftenposten*, part 2, April 14, pages 4–5.

Engdahl, O. (2015). White-collar crime and first-time adult-onset offending: Explorations in the concept of negative life events as turning points, *International Journal of Law, Crime and Justice*, 43 (1), 1–16.

Eriksen, B. (2016). Arbeidstakers rett til å varsle om "kritikkverdige forhold" etter arbeidsmiljøloven § 2–4 (1) (Employees right to blow the whistle about "critical conditions" according to labor protection law), Ph.D thesis, University of Bergen, Norway.

Eriksen, B. (2017). Ordfører e-post eskalerer kommunekonflikten (Mayor's email escalates municipality conflict), *Agderposten*, September 9, page 25.

Eriksen, T.S. (2010). *Arven etter Ole Christian Bach: Et justismord (The legacy of Ole Christian Bach: A miscarriage of justice)*, Oslo: Norgesforlaget.

Fahsing, I.A. (2016). The making of an expert detective: Thinking and deciding in criminal investigations, doctoral dissertation, Department of Psychology, University of Gothenburg, Sweden.

Fahsing, I.A., and Ask, K. (2013). Decision making and decisional tipping points in homicide investigations: An interview study of British and Norwegian detectives, *Journal of Investigative Psychology and Offender Profiling*, 10 (2), 155–165.

Fahsing, I.A. and Ask, K. (2016). The making of an expert detective: The role of experience in English and Norwegian police officers' investigative decision-making, *Psychology, Crime & Law*, 22 (3), 203–223.

Fanelli, A. and Misangyi, V.F. (2006). Bringing out charisma: CEO charisma and external stakeholders, *Academy of Management Review*, 31 (4), 1049–1061.

Farquhar, J.D. and Rowley, J. (2009). Convenience: A services perspective, *Marketing Theory*, 9 (4), 425–438.

Farrell, B.R. and Healy, P. (2000). White-collar crime: A profile of the perpetrator and an evaluation of the responsibilities for its prevention and detection, *Journal of Forensic Accounting*, 1, 17–34.

FBI (2010). *Yusuf Acar, the former acting Chief of Security Officer for the District of Columbia's Office of the Chief Technology Officer (OCTO)*, www.fbi.gov/washingtondc/pressreleases/2010/wfo081210a.htm, downloaded January 10, 2015.

Fehr, R., Yam, K.C. and Dang, C. (2015). Moralized leadership: The construction and consequences of ethical leader perceptions, *Academy of Management Review*, 40 (2), 182–209.

Felson, M. and Boba, R.L. (2017). *Crime and Everyday Life*, chapter 12: "White-collar crime", Thousand Oaks, CA: Sage Publications.

Fjellheim, S. (2007). Waages selvmål (Waages self hurt), *Nordlys*, May 10, page 15.

Flydal, E.F. (2010). Dekknavn: "Joe" (Secret name: "Joe"), *Dagbladet*, May 11.

Flydal, E.F. (2011). SOS Rasisme dømt til å betale over 10 millioner kroner (SOS Racism fined 10 million Norwegian kroner), *Dagbladet*, November 10.

Flydal, E.F. (2013a). Mener disse listene knytter SOS Rasismes ledelse til nytt millionjuks (Says these lists connect SOS Racism leadership to new million fraud ), *Dagbladet*, February 7.

Flydal, E.F. (2013b). Tatt for medlemsjuks og dømt til å betale tilbake 17 millioner: Likevel får de titusener i offentlig støtte (Caught for membership fraud and convicted to pay back 17 million: But they get tens of thousands in public funding), *Dagbladet*, February 17.

Flynn, K. (2016). Financial fraud in the private health insurance sector in Australia: Perspectives from the industry, *Journal of Financial Crime*, 23 (1), 143–158.

Fosse, G. and Magnusson, G. (2004). *Mayday Mayday! Kapteinene først i livbåtene! (Mayday Mayday! The captains first in the lifeboats)*, Oslo: Kolofon Publishing.
Friedrichs, D.O. (2002). Occupational crime, occupational deviance, and workplace crime: Sorting out the difference, *Criminal Justice*, 2 (3), 243–256.
Füss, R. and Hecker, A. (2008). Profiling white-collar crime: Evidence from German-speaking countries, *Corporate Ownership & Control*, 5 (4), 149–161.
Galvin, B.M., Lange, D. and Ashforth, B.E. (2015). Narcissistic organizational identification: Seeing oneself as central to the organization's identity, *Academy of Management Review*, 40 (2), 163–181.
Gill, M. and Hart, J. (1997). Exploring investigative policing, *British Journal of Criminology*, 37 (4), 549–567.
Gilley, K.M. and Rasheed, A. (2000). Making more by doing less: An analysis of outsourcing and its effects on firm performance, *Journal of Management*, 26 (4), 763–790.
Glasø, L. and Einarsen, S. (2008). Emotion regulation in leader–follower relationships, *European Journal of Work and Organizational Psychology*, 17 (4), 482–500.
Goldstraw-White, J. (2012). *White-Collar Crime: Accounts of Offending Behavior*, London: Palgrave Macmillan.
Golladay, K.A. (2017). Reporting behaviors of identity theft victims: An empirical test of Black's theory of law, *Journal of Financial Crime*, 24 (1), 101–117.
Gomulya, D. and Mishina, Y. (2017). Signaler credibility, signal susceptibility, and relative reliance on signals: How stakeholders change their evaluative processes after violation of expectations and rehabilitative efforts, *Academy of Management Journal*, 60 (2), 554–583.
Gottfredson, M. and Hirschi, T. (1990). *A General Theory of Crime*, Redwood City, CA: Stanford University Press.
Gottschalk, P. (2014). *Financial Crime and Knowledge Workers: An Empirical Study of Defense Lawyers and White-Collar Criminals*, New York: Palgrave Macmillan.
Gottschalk, P. (2015). Private investigations of white-collar crime suspicions: A qualitative study of the blame game hypothesis, *Journal of Investigative Psychology and Offender Profiling*, 12, 231–246.
Gottschalk, P. (2016a). Limits to private internal investigations of white-collar crime suspicions: The case of Scandinavian bank Nordea in tax havens, *Cogent Social Sciences*, 2: 12545839.
Gottschalk, P. (2016b). Blame game and rotten apples in private investigation reports: The case of Hadeland and Ringerike Broadband in Norway, *Journal of Investigative Psychology and Offender Profiling*, 13, 91–109.
Gottschalk, P. (2016c). *Explaining White-Collar Crime: The Concept of Convenience in Financial Crime Investigations*, London: Palgrave Macmillan.
Gottschalk, P. (2016d). Private policing of financial crime: Key issues in the investigation business in Norway, *European Journal of Policing Studies*, 3 (3), 292–314.
Gottschalk, P. (2017). Convenience in white-collar crime: Introducing a core concept, *Deviant Behavior*, 38 (5), 605–619.
Gottschalk, P. and Rundmo, T. (2014). Crime: the amount and disparity of sentencing: A comparison of corporate and occupational white collar criminals, *International Journal of Law, Crime and Justice*, 42, 175–187.
Gottschalk, P. and Smith, C. (2016). Detection of white-collar corruption in public procurement in Norway: The role of whistleblowers, *International Journal of Procurement Management*, 9 (4), 427–443.
Gottschalk, P. and Tcherni-Buzzeo, M. (2017). Reasons for gaps in crime reporting: The case of white-collar criminals investigated by private fraud examiners in Norway, University of New Haven, Criminal Justice Faculty Publications, no. 42.

Gray, V.C. and Evans, J. (2008). Report of investigation submitted by the Council of the District of Columbia Office of Tax and Revenue Investigation Special Committee, issued by Cutler Pickering Hale and Dorr LLP, Washington, DC.

Green, B.A. and Podgor, E. (2013). Unregulated internal investigations: Achieving fairness for corporate constituents, *Boston College Law Review*, 54 (1), 73–126.

Green, J. and Plungis, J. (2014). GM picks former Lehman investigator Valukas to lead probe, *Bloomberg*, March 10, www.bloomberg.com/news/2014-03-10/gm-picks-for mer-lehman-investigator-valukas-to-lead-probe.html, downloaded December 2, 2014.

Haakaas, E. (2015). Aktor krever fem års fengsel for heleri og hvittvasking (The prosecutor asks for five years prison for money laundering), *Aftenposten*, October 14, page 12.

Haakaas, E. (2017). *Svartmaling: Kriminelle bygger Norge (Black painting: Criminals build Norway)*, Oslo: Kagge Publishing.

Haines, F. (2014). Corporate fraud as misplaced confidence? Exploring ambiguity in the accuracy of accounts and the materiality of money, *Theoretical Criminology*, 18 (1), 20–37.

Hald (2007). Granskingsrapport: Ledelse og styring av Øyestad helselags boligstiftelse Furuheim (Investigation report: Leadership and management of Øyestad health center housing foundation), Hald, Arendal, Norway.

Hambrick, D.C., Misangyi, V.F. and Park, C.A. (2015). The quad model for identifying a corporate director's potential for effective monitoring: Toward a new theory of board sufficiency, *Academy of Management Review*, 40 (3), 323–344.

Hamilton, Stewart and Alicia Micklethwait (2006), *Greed and Corporate Failure: The Lessons from Recent Disasters*, Basingstoke, UK: Palgrave Macmillan.

Hansen, L.L. (2009). Corporate financial crime: Social diagnosis and treatment, *Journal of Financial Crime*, 16 (1), 28–40.

Hansen, L.L. (2014). "Gossip boys": Insider trading and regulatory ambiguity, *Journal of Financial Crime*, 21 (1), 29–43.

Haugaland (2016). Court case number 15-064394MED/HAUG, dated November 2, *Haugaland tingrett*, district court judge Signe M. Lundegård, co-judges Tove Elin Aksdal and Rune Eriksson, prosecutor Hallvard Gardshol Bjørndal, defendants Kjell Gunnar Larsen (attorneys John Christian Elden and Erik Lea), Trond Thorbjørnsen (attorney Bendik Falch-Koslung), Henrik Ormåsen (attorney Odd Eirik Osmundsen), Bjarne Stokke (attorney Håkon Velde Nordstrøm), Anne Elisabeth Hansen (attorney Ingrid Lauvås), Kenneth Fuglemsmo (attorney Arve Opdahl), Jan Erik Skretteberg (attorney Bjørn Ole Vikse) and Bård Eskild Frantzen (attorney Espen Andre Solberg), 341 pages.

Haverstick, M.H., Seiberling, M.E., Stengel, T.M., Madden, A.R. and Damiani, S.T. (2014). Supplement to Investigative Report to the Board of School Directors for the Coatesville Area School District, issued by Conrad O'Brien, http://casd.schoolwires.net/cms/lib8/PA01916452/Centricity/Domain/513/Supplement to the Conrad OBrien Investigative Report.pdf, 66 pages.

Heath, J. (2008). Business ethics and moral motivation: A criminological perspective, *Journal of Business Ethics*, 83, 595–614.

Hestnes, M. (2017). Hvorfor avdekket ikke revisor underslaget i Hadeland og Ringerike Bredbånd? (Why did the auditor not detect embezzlement at Hadeland and Ringerike Broadband?), MSc thesis, BI Norwegian Business School, Oslo.

Higgins, E.T. (1997). Beyond pleasure and pain, *American Psychologist*, 52, 1280–1300.

Hirschi, T. and Gottfredson, M. (1987). Causes of white-collar crime, *Criminology*, 25 (4), 949–974.

Gjørv, A.B., and Lund, A.S. (2013). Rapport til styret i DNB ASA (Report to the Board at DNB), Hjort, Oslo, September 11.

Hoffmann, J.P. (2002). A contextual analysis of differential association, social control, and strain theories of delinquency, *Social Forces*, 81 (3), 753–785.

Hofoss, E. (2013). Ble tatt for medlemsjuks: Nå lager de blad for romfolk (Were caught for membership fraud: Now they make magazine for rom people), *Aftenposten*, June 15, page 4.

Hofstede, G., Neuijen, B., Ohayv, D.D. and Sanders, G. (1990). Measuring organizational cultures: A qualitative and quantitative study across twenty cases, *Administrative Science Quarterly*, 35 (2), 286–316.

Holler, K.R. (2017). Riksadvokaten: Der bliver ikke rejst straffesag mod Carl Holst (Attorney General: There will be no prosecution against Carl Holst), *Danmarks Radio*, March 31.

Holtfreter, K. (2005). Is occupational fraud "typical" white-collar crime? A comparison of individual and organizational characteristics, *Journal of Criminal Justice*, 33, 353–365.

Holtfreter, K., Reisig, M.D. and Blomberg, T.G. (2005). Consumer fraud victimization in Florida: An empirical study, *St. Thomas Law Review*, 18, 761–788.

Holtfreter, K., Reisig, M.D., Piquero, N.L. and Piquero, A.R. (2010). Low self-control and fraud: Offending, victimization, and their overlap, *Criminal Justice and Behavior*, 37 (2), 188–203.

Holtfreter, K., Reisig, M.D. and Pratt, T.C. (2008). Low self-control, routine activities, and fraud victimization, *Criminology*, 48 (1), 189–219.

Huff, M.J. and Bodner, G.E. (2013). When does memory monitoring succeed versus fail? Comparing item-specific and relational encoding in the DRM paradigm, *Journal of Experimental Psychology: Learning, Memory, and Cognition*, 39 (4), 1246–1256.

Huff, R., Desilets, K. and Kane, J. (2010). *The National Public Survey on White Collar Crime*, Fairmont, WV: National White Collar Crime Center.

Hultgren, G. (2012), Seks års fengsel for Christer Tromsdal (Six years prison for Christer Tromsdal), *Dagbladet*, November 2, www.dagbladet.no/2012/11/02/nyheter/christer_tromsdal/krim/2415991.

Hvistendahl, J., Sandli, E. and Flydal, E.F. (2014). Vi fant mer penger enn hva det er normalt å ha hjemme (We found more money than what is normal to have at home), *Dagbladet*, April 28.

Høyesterett (2011). Case HR-2011-00344-A (number 2011/1479), *Høyesterett* (Supreme Court), February 15.

Imran, M.K., Bilal, A.R., Aslam, U. and Rahman, U.U. (2017). Knowledge management strategies: An organizational change perspective, *Journal of Enterprise Information Management*, 30 (2), 335–351.

Inspector General (2012). Final investigation report of sub-recipient Padakhep Manabik Unnayan Kendra (PMUK) – Bangladesh, Office of the Inspector General, report GF-IG-11-025, www.theglobalfund.org/.../OIG_GFOIG11025InvestigationBangladesh_Report_en.pdf, 32 pages.

Itzkovich, Y. and Heilbrunn, S. (2016). The role of co-workers' solidarity as an antecedent of incivility and deviant behavior in organizations, *Deviant Behavior*, 37 (8), 861–876.

Iver, N. and Samociuk, M. (2006). *Fraud and Corruption: Prevention and Detection*, Farnham, UK: Gower Publishing.

Johnsen, G.J. (2017a). Hva, "leverte" Dale Eiendomsutvikling? (What did Dale Property Development "deliver"?), *Stavanger Aftenblad*, February 15.

Johnsen, G.J. (2017b). Hadde en lignende sak blitt avdekket i et privat selskap ville dette raskt blitt anmeldt av ledelsen (Had a similar case been detected in a private company, it would immediately be reported by management), *Stavanger Aftenblad*, June 20.

Johnson, R.A. (2005). Whistleblowing and the police, *Rutgers University Journal of Law and Urban Policy*, 1 (3), 74–83.

Johnson, S.D. and Groff, E.R. (2014). Strengthening theoretical testing in criminology using agent-based modeling, *Journal of Research in Crime and Delinquency*, 51 (4), 509–25.

Johnson, J.W. and Payne, J. (1986). The decision to commit a crime: An information-processing analysis, in Cornish, D. and Clark, R. (editors), *The Reasoning Criminal: Rational Choice Perspectives of Offending*, New York: Springer Verlag, pages 170–185.

Johnson, G.G. and Rudesill, C.L. (2001). An investigation into fraud prevention and detection of small businesses in the United States: Responsibilities of auditors, managers, and business owners, *Accounting Forum*, 25 (1), 56.

Jones, P. (2004) *Fraud and Corruption in Public Services: A Guide to Risk and Prevention*, Farnham, UK: Gower.

Jones, S. (2014). Internal report details GM ignition coverup, *World Socialist Web Site*, June 14, www.wsws.org/en/articles/2014/06/14/genm-j14.html, downloaded December 2, 2014.

Jonnergård, K., Stafsudd, A. and Elg, U. (2010). Performance evaluations as gender barriers in professional organizations: A study of auditing firms. *Gender, Work and Organization*, 17, 721–749

Judge, T.A., Piccolo, R.F. and Kosalka, T. (2009). The bright and dark sides of leader traits: A review and theoretical extension of the leader trait paradigm, *The Leadership Quarterly*, 20, 855–875.

Kamerdze, S., Loughran, T., Paternoster, R. and Sohoni, T. (2014). The role of affect in intended rule breaking: Extending the rational choice perspective, *Journal of Research in Crime and Delinquency*, 51 (5), 620–654.

Kang, E. and Thosuwanchot, N. (2017). An application of Durkheim's four categories of suicide to organizational crimes, *Deviant Behavior*, 38 (5), 493–513.

Kempa, M. (2010). Combating white-collar crime in Canada: Serving victim needs and market integrity, *Journal of Financial Crime*, 17 (2), 251–264.

Kennedy, D.B. (2013). Applications of forensic sociology and criminology to civil litigation, *Journal of Applied Social Science*, 7 (2), 233–247.

Kerik, B.B. (2005). *From jailer to jailed: My Journey from Correction and Police Commissioner to Inmate #84888-054*, New York: Threshold Editions.

Kessler, R. (2012). *The Secrets of the FBI*, New York: Broadway Paperbacks, Random House.

Khanna, V., Kim, E.H. and Lu, Y. (2015). CEO connectedness and corporate fraud, *The Journal of Finance*, 70 (3), 1203–1252.

Killinger, B. (2010). *Integrity: Doing the Right Thing for the Right Reason*, Canada: McGill University, Queen's University Press.

Kim, W.C. and Mauborgne, R. (2003). Tipping point leadership, *Harvard Business Review*, 81 (4), 60–69.

Kleppe, M.K. (2015). Tromsdal: Der er han skurken som lurte de gamle menneskene (There is the crook who cheated old people), *Dagens Næringsliv*, January 8, www.dn.no/nyheter/2015/01/08/1336/Kriminalitet/tromsdal-der-er-han-skurken-som-lurte-de-gamle-menneskene.

Kommunerevisjonen (2006). Granskingsrapport 1 Undervisningsbygg (Investigation report 1 about school buildings in Oslo City), Kommunerevisjonen, Oslo, Norway.

Koppen, M.V., Poot, C.J. and Blokland, A.A.J. (2010). Comparing criminal careers of organized crime offenders and general offenders, *European Journal of Criminology*, 7 (5), 356–374.

Kouchaki, M. and Desai, S.D. (2015). Anxious, threatened, and also unethical: How anxiety makes individuals feel threatened and commit unethical acts, *Journal of Applied Psychology*, 100 (2), 360–375.

KPMG (2016). Politiets utlendingsenhet: Faktaundersøkelse og vurdering (The Police Immigration Unit: Examination of facts and assessment), KPMG, Oslo, September 29.

Krippendorff, K. (1980). *Content Analysis: An Introduction to its Methodology*, Beverly Hills, CA: Sage.

Kristensen, M.F. (2016). Evaluering av en granskning [advokatundersøkelse]: Region Syddanmark – Undersøgelse af hændelsesforløbet vedrørende tilretning og ændring af fakturatekst fra ekstern leverandør ['Carl Holst-undersøkelsen'] (Evaluation of an investigation [attorney investigation]: Region Syddanmark – Investigation of events for changes in invoice text from external vendor ['Carl Holst investigation']), master of management report in the master class "Financial Crime – Leadership and Corporate Social Responsibility", Spring term 2016, BI Norwegian Business School, Oslo.

Lampe, K. and Johansen, P.O. (2003). *Criminal Networks and Trust*, third annual meeting of the European Society of Criminology, Helsinki, 29 August.

Langton, L. and Piquero, L.N. (2007). Can general strain theory explain white-collar crime? A preliminary investigation of the relationship between strain and select white-collar offenses, *Journal of Criminal Justice*, 35, (1), 1–15.

Laursen, M.T. (2015). Holsts advokat forlanger undersøgelse af lekage (Holst's lawyer demands inquiry into leakage), *Jydske Vestkysten*, November 10.

Leap, T.L. (2007). *Dishonest Dollars: The Dynamics of White-Collar Crime*, Ithaca, NY: Cornell University Press.

Leasure, P. and Zhang, G. (2017). "That's how they taught us to do it": Learned deviance and inadequate deterrents in retail banking, *Deviant Behavior*, published online February, 28 http://dx.doi.org/10.1080/01639625.2017.1286179.

Lee, G. and Fargher, N. (2013). Companies' use of whistle-blowing to detect fraud: An examination of corporate whistle-blowing policies, *Journal of Business Ethics*, 114, 283–295.

Lee, F. and Robinson, R.J. (2000). An attributional analysis of social accounts: Implications of playing the blame game, *Journal of Applied Social Psychology*, 30 (9), 1853–1879.

Lemieux, V. (2003). Criminal networks, Royal Canadian Mounted Police, Ottawa, Canada.

Leonard, W.N. and Weber, M.G. (1970). Automakers and dealers: A study of criminogenic market forces, *Law and Society Review*, 4 (3), 407–424.

Leonard-Barton, D. (1992). Core capabilities and core rigidities: A paradox in managing new product development, *Strategic Management Journal*, 13 (1), 111–125.

Lewis, C., Brooks, G., Button, M., Shepherd, D. and Wakefield, A. (2014). Evaluating the case for greater use of private prosecutions in England and Wales for fraud offences, *International Journal of Law, Crime and Justice*, 42 (1), 3–15.

Li, S. and Ouyang, M. (2007). A dynamic model to explain the bribery behavior of firms, *International Journal of Management*, 24 (3), 605–618.

Liang, L.H., Lian, H., Brown, D.J., Ferris, D.L., Hanig, S. and Keepoing, L.M. (2016). Why are abusive supervisors abusive? A dual-system self-control model, *Academy of Management Journal*, 59 (4), 1385–1406.

Liu, G. and Ren, H. (2017). Ethical team leadership and trainee auditors' likelihood of reporting client's irregularities, *Journal of Financial Crime*, 24 (1), 157–175.

Liu, D., Ray, G. and Whinston, A.B. (2010). The interaction between knowledge codification and knowledge-sharing networks, *Information Systems Research*, 21 (4), 892–906.

Liu, X.L., Liang, P.P., Li, K.C. and Reder, L.M. (2014). Uncovering the neural mechanisms underlying learning from tests, *PLoS ONE*, 9, e92025.

Logan, M.W. (2015). Coping with imprisonment: Testing the special sensitivity hypothesis for white-collar offenders, dissertation in partial fulfilment of Ph.D requirements, Department of Criminal Justice, University of Cincinnati, Clifton, OH.

Lokanan, M.E. (2017). The demographic profile of victims of investment fraud, *Journal of Financial Crime*, 21 (2), 226–242.

Lomas, P. and Kramer, D.J. (2013). *Corporate Internal Investigations*, Oxford: Oxford University Press.

Lord, N. (2016). Establishing enforcement legitimacy in the pursuit of rule-breaking "global elites": The case of transnational corporate bribery, *Theoretical Criminology*, 20 (3), 376–399.

Luo, Y. (2002). Contract, cooperation, and performance in international joint ventures, *Strategic Management Journal*, 23 (10), 903–919.

Machen, M.J. and Richards, R.E. (2004). The use of fraud examiners in the battle against occupational fraud and abuse, *The Journal of Investment Compliance*, Winter, 67–71.

Mai, H.T.X. and Olsen, S.O. (2016). Consumer participation in self-production: The role of control mechanisms, convenience orientation, and moral obligation, *Journal of Marketing Theory and Practice*, 24 (2), 209–223.

Mann, K., Wheeler, K. and Sarat, A. (1979). Sentencing the white collar defender, *American Criminal Law Review*, 17, 479–500.

Mannheimer Swartling (2016), Governance review: Report to Nordea Bank AB, Mannheimer Swartling, Stockholm, 20 pages.

Maslow, A.H. (1943). A theory of human motivation, *Psychological Review*, 50, 370–396.

McClelland, P.L., Liang, X. and Barker, V.L. (2010). CEO commitment to the status quo: Replication and extension using content analysis, *Journal of Management*, 36 (5), 1251–1277.

McDonald, M.L. and Westphal, J.D. (2003). Getting by with the advice of their friends: CEOs' advice networks and firms' strategic responses to poor performance, *Administrative Science Quarterly*, 48, 1–32.

McElwee, G. and Smith, R. (2015). Exploring criminal and illegal enterprise: New perspectives on research, policy and practice, *Contemporary Issues in Entrepreneurship Research*, 5, 3–22.

McInish, T.H., Frino, A. and Sensenbrenner, F. (2011). Strategic illegal insider trading prior to price sensitive announcements, *Journal of Financial Crime*, 18 (3), 247–253.

McIver, D., Lengnick-Hall, C.A., Lengnick-Hall, M.L. and Ramachandran, I. (2013). Understanding work and knowledge management from a knowledge-in-practice perspective, *Academy of Management Review*, 38 (4), 597–620.

Meerts, C. (2014). Empirical case studies of corporate security in international perspective, in Walby, K. and Lippert, R.K. (editors), *Corporate Security in the 21st Century: Theory and Practice in International Perspective*, Basingstoke, UK: Palgrave Macmillan, 97–115.

Meldalen, S.G. (2015). Når noen hører ordet "stråmann", høres det skummelt ut (When someone hears the word "straw man", it sounds scary), *Dagbladet*, January 8, www.dagbladet.no/2015/01/08/nyheter/innenriks/christer_tromsdal/bedrageri/37075845/.

Mertens, W., Recker, J., Kohlborn, T. and Kummer, T.F. (2016). A framework for the study of positive deviance in organizations, *Deviant Behavior*, 37 (11), 1288–1307.

Miceli, M.P., Near, J.P. and Dworkin, T.M. (2009). A word to the wise: How managers and policy-makers can encourage employees to report wrongdoing, *Journal of Business Ethics*, 86, 379–396.

Michel, P. (2008). Financial crimes: The constant challenge of seeking effective prevention solutions, *Journal of Financial Crime*, 15 (4), 383–397.

Miller, S. (2010). What makes a good internal affairs investigation? *Criminal Justice Ethics*, 29 (1), 29–40.

Mitchell, V.L. (2006). Knowledge integration and information technology project performance, *MIS Quarterly*, 30 (4), 919–939.

Montella, E.C. (2016). *Full Circle: A Memoir of Leaning In Too Far and the Journey Back*, Sanibel, FL: Triple M Press.

Morgan, M. and Nix, W. (2003). CPA perceptions of the marketability, career enhancements and quality of services of certified fraud examiners, *Southern Business and Economic Journal*, 3 (34), 31–50.

Moyes, G.D. and Baker, C.R. (2003). Auditor's beliefs about the fraud detection effectiveness of standard audit procedures, *Journal of Forensic Accounting*, 4, 199–216.

Mæland, M. (2016a). *Anmodning fra Stortingets kontroll- og konstitusjonskomité vedrørende DNB (Request from the Parliament's Control og Constitution Committee regarding DNB)*, brev datert 30. september fra Det kongelige nærings- og fiskeridepartement til Kontroll- og konstitusjonskomiteen på Stortinget (letter dated September 30 from the Royal Industry and Fishery Department to the Control and Constitution Committee in the Parliament).

Mæland, M. (2016b). *DNBs rolle i etableringen av selskaper på Seychellene (DNB's role in etablishing companies in the Seychelles)*, brev datert 4. november fra Det kongelige nærings- og fiskeridepartement til Kontroll- og konstitusjonskomiteen på Stortinget (letter dated November 4 from the Royal Industry and Fishery Department to the Control and Constitution Committee in the Parliament).

Møller, O. (2016). Kemperegning for Carl Holst-undersøgelse på vej (Large bill for Carl Holst investigation on its way), *TV Syd*, February 3.

Naylor, R.T. (2003). Towards a general theory of profit-driven crimes, *British Journal of Criminology*, 43, 81–101.

Nemeth, K.L. and Azzouzi, N. (2015). Redegørelse på vegne tidligere regionrådsformand Carl Holst i anledning af advokatundersøgelser gennemført af Kromann Reumert på vegne Region Syddanmark "Undersøgelse af hændelsesforløbet ved tilretningen og ændring af fakturatekst fra ekstern leverandør" (Statement on behalf of former regional governor Carl Holst in connection with legal investigation conducted by Kromann Reumert on behalf of the Region Syddanmark "Examination of the course of events during the adjustment and change of invoice text from external supplier"), issued by Nemeth & Sigetty, Frederiksgade, Copenhagen.

Nesti, L. (2014). The 2010 "Agreement on mutual enforcement of debarments decisions" and its impact for the fight against fraud and corruption in public procurement, *Journal of Public Procurement*, 14 (1), 62–95.

Niland, K. (2014). GM lawyers under federal criminal investigation for allegedly concealing ignition switch evidence, *RightingInjustice*, August 26, www.rightinginjustice.com/news/2014/08/26/gm-lawyers-under-federal-criminal-investigation-for-allegedly-concealing-ignition-switch-evidence/.

Nordea (2016). *Report on Investigation of Nordea Private Banking in Relation to Offshore Structures*, Nordea Group Compliance and Group Operational Risk, Stockholm, www.nordea.com, 12 pages.

NTB (2012a). SOS Rasisme ber om lukkede dører (SOS Racism ask for closed doors), October 14, page 9. Daily Norwegian newspaper *Aftenposten*.

NTB (2012b). Dømt til å betale tilbake statstilskudd (Convicted to pay back government grant), *Aftenposten*, October 18, page 13. Daily Norwegian newspaper Aftenposten.

NTB (2015a). Økokrim ber om seks års fengsel for Tromsdal (Økokrim asks for six years prison for Tromsdal), *Klassekampen*, March 2, www.klassekampen.no/article/20150320/NTBO/928007743.

NTB (2015b). Danmarks forsvarsminister går av (Danish defense minister resigns), *Dagens Næringsliv*, September 29.

O'Connor, T.R. (2005). Police deviance and ethics, 1: from *MegaLinks in Criminal Justice*, http://faculty.ncwc.edu/toconnor/205/205lect11.htm, downloaded February 19, 2009.

Olsen, A.B. (2007). *Økonomisk kriminalitet: avdekking, gransking og forebygging (Financial crime: detection, investigation and prevention)*, Oslo: Universitetsforlaget.

Oslo tingrett (2015). Case number 14-035631MED-OTIR/05, *Oslo tingrett* (Oslo district court), June 19.

Osterburg, J.W. and Ward, R.H. (2014). *Criminal Investigation: A Method for Reconstructing the Past*, 7th edition, Waltham, MA: Anderson Publishing.

Otusanya, O.J. (2012). An investigation of the financial criminal practices of the elite in developing countries: Evidence from Nigeria, *Journal of Financial Crime*, 19 (2), 175–206.

Øvrebø, T. (2004). Nyhetsproduksjon – kjønn og makt: En studie av endring i Dagsavisen 2000–2003 (News production – sex and power: A study of change in *Dagsavisen* 2000–2003), thesis for master's degree in Media Science, University of Oslo, Oslo.

Passas, N. (2007). Corruption in the procurement process/outsourcing government functions: Issues, case studies, implications, Report to the Institute for Fraud Prevention, shortened version by W. Black, www.theifp.org/researchgrants/procurement_final_edited.pdf, 33 pages.

Patrucco, A.S., Luzzini, D. and Ronchi, S. (2017). Research perspectives on public procurement: Content analysis of 14 years of publications in the Journal of Public Procurement, *Journal of Public Procurement*, 16 (2), 229–269.

Peltier-Rivest, D. (2009). An analysis of the victims of occupational fraud: A Canadian perspective, *Journal of Financial Crime*, 16 (1), 60–66.

Pennsylvania (1974). Report on the police corruption and the quality of law enforcement in Philadelphia, The Pennsylvania Crime Commission, March, www.ncjrs.gov/App/publications/abstract.aspx?ID=25640, 456 pages.

Petrocelli, M., Piquero, A.R. and Smith, MR. (2003). Conflict theory and racial profiling: An empirical analysis, *Journal of Criminal Justice*, 31, 1–11.

Pettersen, E., Nedkvitne, S. and Svendsen, R.H. (2015). Angrende Drevland dømt for underslag (Regretful Drevland convicted of embezzlement), *NRK*, March 10.

Pickett, K.H.S. and Pickett, J.M. (2002). *Financial Crime Investigation and Control*, New York: John Wiley & Sons.

Pillay, S. and Kluvers, R. (2014). An institutional theory perspective on corruption: The case of a developing democracy, *Financial Accountability & Management*, 30 (1), 95–119.

Piquero, N.L., Schoepfer, A. and Langton, L. (2010). Completely out of control or the desire to be in complete control? How low self-control and the desire for control relate to corporate offending, *Crime and Delinquency*, 56 (4), 627–647.

Piquero, N.L. (2012). The only thing we have to fear is fear itself: Investigating the relationship between fear of falling and white-collar crime, *Crime and Delinquency*, 58 (3), 362–379.

Piquero, N.L. and Benson, M.L. (2004). White-collar crime and criminal careers: Specifying a trajectory of punctuated situational offending, *Journal of Contemporary Criminal Justice*, 20, 148–165.

Police (2014). Etterretningsdoktrine for politiet (Intelligence doctrine for the police), Norwegian Police Directorate, Oslo.

Pontell, H.N., Black, W.K. and Geiss, G. (2014). Too big to fail, too powerful to jail? On the absence of criminal prosecutions after the 2008 financial meltdown, *Crime, Law and Social Change*, 61 (1), 1–13.

Powers, W., Troubh, R.S. and Winokur, H.S. (2002). Report of investigation by the Special Investigative Committee of the Board of Directors of Enron Corp., issued by Wilmer, Cutler & Pickering, February 1.

Pratt, T.C. and Cullen, F.T. (2005). Assessing macro-level predictors and theories of crime: A meta-analysis, *Crime & Justice*, 32, 373–450.
Punch, M. (2003). Rotten orchards. "Pestilence", police misconduct and system failure, *Policing and Society*, 13 (2) 171–196.
Puranam, P., Alexy, O. and Reitzig, M. (2014). What's "new" about new forms of organizing? *Academy of Management Review*, 39 (2), 162–180.
PwC (1991). Report on Sandstorm SA under section 41 of the Banking Act 1987, PricewaterhouseCoopers, http://file.wikileaks.info/leak/sandstorm-bcci-report-1881.pdf, 22 + 28 = 50 pages.
PwC (2014). Hadeland og Ringerike Bredbånd. Rapport – gransking (Hadeland and Ringerike Broadband. Report – investigation), PricewaterhouseCoopers, Oslo.
Reed, G.E. and Yeager, P.C. (1996). Organizational offending and neoclassical criminology: Challenging the reach of a general theory of crime, *Criminology*, 34 (3), 357–382.
Region Syddanmark (2015a). Sagsnr. 14/25585 Undersøgelser af interne forhold (Investigation of internal issues), www.regionsyddanmark.dk.
Region Syddanmark (2015b). Kommisorium for undersøkelse af sagsforløb vedr. tilretning og anonymisering af faktura (Mandate for investigation of case events regarding handling and anonymizing of invoice), www.regionsyddanmark.dk.
Reisig, M.D. and Holtfreter, K. (2013). Shopping fraud victimization among the elderly, *Journal of Financial Crime*, 20 (3), 324–337.
Rendal, S. and Westerby, T. (2010). Hvilke forventninger har revisor i forhold til brukere av finansiell informasjon når det gjelder revisors plikter til forebygging og avdekking av misligheter? (What expectations does the auditor have in relation to users of financial information concerning auditor responsibility for prevention and detection of misconduct?), MSc thesis, BI Norwegian Business School, Oslo.
Risa, E. (2017). Full etterforsking etter nye Dale-avhør (Full investigation after recent Dale interviews), *Stavanger Aftenblad*, August 15.
Risa, E., Aass, H.P., Nedrebø, R., Heimsvik, O. and Christensen, P. (2017a). Luftslottet (The castle in the air), *Stavanger Aftenblad*, Magasinet (Magazine), January 28, pages 1–21.
Risa, E., Aas, H.P. and Heimsvik, O. (2017b). Dale-ansatt reiste for over 400,000 kr (Dale employee travelled for more than 400,000 kroner), *Stavanger Aftenblad*, January 31, page 1 and pages 4–5.
Ritzau, A. (2016). Carl Holst genopstiller: Lokalformand går af i protest (Carl Holst runs again: Local chairman leaves in protest), *Børsen*, February 11.
Rogaland Revisjon (2015). Forvaltningsrevisjon/selskapskontroll av Dale Eiendomsutvikling AS (Public audit/company control of Dale Property Development Ltd), Rogaland fylkeskommune (Rogaland county), October, 82 pages.
Rostami, A., Melde, C. and Holgersson, S. (2015). The myth of success: The emergence and maintenance of a specialized gang unit in Stockholm, Sweden, *International Journal of Comparative and Applied Criminal Justice*, 39 (3), 199–217.
Ryan, K. (1994). Technicians and interpreters in moral crusades: The case of the drug courier profile, *Deviant Behavior*, 15 (3), 217–240.
Sampson, R.J., Raudenbush, S.W. and Earls, F. (1997). Neighborhoods and violent crime: A multilevel study of collective efficacy, *Science*, 277, 918–924.
Sari, Y.K., Shaari, Z.H. and Amar, A.B. (2017). Measurement development of customer patronage of petrol station with convenience store, *Global Business and Management Research: An International Journal*, 9 (1), 52–62.

Schneider, S. (2006). Privatizing economic crime enforcement: Exploring the role of private sector investigative agencies in combating money laundering, *Policing & Society*, 16 (3), 285–312.

Schneider, F. and Williams, C.C. (2013). *The Shadow Economy*, London: Institute of Economic Affairs.

Schoepfer, A. and Piquero, N.L. (2006). Exploring white-collar crime and the American dream: A partial test of institutional anomie theory, *Journal of Criminal Justice*, 34, 227–235.

SEC (2002). Report of investigation pursuant to section 21 (a) of the Securities Exchange Act of 1934: Motorola, Inc., U.S. Securities and Exchange Commission, www.sec.gov/litigation/investreport/34-46898.htm.

SEC (2013). Enforcement manual, Securities and Exchange Commission, Division of Enforcement, www.sec.gov/divisions/enforce/enforcementmanual.pdf, 141 pages.

Shadnam, M. and Lawrence, T.B. (2011). Understanding widespread misconduct in organizations: An institutional theory of moral collapse, *Business Ethics Quarterly*, 21 (3), 379–407.

Shen, W. (2003). The dynamics of the CEO–board relationship: An evolutionary perspective, *Academy of Management Review*, 28 (3), 466–476.

Short, J.L., Toffel, M.W. and Hugill, A.R. (2016). Monitoring global supply chains, *Strategic Management Journal*, 37 (9), 1878–1897.

Sidley (2010). Report of investigation regarding procurement practices at the office of the chief technology officer of the District of Columbia, Sidley Austin LLP, July 14 (draft), 60 pages, http://assets.bizjournals.com/cms_media/washington/pdf/Sidley%20Report.pdf.

Silverstone, H. and Sheetz, M. (2003). *Forensic Accounting and Fraud Investigation for Non-experts*. Hoboken, NJ: Wiley.

Silvola, N.M., Jonassen, T.H. and Grønneberg, A. (2014). Aschehoughs finansdirektør dømt for underslag (Aschehoug's finance director sentenced for embezzlement), *Dagbladet*, December 3.

Skjæveland, K. (2017). Kunnskapsløs prosjektstyring (Lacking knowledge in project monitoring), *Stavanger Aftenblad*, February 1, page 21.

Sjølie, H.P. (2008). Søppel og skrot (Garbage and trash), *Klassekampen*, May 29.

Slyke, S.V. and Bales, W.D. (2012). A contemporary study of the decision to incarcerate white-collar and street property offenders, *Punishment & Society*, 14 (2), 217–246.

Soltes, E. (2016). *Why They Do It: Inside the Mind of the White-Collar Criminal*, New York: Public Affairs Books.

Sonnier, B.M., Lassar, W.M. and Lassar, S.S. (2015). The influence of source credibility and attribution of blame on juror evaluation of liability of industry specialist auditors, *Journal of Forensic & Investigative Accounting*, 7 (1), 1–37.

Stadler, W.A. and Benson, M.L. (2012). Revisiting the guilty mind: The neutralization of white-collar crime, *Criminal Justice Review*, 37 (4), 494–511.

Stadler, W.A., Benson, M.L. and Cullen, E.T. (2013). Revisiting the special sensitivity hypothesis: The prison experience of white-collar inmates, *Justice Quarterly*, 30 (6), 1090–1114.

Steffensmeier, D. and Allan, E. (1996). Gender and crime: Toward a gendered theory of female offending, *Annual Review of Sociology*, 22, 459–487.

Stewart, N. and Nakamura, D. (2007). Two more D.C. tax workers removed, *Washington Post*, November 10.

Suddaby, R. (2014). Editor's comments: Why theory? *Academy of Management Review*, 39 (4), 407–411.

Sundström, M. and Radon, A. (2015). Utilizing the concept of convenience as a business opportunity in emerging markets, *Organizations and Markets in Emerging Economies*, 6 (2), 7–21.

Supernor, H. (2017). Community service and white-collar offenders: The characteristics of the sanction on factors determining its use among a sample of health-care offenders, *Journal of Financial Crime*, 24 (1), 148–156.

Sutherland, E.H. (1939). White-collar criminality, *American Sociological Review*, 5, 1–12.

Sutherland, E.H. (1949). *White-Collar Crime*, New York: Holt, Rinehart & Winston Publishing.

Sutherland, E.H. (1983). *White-Collar Crime – The Uncut Version*, New Haven, CT: Yale University Press.

Suurballe, M.H. (2017). Straffesag om lækage i Carl Holst-sagen er droppet (Criminal proceedings concerning the leakage in the Carl Holst case are dropped), *Danmarks Radio*, August 29.

Swart, J. and Kinnie, N. (2003). Sharing knowledge in knowledge-intensive firms, *Human Resource Management Journal*, 13 (2), 60–75.

Sykes, G.M. and Matza, D. (1957). Techniques of neutralization: A theory of delinquency, *American Sociological Review*, 22 (6), 664–670.

Szalma, J.L. and Hancock, P.A. (2013). A signal improvement to signal detection analysis: Fuzzy SDT on the ROCs, *Journal of Experimental Psychology: Human Perception and Performance*, 39 (6), 1741–1762.

Sørhus, T.S. and Wold, C. (2012). Statsbudsjettet kap. 254 post 70: Vedtak om krav om tilbakebetaling av tilskudd og reduksjon i beregningsgrunnlaget for tilskudd for 2013 og 2014 (Government budget chapter 254 item 70: Decision concerning requirement for back payment of subsidy and reduction in the computational foundation for support in 2013 and 2014), Vox, Nasjonalt fagorgan for kompetansepolitikk (National expert organ for competence polity), December 10.

Tanum, A.C. (2016a). DNB Luxembourg: Redegjørelse fra styret (DNB Luxembourg: Statement from the board), issued by DNB, Oslo, April 11.

Tanum, A.C. (2016b). DNB Luxembourg: Svar på departementets oppfølgingsspørsmål (DNB Luxembourg: Answers to the ministry's follow-up questions), issued by DNB, Oslo, September 16.

Telep, C.W. and Weisburd, D. (2012). What is known about the effectiveness of police practices in reducing crime and disorder? *Police Quarterly*, 15 (4), 331–357.

Tingstad, T. (2016). Styrene mangler mot, ikke kunnskap (Boards lack courage, not knowledge), *Dagens Næringsliv*, September 17, page 28.

Tjørholm, O. (2016). Det katolske medlemsjukset er fortsatt juks (Catholic membership cheating is still cheating), *Aftenposten*, December 5, pages 12–13.

Tonoyan, V., Strohmeyer, R., Habib, M. and Perlitz, M. (2010). Corruption and entrepreneurship: How formal and informal institutions shape small firm behavior in transition and mature market economies, *Entrepreneurship: Theory & Practice*, 34 (5), 803–831.

Trahan, A. (2011). Filling in the gaps in culture-based theories of organizational crime, *Journal of Theoretical and Philosophical Criminology*, 3 (1), 89–109.

Trahan, A., Marquart, J. and Mullings, J. (2005). Fraud and the American dream: Toward an understanding of fraud victimization, *Deviant Behavior*, 26 (6), 601–620.

Treadway, D.C., Adams, G.L., Ranft, A.L., and Ferris, G.R. (2009). A meso-level conceptualization of CEO celebrity effectiveness, *The Leadership Quarterly*, 40 (4), 554–570.

Trenskow, K. and Mosbek, J.L. (2015). *Region Syddanmark: Undersøgelse af hændelsesforløbet vedrørende tilretning og ændring af fakturatekst fra ekstern leverandør (Region Syddanmark: Investigation of events regarding handling and change of invoice text from external vendor)*, Kromann and Reumert, Copenhagen.

Uhl-Bien, M. and Carsten, M.K. (2007). Being ethical when the boss is not, *Organizational Dynamics*, 36 (2), 187–201.

UNODC (2006). The integrity and accountability of the police: Criminal justice assessment toolkit, United Nations Office of Drugs and Crime (UNODC), Vienna International Center, Vienna, Austria, www.unodc.org.

Vadera, A.K. and Aguilera, R.V. (2015). The evolution of vocabularies and its relation to investigation of white-collar crimes: An institutional work perspective, *Journal of Business Ethics*, 128, 21–38.

Vadera, A.K., Aguilera, R.V. and Caza, B.B. (2009). Making sense of whistleblowing's antecedents: Learning from research on identity and ethics programs, *Business Ethics Quarterly*, 19 (4), 553–586.

Valukas, A.R. (2010). In regard Lehman Brothers Holdings Inc. to United States Bankruptcy Court in Southern District of New York, issued by Jenner & Block, March 11, 239 pages, www.nysb.uscourts.gov/sites/default/files/opinions/188162_61_opinion.pdf.

Valukas, A.R. (2014). Report to board of directors of General Motors Company regarding ignition switch recalls, issued by Jenner & Block, May 29, 325 pages, www.beasleyallen.com/webfiles/valukas-report-on-gm-redacted.pdf.

Veiga, J., Lubatkin, M., Calori, R. and Very, P. (2000). Measuring organizational culture clashes: A two-nation post-hoc analysis of a cultural compatibility index, *Human Relations*, 53 (4), 539–57.

Vierdal (2012). Rapport til Stavanger tingrett: Lundegruppen konkursbo med datterselskaper og deleide selskaper (Report to Stavanger district court: Lunde group bankruptcy with subsidiaries and part-owned companies), Vierdal, Stavanger, Norway.

Walker, K. (2010). A systematic review of the corporate reputation literature: Definition, measurement, and theory, *Corporate Reputation Review*, 12 (4), 357–387.

Warhuus, C. (2011), Finding fraud: The role of auditing in the detection of white-collar crime, MSc thesis, BI Norwegian Business School, Oslo.

Warshaw, E.A. (2015). "Obviously, we're all oil industry": The criminogenic structure of the offshore oil industry, *Theoretical Criminology*, 19 (3), 376–395.

Weick, K. (1989). Theory construction as disciplined imagination, *Academy of Management Review*, 14 (4), 516–531.

Weick, K.E., Sutcliffe, K.M. and Obstfeld, D. (2005). Organizing and the process of sensemaking, *Organization Science*, 16 (4), 409–421.

Wells, J.T. (2003). The fraud examiners, *Journal of Accountancy*, October, 76–80.

Wells, J.T. (2007). *Fraud Casebook: Lessons from the Bad Side of Business*, Hoboken, NJ: Wiley & Sons.

Welsh, D.T., Oronez, L.D., Snyder, D.G. and Christian, M.S. (2014). The slippery slope: How small ethical transgressions pave the way for larger future transgressions, *Journal of Applied Psychology*, 100 (1), 114–127.

Welter, F., Baker, T., Audretsch, D.B. and Gartner, W.B. (2017). Everyday entrepreneurship: A call for entrepreneurship research to embrace entrepreneurial diversity, *Entrepreneurship: Theory and Practice*, 41 (3), 323–347.

Wensink, W. and Vet, J.M. (2013). Identifying and reducing corruption in public procurement in the EU, https://ec.europa.eu/anti-fraud/sites/antifraud/files/docs/body/identifying_reducing_corruption_in_public_procurment_en.pdf

Wickens, T.D. (2001). *Elementary Signal Detection Theory*, New York: Oxford University Press.

Wiersholm (2012). Granskingsrapport til styret i Unibuss (Report of investigation to the board at Unibuss), Wiersholm, Oslo.

Wijnen, P. (2017). Police Immigration Unit downsizes by 60–80 persons, *Norway Today*, posted May 4.

Wikborg, M.I. and Stensland, K.E. (2016). DNB Luxembourg: redegjørelse for styret – oppfølgingsspørsmål (DNB Luxembourg: Statement from the Board – Follow-up questions), Det kongelige nærings- og fiskeridepartement (The Royal Industry and Fishery Department), Oslo, April 12.

Wilberg, E. and Gottschalk, P. (2014). Media role in white-collar crime detection in Norway, *Journal of International Doctoral Research*, 3 (1), 105–125.

Wildman, J.L., Salas, E. and Scott, C.P.R. (2014). Measuring cognition in teams: A cross-domain review, *Human Factors*, 56 (5), 911–941.

Williams, C.C. (2006). *The Hidden Enterprise Culture: Entrepreneurship in the Underground Economy*, Cheltenham, UK: Edward Elgar Publishing.

Williams, H.E. (2006). *Investigating White-Collar Crime*, Springfield, IL: Charles C. Thomas.

Williams, J.W. (2005). Governability matters: The private policing of economic crime and the challenge of democratic governance, *Policing & Society*, 15 (2), 187–211.

Williams, J.W. (2008). The lessons of Enron: Media accounts, corporate crimes, and financial markets, *Theoretical Criminology*, 12 (4), 471–499.

Williams, J.W. (2014). The private eyes of corporate culture: The forensic accounting and corporate investigation industry and the production of corporate financial security, in Walby, K. and Lippert, R.K. (editors), *Corporate Security in the 21st Century: Theory and Practice in International Perspective*, Basingstoke, UK: Palgrave Macmillan, 56–77.

Wilmer and PwC (2003). Report of investigation by the special investigative committee of the Board of Directors of WorldCom Inc., Wilmer, Cutler & Pickering (Counsel) and PricewaterhouseCoopers LLP (Accounting Advisors), www.sec.gov/Archives/edgar/data/723527/000093176303001862/dex991.htm, downloaded February 8, 2015, 345 pages.

WilmerHale and PwC (2008). Report of investigation submitted by the Council of the District of Columbia, Wilmer Cutler Pickering Hale and Dorr LLP (Counsel) and PricewaterhouseCoopers LLP (Forensic Accounting Advisors), www.dcwatch.com/govern/otr081215.pdf, downloaded February 8, 2015, 126 pages.

Wood, J. and Alleyne, E. (2010). Street gang theory and research: Where are we now and where do we go from here? *Aggression and Violent Behavior*, 15, 100–111.

Wright, A. (2006). *Organised Crime*, Cullompton, UK: Willan Publishing.

Zagorin, P. (2001). Francis Bacon's concept of objectivity and the idols of the mind, *British Journal of Historical Science*, 34 (4), 379–393.

Zahra, S.A., Priem, R.L. and Rasheed, A.A. (2007). Understanding the causes and effects of top management fraud, *Organizational Dynamics*, 36 (2), 122–139.

Zipparo, L. (1999). Factors which deter public officials from reporting corruption, *Crime, Law & Social Change*, 30 (3), 273–287.

# INDEX

Note: Indicators in in **bold** refer to tables.

Aas, P. et al. 140, 141, 143
abductive reasoning 86
Acar, Y. (OCTO) 36–7, 77, 170–2
accountability 10, 21, 27, 34, 139; at General Motors 187
Adler, P.S. 56
Advanced Integral Technologies Corporation (AITC) 36–7
*Aftenposten* 124
agency theory 29, 51, 55, 120, 140; and blaming 139; and CEOs 144; DNB bank case 124, 129–30
Agnew, R. 32, 50, 57, 58
Aguilera, R.V. 51, 55, 131
Albrecht, C.C. et al. 65, 67
Alderson, J. (whistleblower) 76
Allan, E. 20
Alleyne, E. 24, 25
American dream theory 50
Anchor Glass Container Corporation 32
Anders, S.B. 90
Andersen, J.J. 9, 124
Andersen, Ø. 131
anti-money laundering (AML) 127, 147
Arjoon, S. 24, 57, 58
Arnulf, J.K. 2
Aschehoug Publishing **28**, 29
Ashfort, B.E. 56
Ashkanasy, N.M. 19, 22

Ask, K. 160, 161, 162, 163
Association of Certified Financial Crime Specialists (ACFCS) 88–90
Association of Certified Fraud Examiners (ACFE) 90–2; crime estimates 46–7
attribution theory 54, 149, 191
Atwater, K. 75, 77, 131, 132
auditing 64–5, 84, 108; efficacy 65, 196; lack of alertness 72–4, 109; responsibility 66; role and expectations 67; and skepticism 67, 73
Australia 34
Azzouzi, N. 152–8

backdating 129, 146–7, 149, 150
Baird, J.E. 53
Baker, C.R. 65, 67
Bales, W.D. 139
bank fraud 26, 39, 41, 112–3; and neutralization 43, **44**; and whistleblowing 75–6
Bank of Credit and Commerce International (BCCI) 197–8
Bank of England 197–8
Barney, J.B. 52
Barra, M. (General Motors) 149, 185, 190
BDO **98**, **99**, **102**, **103**; Betanien Foundation 41, 106–7; Coatesville Area School District 192–3
Beasley, M.S. 64

behavioral willingness (deviance) 20, 25, **28**, 30, 45, 48, 49, 94–5, **97**, 115; and criminal entrepreneurship 27–8; and cultural transmission 30; and detection 31, 32; different association 6–7, 25, 52, 107, 182; and empathy 32; increasing 56–9; and neutralization techniques 46, 109, 112, 119, 168; organizational dynamics 26, 27; and organizational opportunity 140; payback intention 110; for personal enrichment 134, 135; and personality disorders 31–2; and self-control 30–1, 53, 109, 113; sense of entitlement 184; theories 52–3; win-win situations 108
Belfort, Jordan 199–201
Bendahan, S. et al. 122
Bendiktsson, M.O. 76
Bennet, P.R. (Refco Inc.) 21
Benson, M.L. 2, 5, 7–8, 11, 14, 45, 49, 51, 55, 57, 58, 115, 122, 168
Berglihn, H. 29
Berkley Research Group 160, 196
Berry, L.L. et al. 19, 140
Betanien Foundation 28, 29, 41, **97**, 106–7
Bjørkelo, B. et al. 74, 75, 76, 78, 131, 132
Bjørndal, B. 44
blame game theory 54, 138–9, 148–9; and decision-making 161; DNB bank case 127; General Motors case 191–2; Lehman Brothers case 180; at Motorola Sales 194; Nordea Bank case 148–9; Norwegian police case 131, 139–40; self-blame 149
Blickle, G. 2, 17, 31, 57
Blomhoff, A. (Betanien) 28, 29, 41, **97**, 106–7
Boba, R.L. 26
Bodner, G.E. 1, 68
Bond, G.D. 72
Bosse, D.A. 29, 124, 129
Breen, K.M. 160, 182–4
bribery *see* corruption
Brightman, H.J. 57
Brodahl, N. 74
Brody, R.G. 32
Brooks, G. 3, 81, 82, 86, 93, 123, 124, 131, 138, 145, 161
Brorson, L. (Hadeland Broadband) **28**, 29, **97**, 108–9
Brynhildsen, R. (Woldsdal Public Relations) 43, 45
Buanes, F. 42
Bucy, P.H. et al. 55, 57
Button, M. 3, 81, 82, 86, 93, 123, 124, 131, 138, 145, 161

Callan, E.M. (Lehman Brothers) 11, 180–1
Campbell, F. 63
Canada: occupational crime 34–5; victims 36
Carson, D. 81, 94
Carsten, M.K. 23
cartels 10
Ceccato, V. 122
CEOs 23, 25, 28, 48, 76, **97**, **98**, **99**, **101**, 120, 196; and corruption 114; and embezzlement 41, 106–7; and goal orientation 21, 121; and leadership 111; mundane offenders and serious predators 122; narcissism 121–2; and power 122; organizational opportunity 140–4; tipping points **164**, **165**
Certified Financial Crime Specialists (CFCS) 88–90
certified public accountants (CPAs) 66
Chang, J.J. et al. 57
Chattopadhyay, P. et al. 21
Cheney, D. 76
Chokshi, N. 47
Chrisman, J.J. et al. 55
Coatesville Area School District (CASD) 192–4
Coburn, N.F. 86
Cohen, L.E. 26, 52
collective efficacy 31
Collier, J.E. 3, 140
Comey, J.B. 53, 58
Como, R. (Coatesville Area School District) 193–4
concealment 83; and increasing opportunity 54–8; in occupational crime 45
confidentiality 88, 96, 166; DNB case 127
consumer fraud 35
content analysis 3, 15, 117; and decision-making 160, 161, 162
contract theory 52
convenience theory 2–3, 5, 8, 18, 45–6, 179, 181; CEOs 48, 120–2; convenience orientation 18–9, 48; and conviction 17; and decision-making 161; dimensions 3; implications 94–5; and misconduct 128–9; occupational crime 32–45; perceived convenience 19; and police corruption 168–9; report findings 97; research propositions 54–9; theory development 19–20; and wealth secrecy 148; *see also* behavioral willingness; financial motive; organizational opportunity

conviction 96, **99**, 108–9; and convenience theory 17, 115; feeling of innocence and neutralization 11; lack of prosecution 181, 182; sensitivity testing 14–5; special resilience hypothesis 15–6; special sensitivity hypothesis 11–3, 16; and victimization 13, 14
core competences theory 52
corporate crime 7, 10, 41, 118; DNB bank 123–30; *see also* organizational dynamics; organizational opportunity
corporation, as offender 7
corruption 83; by CEOs 122; and corporate crime 10; and criminal entrepreneurship 27; and occupational crime 36–7, **97**, 114–5; police 168–9; and whistleblowing 75–6, 133
court documents 38, 40, 116–7, 119
Cowen, A.P. et al. 121
Craig, J.M. 30, 32
Cullen, F.T. 14, 50, 52, 57, 58
cultural transmission 30
Cutler, D. (fraud examiner) 90

*Dagbladet* 116
Dahle, D.Y. 44
Dale Property Development 140–4
data/information collection 38–9, 81, 83–4, 87, 135–6, 185, 190
Dawson, G.S. et al. 129
Dean, G. et al. 160
Dearden, T.E. 2, 8–9, 26
deception 72
decision-making 94, 137, 150, 171–2, 181, 187; and agency theory 51; by CEOs 120, 122, 140; and convenience theory 18, 48, 128; and knowledge 83, 165; and organizational structure 186; recall 190; on report disclosure 162–3; and signal detection theory 69, 71, 72; tipping points 159–61
Deloitte 98, 99, 100, 101, 102, 103, 104, 105; Hadeland Broadband case 108
Denmark (Carl Høst case) 150–9
Desai, S.D. 20
detection risk 31, 49; *see also* signal detection
deterrence 26, 53, 57, 85
developing countries 35
deviance *see* behavioral willingness
Dhami, M.K. 11, 14
differential association 6–7, 25, 52; at Lehman Brothers 182

disclosure 3, 55, 91; cases 97–106; and decision-making 162–3; by media 108; prohibited 194; *see also* whistleblowing
Distriktsrevisjonen **101**, **105**, 111–2
DNB bank, Panama Papers 123–5; blame game hypothesis 127–8, 138–9; convenience analysis 128–9; information flow 128; internal investigation 125–6; investigation process 126–7; principal-agent analysis 129–30; reputation damage 128
Donk, D.P. 186
double-bind leadership **97**, 111–2
Dowler, K. 31
Drage, K. 67
*Drammen tingrett* 41
Drevland, O.A. (embezzler) 42–3
Dugstad, L. 137
Dupont, B. 85
Durkheim, É. 32

Earl, M. 165
Ebbers, B. (WorldCom) 175–7
Eberly, M.B. 54
economic dimension *see* financial motive
Eddleston, K.A. 27
Edelbacher, M. et al. 33, 42
Eidsvig, Bishop B. (Oslo Catholic diocese) 25, 118
Einarsen, S. 53
Eisenhardt, K.M. 51, 120
Ekeberg, E. 146, 148
email searching 38, 83, 123, 126, 153, 159, 185
embezzlement: in criminal entrepreneurship 27, 28–9; impact of empathy 32; investigations 37–40, 170–2; occupational crime 35, 37–40, **97**, 106–9; signal detection 72–3; victims 41, 42–3
empathy 32
Engdahl, O. 17, 53
Enron Corporation 76, 166–8
entrepreneurship 27, 28; and deviance 27–8; and the shadow economy 28; theory 52
ethics: breaches, and whistleblowing 77; and organizational dynamics 23, 24; slippery slope theory 53

Fahsing, I.A. 86, 160, 161, 162, 163
family firms 27, 29; victims 41–2
Fanelli, A. 48, 121, 144
Fargher, N. 95
Farquhar, J.D. 3, 140
Farrell, B.R. 66

Fastow, A. (Enron Corporation) 166–8
fear of falling 20, 22, 49, 50, 110, 168
Federal Bureau of Investigation (FBI) 36, 40, 46, 84, 201
Fehr, R. et al. 78, 133
Felson, M. 26, 52
financial motive 4, 19, 45, 48–9, 109; American dream 50; crime forces theory 50; expansion desire 107; fear of falling 20, 22, 49, 50, 110, 168, 169; goal orientation 21, 49; greed **28**, 45, **97**, 106, 113, 114, 167, 177; increasing opportunities 55–8; power **97**, 111, 118–9, 122; profit-driven 50, 51, 57; social concerns 50; strain 49–50, 57
Flynn, K. 34
forensic accounting 37, 81, 85, 88, 91, **98, 100**, 193
Fosse, S.S. 29
Frantzen, B.E. (SOS Racism) 116, 117
Friedrichs, D.O. 33, 34
Furuheim Housing Foundation **99, 103**, 107–8, **164**
Füss, R. 2, 57

Galvin, B.M. et al. 48, 56, 121–2
Garrison, J.A. (whistleblower) 76–7
Gausi, K. 107–8
Gee, J. 81, 82, 123, 131
gender 9, 36
General Motors 184–5; blame theory 191–2; internal investigation 185–91
Gerbeshi, I. (Wara Painting Service) 41–2
Gill, M. 2, 69, 88, 93, 123
Gilley, K.M. 52
Glasø, L. 53
goal orientation 10, 49, 56, 121; of CEOs 21, 121; and internal investigations 81, 87, 92; and strain 50
Goldstraw-White, J. 49, 57
Golladay, K.A. 35
Gomulya, D. 69
Gottfredson, M. 46, 49, 53, 57, 58, 184
Gottschalk, P. 2, 3, 10, 11, 13, 17, 18, 33, 45, 48, 49, 68, 82, 94, 96, 97, 115, 116, 123, 124, 127, 128, 129, 131, 134, 138, 149, 160, 161, 162, 166, 178, 179
grant fraud 117, **165**, 195
greed **28**, 45, 57, **97**, 106, 113, 114, 177
Green, B.A. 86, 131
Green, J. 185

Greenhouse, B. (whistleblower) 76
Groff, E.R. 58
guardianship 13, 26, 31, 52
Guberman, P.A. 160, 182–4

Haakaas, E. 41, 42
*Hadeland* 108
Hadeland Broadband **28**, 29, 73, **97**, 108–9, **164**
Haines, F. 55
Hald 108
Hambrick, D.C. et al. 144
Hamilton, S. 57
Hancock, P.A. 1, 68, 71–2
Hansen, L.L. 33, 45, 56, 57
Hart, J. 2, 69, 88, 93, 123
Haverstick, M.H. et al. 192–3
Healy, P. 66
Heath, J. 33, 56
Hecker, A. 2, 57
Heilbrunn, S. 23
Helsingeng, A. 41
Henriksen, I. (Romerike Water Supply) **97**, 111–2
Hestnes, M. 72–3
Higgins, E.T. 3, 140
Hirschi, T. 46, 49, 53, 57, 58, 184
Hjort (law firm) 125–30
Hoffmann, J.P. 24, 25
Hofstede, G. et al. 186
Holler, K.R. 159
Holst, C. (Southern Denmark): case description 151–2; defense 154–5; information retrieval 152–3; investigation consequences 158–9; investigation process 153–8
Holtfreter, K. 34, 35, 36, 47
Høyesterett 43
Huff, M.J. 1, 68
Huff, R. et al. 47
Hultgren, G. 44
Hyman, H.F. (whistleblower) 76–7
hypothesis testing 86

identity theft 35–6
Imran, M.K. et al. 165
informal economy *see* shadow economy
innocence, self-perception 11
institutional collapse 23, 25, 51
insurance sector 34, 84, 87
investment fraud 36, 75, 88, 167
ISA 200 73
Itzkovich, Y. 23
Iver, N. 67

Jenner & Block 184, 185
Johansen, P.O. 52
Johnsen, G.J. 141
Johnson, G.G. 66
Johnson, R.A. 74, 132
Johnson, S.D. 58
Jones, P. 66
Jones, S. 191, 192
Jonnergård, K. 49, 121, 168
journalists *see* media
Judge, T.A. et al. 52

Kamerdze, S. et al. 57
Kang, E. 6, 10, 21, 27, 28, 32, 33, 34, 47
Kempa, M. 34, 36
Kennedy, D.B. 90
Kerik, B.B. 11, 15–6
Kessler, R. 84
Khanna, V. et al. 120
Kidwell, R.E. 27
Kim, W.C. 161
Kimes, S.E. 3, 140
Kinnie, N. 24
Kleppe, M.K. 44
Kluvers, R. 23, 51
knowledge 19, 48, 51, 81; categories 83; and decision-making 163, 165; and lack of communication 187–8
Kommunerevisjonen **100**, **102**, **104**, **105**, 113
Kouchaki, M. 20
KPMG **99**, **101**, **103**, **104**, 134–9
Kramer, D.J. 82
Krippendorff, K. 15, 117, 162
Kristensen, M.F. 156, 157, 158
Kromann & Reumert 150–3, 157
Kwon, S.W. 56

Lampe, K. 52
Langton, L. 49, 58
Larsen, K.G. (SOS Racism) 116–20
Laursen, M.T. 153
law enforcement 84; consequences 162; efficacy 31; privatization **98–102**, 145, 150
Lawrence, T.B. 23, 51
Lay, K. (Enron Corporation) 166–8
leadership 135–6; destructive 56; double-bind **97**, 111–2; and obedience theory 23, 53
Leap, T.L. 20, 23
Leasure, P. 2, 7, 8, 10, 26, 35
Lee, F. 54, 127, 139, 149, 161, 179
Lee, G. 95

legal services: DNB bank scandal 125–9; Host case 150–9; and integrity 190; lack, in the GM case 189; Lunde Group case 110; Nordea Bank scandal 144–50
Lehman Brothers 56, 178–82, 184
Leite, H. (Unibuss) **97**, 114–5
Lemieux, V. 52
Leonard, W.N. 50
Leonard-Barton, D. 52
Lewis, C. et al. 123
Li, S. 55
Liang, L.H. et al. 31
Lissack, M. (whistleblower) 75–6
Liu, G. 81
Liu, X.L. 1, 68
LJM Cayman 167–8
Logan, M.W. 12, 14, 15
Lokanan, M.E. 36
Lomas, P. 82
Lord, N. 122
loyalty: and deviance 119; and social dominance 52; and whistleblowing 77–8, 133, 135–6
Lunde, J. (Lunde Group) **97**, **100**, 109–10
Luo, Y. 52
Luxembourg 147, 148; DNB Luxembourg 125–30

Machen, M.J. 33, 91, 123
Mæland, M. 125, 129
Mai, H.T.X. 18, 48, 140
Mann, K. et al. 12, 13
Mannheimer Swartling **100**, **104**, 145, 146–50
Marxism 54
Matza, D. 11, 24, 46, 49, 54, 57, 58, 119, 184
Mauborgne, R. 161
McClelland, P.L. et al. 15, 117, 162
McElwee, G. 28
McInish, T.H. et al. 45
McIver, D. et al. 163, 165
media / journalists 60–1; and disclosure 108, 115–7, 124–5, 140, 150–1; news organizations 63–4; signal alertness 70; specialized *vs.* regular 62–3
Meerts, C. 85, 86
Meldalen, S.G. 44
Mertens, W. et al. 30
Miceli, M.P. et al. 77
Michel, P. 55, 121
Micklethwait, A. 57
Miller, S. 131
Misangyi, V.F. 48, 121, 144

misappropriation of funds 23, 35, **97**; Furheim Housing Foundation 107–8; Save the Children 195–6
Mishina, Y. 69
Mitchell, V.L. 188
Møller, O. 153
Molloy, E. 186
Montella, E.C. 11, 180
Morgan, M. 90
Morgan Stanley 26
Mosbek, J.L. 151, 152–8
Mossack Fonseca 124, 146
Motorola Sales 194
Moyes, G.D. 65, 67
mundane offenders 122
Murud, F. (School Buildings) **97**, 112–4

Nakamura, D. 37
narcissism 56, 121–2
National Future Association (NFA) 196
National Police Immigration Unit (Norway) 131, 133–40
National Whistleblowers Center (NWC) 76
National White Crime Collar Center 47
Naylor, R.T. 51, 121
negative life events 32, 53
negative task-related words 1, 68
Nemeth, K.L. 152–8
network theory 52
neutralization techniques 24–5, 54, 57, 58, 168; and conviction 11; dilemmas 119; in occupational crime 43, **44**, 46, 109; in religious organizations 24–5; sense of entitlement 184
Niland, K. 192
Nix, W. 90
Nordea Bank 129, 144–6; blame game theory 148–9; internal investigation 146–8; limits of the investigation 149–50
Norway 47; auditing 66–7, 72–3; certified fraud examiners 92; corporate crime 123–30; Dale Property Development case 140–4; decision-making, tipping points 159–65; DNB bank case 123–30; financial crime in 46; investigating bureaus 44, 84; investigation reports 98–122; occupational crime 40–5; Police Immigration Unit 130–4; sources of detection 60, 63, 68, 70

obedience theory 23, 53
occupational crime 9–10, 32–3, 47; characteristics 33–4; and concealment 45; corruption 36–7, 114–5; and deviance 27; and embezzlement 35, 37–40, 106–9, 170–2; and neutralization 43, **44**, 46; offenders 36–40; type of harm 34–5; victims 35–6, 40–5
O'Connor, T.R. 56
offence/offender-based perspective 7–9
Office of the Chief Technology Officer (OCTO) 36, 170–2
Økokrim **44**, 84; DNB bank case 129
Olsen, A.B. 67, 140
Olsen, S.O. 18, 48
Olstad, T. 67
opportunity *see* organizational opportunity
organizational culture 23; at General Motors 186–7
organizational dynamics: differential association 25; ethics 23; institutional collapse 23; negative 25; neutralization theory 24–5; slippery slope theory 24
organizational opportunity 8, 22, 45, 48, 49, 94, **97**, 121; agency theory 51; contract theory 52; core competences theory 52; double-bind leadership 111–2; dynamics 22, 23–5; economic and behavioral dimension impact 20; and entrepreneurship 27–30, 52; exclusive responsibility/control 28, **97**, 106, 109, 177; institutional theory 51; and management control 26–7; manipulation 168; and misconduct 140–4; network theory 52; and occupational crime 37, 106, 108, 110; outsourcing theory 52; partnership theory 51–2; position in the company 108, 119; procurement of goods and services 113; resource mobilization theory 52; routine activity theory 26, 52; social dominance theory 52; tax fraud 37–40, 172–4
Oslo tingrett 43
Osterburg, J.W. 81, 145
Otusanya, O.J. 35
outsourcing theory 52
Ouyang, M. 55
Øvrebø, T. 63

Padakhep Manabik Unnayan Kendra (PMUK) 195–6
Panama Papers: DNB bank **98**, 123–30; Nordea Bank **100**, 144–50
panic, moral 21
partnership theory 51–2
Passas, N. 58
Patrucco, A.S. et al. 15, 117, 162
Peltier-Rivest, D. 34, 35, 36

Pennsylvania Crime Commission 168–9
perceptual sensitivity 1, 2, 68, 71, 199
Peregrine Financial Group 196
Perri, F.S. 32, 57
personality disorders 31–2
Petrocelli, M. et al. 54, 58
Pettersen, E. 43
Philadephia Police Department 168–9
Phillips, R.A. 29, 124, 129
Pickett, J.M. 55
Pickett, K.H.S. 55
Pillay, S. 23, 51
Piquero, N.L. 2, 5, 20, 30, 49, 50, 57, 58, 168
Plungis, J. 185
Podgor, E. 86, 131
police investigation 2, **60**, 62, 96, 109, 116, 141, 156; competence 68; detective decision-making 159–60; limits 162; performance 31; *vs.* private 92–4; on public water works 111; signal detection 70; of tax evasion 41
Pontell, H.N. et al. 5, 19, 49, 129, 139, 178–9, 182
power 9, **97**, 111, 118–9; and CEO crime 122; and decision-making 186; and organizational opportunity 94; political 179
Powers, W. et al. 160, 166, 167
Pratt, T.C. 50, 52, 57, 58, 192
predatory crime 26, 51, 121, 122
Price Waterhouse Coopers (PWC): and embezzlement 29, 109, 176; Sandstorm case 197–8; and tax fraud 37–40, 173, 175
prison sentences *see* conviction
private investigation 1, 39; certified examiners 90–2; challenges 83–4; competence 68–9, 199; confidence in knowledge 81–2; definition 87–8; external 84; information collection 82–3, 94; internal 80–1, 146–8; limits 145, 149–50; Nordea bank 144–50; organizations 84; *vs.* police 92–4; reasons for 85–7; reliability of sources 78; reports, key issues 98–106; specialists (ACFCS) 88–90
profit-driven crime 50, 51, 57, 121
psychopathy 31
Punch, M. 56

Quorum Health Services 76

Radon, A. 3, 17, 18, 48, 140
Rasheed, A. 52
rational choice theory 24, 52, 57

Refco Inc. 21
regional public management (Holst case) 150–9
Reisig, M.D. 35
religious organizations: embezzlement 28, 41, **97**, 106–7; neutralization theory 24–5
Ren, H. 81
Rendal, S. 67
reports 3–4
reputational damage 12, 85, **98**, 162; DNB bank case 127, 128
resilience 10, 11, 15–6, 17
resource mobilization theory 52
retaliation 94; fear 186; and whistleblowing 75, 76, 77, 78, 132
Richards, R.E. 33, 91, 123
Risa, E. et al. 140–1, 142–3
Ritzau, A. 158
Robinson, R.J. 54, 127, 139, 149, 161, 179
Romerike Water Supply 111–2
Røn, J. 159
Rostami, A. et al. 23
routine activity theory 26, 52
Rowley, J. 3, 140
Rudesill, C.L. 66
rule-based management 121
Rundmo, T. 33
Ryan, K. 27

Samociuk, M. 67
Sampson, R.J. et al. 31
Sandstorm 197–8
Sari, Y.K. et al. 18, 140
SAS No. 82 66
SAS No. 99 65
Save the Children USA (SCUSA) 195–6
Schatvet, M. (Aschehoug) **28**, 29
Schneider, F. 28, 42, 47
Schneider, S. 3, 80, 123, 131, 138, 145
Schoepfer, A. 50, 58
School Buildings **97**, 112–4
Schütte, N. 31
Scotland 63
Securities and Exchange Commission (SEC) 88, 177, 194
self-control 26, 46, 58; and crime victims 35, 36; and empathy 32; and willingness 30–1, 53, 57, 109, 184
self-interest 8, 20, 129
self-reports 69; by prison inmates 14–5; in the UK 89
Shadnam, M. 23, 51
shadow economy 28, 33, 42, 46–7
Sheetz, M. 65, 67

Shen, W. 48, 121, 144
shopping fraud 35
Sidley 36–7, 77, 170–2
signal detection 1, 199; auditing 64–7; competence 2, 68, 156; and deception 72; fuzzy 72; lack 72–4; pattern recognition 69–70; perceptual sensitivity 1, 2, 68; performance evaluation 71; reliance 69; screening theory 69; source reliability levels 78–9; susceptibility 69; threshold level 68
Silverstone, H. 65, 67
Silvolva, N.M. et al. 29
Simpson, S.S. 8, 45, 49, 51, 55, 57, 58, 168
Skilling, J. (Enron Corporation) 166–8
Skjæveland, K. 142
slippery slope theory 22, 24, 25, 53; at Lehman Brothers 182
Slyke, S.V. 139
Smith, C. 115, 116
Smith, R. 28
social conflict theory 54
social disorganization 7, 23–4, 25, 133–4
social dominance theory 52
Soltes, E. 30
Sonnier, B.M. et al. 127, 149, 191
SOS Racism 115–9
Sparks, R. 31
special resilience hypothesis 10, 11, 15–6, 17
special sensitivity hypothesis 10, 11–5, 16
Staddeland, K.R. (Ugland Shipping) 28, 29
Stadler, W.A. et al. 5, 11, 12, 13, 14
Steffensmeier, D. 20
Stewart, N. 37
strain 45, 49–50, 57
stress 15, 17, 20, 34, 57, 58, 138, 161
subsidy fraud 25, 83, **98**; SOS Racism 115–9
Suddaby, R. 19
suicide 32
*Sunday Times* 197
Sundström, M. 3, 17, 18, 48, 140
Supernor, H. 9, 124
Sushil Bansal 36–7, 170–1
Sutherland, E.H. 2, 3, 5, 6–7, 8, 19, 34, 49, 52, 56, 58, 179, 182
Suurballe, M.H. 159
Swart, J. 24
Sweden (Nordea Bank) 129, 144–50
Sykes, G.M. 11, 24, 46, 49, 54, 57, 58, 119, 184

System of Accounting and Reporting (SOAR) 38–9
Szalma, J.L. 1, 68, 71–2

tax fraud 9, **97**; investigations 37–40, 109–10, 172–5; signal alertness 74; victims 42–3
Tcherni-Buzzeo, M. 3, 49, 82, 96, 97, 162, 166
team cognition 72
Telep, C.W. 31, 49
Thosuwanchot, N. 6, 10, 21, 27, 28, 32, 33, 34, 47
threat 20–1, 45, 49, 55, 57, 58, 59, 167, 182
Tingstad, T. 144
tipping points 159–65
Tjørholm, O. 25, 118
Tonoyan, V. et al. 27
Treadway, D.C. et al. 120
Trenskow, K. 151, 152–8
Tromsdal, C. (bank fraud) 43–4

Ugland Shipping **28**, 29
Uhl-Bien, M. 23
undercover questioning 93
underground economy *see* shadow economy
Unibuss **97**, **102**, 114–5, **165**
United Kingdom: self-reports 89; whistleblowing 137–8
United States 47; certified fraud examiners 90–1; Chief Technology Officers 36–7, 170–2; Coatesville Area School District 192–4; Enron Corporation 166–8; General Motors 184–92; Lehman Brothers 178–82; Motorola Sales 194; Peregrine Financial Group 196; Philadelphia Police Department 168–9; Save the Children 195–6; tax fraud 37–40, 172–5; University of Texas 182–4; whistleblowing 75–7, 138; WorldCom Corporation 175–7
University of New Haven 90
University of Texas (UTSW center) 182–4

Vadera, A.K. 51, 55, 74, 75, 131, 132
Valland, G. 42
value-based management 121
Valukas, A.R. 56, 82, 149, 160, 178–82, 184–5, 188, 190–2
Veiga, J. et al. 186
Vet, J.M. 77, 133

victims 20, 33, 47, **60**, 62; banks 43; customers 42–3; in double-bind leadership 111–2; employers 41; fear of reputational damage 85; identity theft 35–6; lack 83; prison inmates 13, 14; shareholders 32, 43–5; of shopping fraud 35; tax revenue 41–2; type and extent of harm 34, 41
Vierdal 110

Walker, K. 188
Walle, L. (Furuheim Housing Foundation) **97**, 107–8
Walters, H. (District of Columbia) 37–40, 172–4
Wara Painting Service 41
war crimes 7
Ward, R.H. 81, 145
Warhuus, C. 64, 66
Wasendorf, R. (Peregrine Financial Group) 196
Watkins, S. (whistleblower) 76
Weber, M.G. 50
Weick, K. 20
Weisburd, D. 31, 49
Wells, J.T. 88, 90, 123
Wells Fargo 26
Welsh, D.T. et al. 24, 53, 57, 58
Welter, F. 27
Wensink, W. 77, 133
Westerby, T. 67
whistleblowing 1, 29, 41, 106, 107; definition 74–5, 132–3; implications 95; and loyalty 77–8, 133; Norwegian scandals 131, 133–40, 146; protection 137–8; reliability 78; reporting to media 62; and retaliation 75, 76, 77, 78, 132
white-collar crime 2, 47; attributes 5–6; behavioral willingness 30–2; business crime 10; conviction 10–7; differential association theory 6–7; at Enron 166–8; and entrepreneurship 27–30; estimation of magnitude 46–7; gender perspectives 9; and occupational crime 9–10; offence/offender-based perspective 7–9; as routine activity 26, 52; source of detection 60–77; *see also* convenience theory; occupational crime; organizational opportunity
Wickens, T.D. 2, 72
Wiersholm 114, 115
Wijnen, P. 133
Wildenthal, K. (University of Texas) 182–4
Wildman, J.L. 72
Williams, C.C. 28, 42, 47
Williams, J.W. 55, 81, 85, 94, 119, 123, 138, 145, 188
Wilmerhale 37–40, 173, 175
witness interviews 38, 39, 40, 94, 147, 174, 185
Woldsdal Public Relations 43
Wood, J. 24, 25
Working Environment Act 134–5, 138
WorldCom Corporation 175–7
Wright, A. 52

Zahra, S.A. et al. 22, 23
Zelin, R.C. 53
Zhang, G. 2, 7, 8, 10, 26, 35
Zipparo, L. 75, 133